WHAT THE CRITICS ARE SAYI
HOW TO SURVIVE YOUR FRESHMAN YEAR

Book of the Year Award finalist, *Foreword* magazine

Recommended Reading, *Positive Teens* magazine

Included in "Ten Good Books for Grads," *Detroit Free Press*

A Top 40 Young Adult book, Pennsylvania School Librarian Association

"Hidden Gem"
        —INGRAM LIBRARY SERVICE

"A guide full of fantastic advice from hundreds of young scholars who've
been there …. a quick and fun read."
        —BOSTON HERALD

"The perfect send-off present for the student who is college bound. The book
manages to be hilarious and helpful. As an added bonus, it's refreshingly free
of sanctimony."
        —THE POST AND COURIER, CHARLESTON, SOUTH CAROLINA

"Honest portrait of the trials and jubilations of college and how to best navi-
gate your own way through."
        —NEXT STEP MAGAZINE

"Explains college to the clueless."
        —COLLEGE-BOUND TEEN

"The advice dispensed is handy, useful, and practical. This book will make
great light reading for an incoming freshman."
        —VOYA

"A great tool for young people beginning an important and often daunting
new challenge, with short and funny, real-world tips."
        —WASHINGTON PARENT

Visit www.hundredsofheads.com to learn more.

PRAISE FOR HUNDREDS OF HEADS® GUIDES:

"Hundreds of Heads is an innovative publishing house ... Its entertaining and informative 'How To Survive ...' series takes a different approach to offering advice. Thousands of people around the nation were asked for their firsthand experiences and real-life tips in six of life's arenas. Think 'Chicken Soup' meets 'Zagats,' says a press release, and rightfully so."

—*ALLEN O. PIERLEONI*
"BETWEEN THE LINES," THE SACRAMENTO BEE

"A concept that will be ... a huge seller and a great help to people. I firmly believe that today's readers want sound bytes of information, not tomes."

—*CYNTHIA BRIAN*
TV/RADIO PERSONALITY, BEST SELLING AUTHOR: CHICKEN SOUP FOR THE GARDENER'S SOUL; BE THE STAR YOU ARE!; THE BUSINESS OF SHOW BUSINESS

"Practical advice...Entertaining reading, as well as a wake-up call to parents who think their kid's experience will mirror their own."

—*THE SEATTLE TIMES*

"The addictive book would make for a great graduation gift or addition to a school library...With many different outlooks on every topic, readers will surely find advice to suit their style and fit their situation, whether they are dealing with office politics or managing e-mail overload."

—*FOREWORD MAGAZINE*

How to Survive Your Freshman Year

WARNING:

This Guide contains differing
opinions. Hundreds of Heads
will not always agree.
Advice taken in combination may
cause unwanted side effects. Use
your Head when selecting advice.

How to Survive Your Freshman Year

Third Edition

by Hundreds of College Students Who Did*

*and some things to avoid, from a few dropouts who didn't

FRANCES NORTHCUTT, Special Editor

Created by
MARK BERNSTEIN & YADIN KAUFMANN

Hundreds of Heads Books, LLC
ATLANTA

Cover photograph by Jupiter Images
Cover and book design by Elizabeth Johnsboen

Library of Congress Control Number: 2007938491

HUNDREDS OF HEADS® books are available at special discounts when purchased in bulk for premiums or institutional or educational use. Excerpts and custom editions can be created for specific uses. For more information, please email sales@hundredsofheads.com or write to:

HUNDREDS OF HEADS BOOKS, LLC
#230
2221 Peachtree Road, Suite D
Atlanta, Georgia 30309

ISBN-10: 1-933512-14-8
ISBN-13: 978-1933512-14-3

Printed in U.S.A.
10 9 8 7 6 5 4 3 2 1

CONTENTS

Introduction

You're so lucky, it's unbelievable: not only are you headed for college, but you get to be a freshman now, in the 21st century. You and your classmates have more choices and opportunities than freshmen have ever had in the history of higher education.

Pretty exciting, right? And maybe pretty stressful, too. You may be leaving your high school friends behind, going away from home for the first time, jumping into a new social scene, and facing a tougher academic environment, among other new challenges. Fortunately, you are not alone. For any dilemma or problem you might face, there are thousands of other students who've been there before you.

Our goal is to help you succeed in the real world of college, and we've gone straight to the source. We've collected advice from all kinds of students, from all kinds of colleges and universities, about every aspect of freshman life. Which classes to take, whom to date, how to overcome the challenge of doing your own laundry—every student in this book has an opinion and plenty of suggestions. You'll hear from frat boys, theater majors, math whizzes, and future teachers. You'll hear from optimists, pessimists, chemists, and artists. You'll find some contributors who sound like the voice of truth and reason; listen to them! You'll find others who seem like they're on a completely different plane. Give them a chance, too—there may be nuggets of wisdom hidden in their crazy stories.

During my decade of guiding college students through their freshman year, I've seen a lot, but even I was surprised by much of what we found when we interviewed students and graduates for this book. The advice you'll find here is funny, triumphant, grateful, regretful, nostalgic, and affectionate, but above all, it's candid and honest. In the end, you'll make your own decisions. Be confident, have fun, and keep reading!

FRAN NORTHCUTT

When we published the first edition of *How to Survive Your Freshman Year* in 2004, we were walking in uncharted territory. We believed—strongly—that kids going off to college would benefit from, and enjoy, a book full of the wisdom and experiences of many hundreds of others who have lived through freshman year and come out with something interesting to say about it. But the enthusiasm with which readers responded surprised even us. The book quickly became the year's best-selling college guide, and it has gone from strength to strength since then.

We've now got 20 books in our Hundreds of Heads® Survival Guide series—including books on getting into college, succeeding in college, and even getting *your kids* into college, as well as marriage, divorce, raising kids, dieting, retirement, and many other wonderful challenges life throws at you.

Other advice books, no matter how smart or expert their authors, are generally limited to the knowledge of only one person. But two heads are better than one, as the old saying goes—and it turns out that hundreds of them are even better. So we interviewed students and graduates from big schools, small schools, Ivies and state universities. Greeks, geeks and jocks weighed in on their college experiences. The results are remarkably universal. From dorm life and roommates to college parties and dating; from choosing your major to implementing helpful study practices; from battling homesickness to avoiding fashion faux pas—it's all here for your educational use. You might even be relieved to know that the things you worry about are, in fact, common concerns among your fellow students.

As you might expect, we heard many different views—and some of those views differed from one another. Are fraternities and sororities a good choice or not? How close should you try to stay with your high school friends? And, of course—to party or not to party? You'll make your own decisions, but you can do it armed with the insights of the people featured on these pages.

And now we're on to the third edition of *HTSYFY*, which is even better (and also much bigger!) than its predecessors. The new version of this indispensable guide features not only updated wisdom from college students across the country, but also expert advice from Frances Northcutt, Honors Adviser at CUNY/Macaulay Honors College. Fran weighs in with invaluable perspective for college freshmen based on her years of advising them as they go through this wonderful and complex new period in their lives.

You're embarking on one of the best experiences of your life. Have fun. Study hard. And know that you've got hundreds of friends to show you the way.

MARK W. BERNSTEIN
YADIN KAUFMANN

Get Ready: What to Take to College

I t is a universal truth that college freshmen leave packing until the last minute. You all put off packing for three reasons. First, it's a big job and you didn't feel like doing it. Fair enough! Second, you couldn't quite believe that the big day would really come. Oops.

And third, you had a gut sense that leaving home just might be harder than you thought during all those years of high school when you couldn't wait to be out on your own. So your subconscious concocted the perfect plan: instead of getting weepy and emotional during this fraught time, you and your loved ones will be stressed out, irritable, and panicked over the chaos of last-minute packing. Brilliant!

Bring your blanket. Make sure it's comfy.

—*CHANA WEINER*
BARNARD COLLEGE
SOPHOMORE

I HAD A BATTERY-CHARGED, PORTABLE BLENDER. It was super. It cost $50. I was dorm shopping with my dad, and I said, "I need that blender." He was like, "You don't need a portable blender for college." I was like, "No, no, Dad, I need that. Take the comforter out of the cart. I need that." So we got it. And I made everything in it. A blender helps make friends.

> —*CASEY*
> *GEORGETOWN UNIVERSITY, SENIOR*

• • • • • • • •

BEST GIFT TO ASK FOR FROM YOUR PARENTS: One really great sleeping bag. You'll use it for everything, from spring break in a hotel room with 20 other people, to backpacking across Europe or the U.S.

> —*WENDY W.*
> *UNIVERSITY OF GEORGIA, GRADUATE*

• • • • • • • •

BRING SOME GOOD PAJAMAS. It's uncomfortable sleeping with other people in the same room, but one thing that helps is to have good pajamas that cover most of your body parts. You can lounge around in them without worrying about how you look.

> —*S.G.*
> *COLUMBIA UNIVERSITY, SENIOR*

Bring good judgment. Having good judgment will help freshmen start off in the right direction.

—*KAMALI BENT*
CORNELL
UNIVERSITY
GRADUATE

• • • • • • • •

LAPTOPS ARE A MUST. If it has wireless Internet, you can take it to Starbucks or the student center to study. This will help you get away from that annoying roommate. Also, it's a huge pain to move a heavy computer into the dorms.

> —*SUSAN MORGENBESSER*
> *PENNSYLVANIA STATE UNIVERSITY, GRADUATE*

BRING LOTS OF BEDDING. Foam "egg crates" are a must. The mattresses at my school are covered in rubber in case you wet the bed or something, so I got a feather bed, and lots of people have foam things. Then you can get a good night's sleep.

—*EDITH ZIMMERMAN*
  WESLEYAN UNIVERSITY, SOPHOMORE

• • • • • • • •

A CASE OF NO-DOZ, Pop-Tarts, and several extra room keys.

—*S.L.M.*
  INDIANA UNIVERSITY, GRADUATE

• • • • • • • •

AN EXCELLENT PAIR OF STUDIO-GRADE headphones for those times when you want to jam but your roommate wants to snooze. You cannot get through college without your music.

—*MARGOT CARMICHAEL LESTER*
  UNIVERSITY OF NORTH CAROLINA AT CHAPEL HILL
  GRADUATE

• • • • • • • •

A TENNIS BALL. It's great to toss around the lounge and in the hallway, and it is a great conversation starter. As you throw the ball around, people come in to toss and the camaraderie begins.

—*DAVE BANVILLE*
  AMERICAN UNIVERSITY, GRADUATE

• • • • • • • •

A SENSE OF SELF: You always have to see where you are and where you want to be in the future. It's something that's always changing.

—*RUTHANN*
  MOUNT HOLYOKE COLLEGE, GRADUATE

Top 10 FRESHMAN FAVORITES

Sleeping Bag

Guitar

Headphones

Blender

Blankie

Photos

Organizer

Cell Phone

Bible

Toothbrush

A PALM or other kind of organizer. It helps.

—*M.A.A.*
GEORGE WASHINGTON UNIVERSITY, SENIOR

• • • • • • • •

A REALLY NICE CHAIR; something you can move, something that folds up. If there are five or six people in a room, everyone is sitting on the floor. But if you bring in your chair, you can keep it for yourself. Or, if there's that girl, give it up to her and you earn bonus points.

—*CHRIS PROVENCHER*
JAMES MADISON UNIVERSITY, FRESHMAN

• • • • • • • •

" Communal showers are gross, so bring shower shoes. Everybody wears them, except my roommate. But at least she took showers! "

—*SIERRA*
CAL POLY SAN LUIS OBISPO, JUNIOR

• • • • • • • •

BRING HEADPHONES. I have a friend who's into white pop music and she lived with a girl from the Bronx who only liked gangsta rap, and they had this huge friction that basically ruined their roommate relationship.

—*ERIC FRIES*
BOSTON UNIVERSITY, GRADUATE

A BOOK BY NIETZSCHE. People might think I was intellectual, introspective and maybe a little dark and mysterious. And it would provide some interesting reading.

> —*R.D.W.*
> *UNIVERSITY OF VIRGINIA, GRADUATE*

• • • • • • • •

MY JOURNAL. It's a companion when you don't have one. It sounds cheesy, but I used mine a lot.

> —*STEPHANIE*
> *UNIVERSITY OF PENNSYLVANIA, SENIOR*

If I could, I'd bring my bed from home.

> —*CESAR*
> *YALE UNIVERSITY*
> *FRESHMAN*

• • • • • • • •

A MAID.

> —*MATT BIGGERSTAFF*
> *EMORY UNIVERSITY, SENIOR*

• • • • • • • •

A NICE TOWEL IS REALLY IMPORTANT. People see you in your towel and you need to look good. Douglas Adams said the towel is the most important piece of equipment in the universe, because you can do so much with it.

> —*TIM JOYCE*
> *GEORGETOWN UNIVERSITY, SENIOR*

• • • • • • • •

I WOULD DEFINITELY BRING A STEREO. I used to listen to Bach when I was studying. It supposedly enhances your learning. I don't know if it's true.

> —*JAKE MALAWAY*
> *UNIVERSITY OF ILLINOIS, GRADUATE*

• • • • • • • •

GET A KICK-ASS MOUNTAIN BIKE to ride between classes—and an even more kick-ass lock.

> —*J.G.*
> *FLORIDA STATE UNIVERSITY, GRADUATE*

A Hot Pot. I hated the food at my college, so every other meal I made *Oodles and Noodles.* You can make tea, coffee, soup—anything, really—in a Hot Pot.

—*ALYSSA*
   JAMES MADISON
   UNIVERSITY
   SOPHOMORE

My photos. They kept me grounded.

—*HANNAH SMITH*
   HARVARD
   UNIVERSITY, JUNIOR

A TRUSTWORTHY ALARM CLOCK. I went through all undergraduate and graduate schools without my own desktop or laptop computer.

I didn't have a car until I started grad school and I didn't have a cell phone until my last semester of grad school. Yes, life would have been much easier if I had all those things, but I was able to make it without them.

> —*HASSAN*
>   *UNIVERSITY OF TULSA, GRADUATE*

. . . .

A TOOTHBRUSH. I wouldn't do well without a toothbrush.

> —*J.P.G.*
>   *UNIVERSITY OF PENNSYLVANIA, SOPHOMORE*

. . . .

A FRISBEE. You can make friends just by going out in the quad and throwing it around. People come by and play.

> —*JOSH STAFFORD*
>   *UNIVERSITY OF VIRGINIA, GRADUATE*

. . . .

I FORGOT MY PILLOW. That didn't work out too well. I had to use a rolled-up towel.

> —*PATRICK*
>   *UNIVERSITY OF RHODE ISLAND, FRESHMAN*

. . . .

CONTRACEPTIVES: You don't want to make the proverbial mistake that you're stuck with for the rest of your life. There's such a thing as taking a reasonable risk or a stupid risk. That covers sex, drug use, everything.

> —*MICHAEL A. FEKULA*
>   *UNIVERSITY OF MARYLAND, GRADUATE*

A TRUNKFUL OF COMFORT

There are many things to fill your old leather trunk with before heading off to college. Comfortable bedding is a must. A soft comforter and a substantial pillow will make your dreams of calculus and Shakespeare that much sweeter. A microwave, some Pyrex, and a few packets of cocoa will help to make cold winter study sessions more bearable. Moreover, a rug or two can help to add a bit of warmth to a dorm room. The greatest things to bring to college, however, won't fit in your trunk. These are things like self-confidence, composure, and respect. Don't be afraid to stick to your guns, hold your morals, and be yourself. College can be a time of becoming someone new, for sure, but that doesn't mean you have to become someone else. If you have respect for yourself, people will have respect for you. Respect for others is also essential.

> —*Drew Hill*
> *Colby College, Junior*

Bring warm clothes if you go to school up north. I'm from Miami and I didn't know what a winter coat was. Now I have a couple, and an umbrella.

> —*Hilary Tress*
> *New York University, Junior*

• • • • • • • •

Freshmen should take a blank slate with them to college; a fresh and clean start. If they did poorly in high school or were nerds, college is the time to change all of that. In college, you determine your future.

> —*Vivian Oriaku*
> *University of Miami, Graduate*

MUSIC ON THE MOVE

AN IPOD IS A MUST HAVE FOR SCHOOL! I use it much more now that I'm at school than I ever did at home. When my roommates are being loud and I'm sitting at my desk, trying to study, my iPod is the only thing that makes it possible. I'm especially grateful for my iPod when my roommate, a big fan of the Backstreet Boys and Enrique Iglesias, starts playing their greatest hits. My headphones go right on and I can pretend he isn't listening to music that stopped being cool in 1999. An iPod is also guaranteed to keep you occupied if, like me, you take a trip home every month or so and have nothing to do on the train.

—*TOBIAS*
HARVARD UNIVERSITY

I USE MY IPOD MOST OFTEN WHEN I'M WALKING FROM CLASS TO CLASS. Whenever people are walking around campus, they're either on their cell phones or listening to their iPods (sad, I know). So, when I don't have anyone to call, I save face with my iPod. That said, be aware of your surroundings when you're listening to your iPod. It's a total faux pas when people say hi to you while you're listening to your iPod and you're too spacey/into your music to notice.

—*ELANA*
UNIVERSITY OF MARYLAND, SENIOR

BRING YOUR IPOD TO PARTIES. It's fairly common for the person with the largest music collection to bring his/her iPod to parties. Hook it up to the host's laptop or iPod docking station so that there is an ample supply of good dance music!

—*RYAN*
BOSTON UNIVERSITY, JUNIOR

I LIKE TO LISTEN TO MUSIC, but I find that I don't actually use my iPod as much as my friends do. Many people listen to music while walking to and from class, but I prefer talking to a friend while walking or saying hi to people I know along the way to class. Some people listen to music while they're studying, whether it's iTunes on their computer or their iPod. I actually find it difficult to study with music playing and prefer to study in quiet. I find that I listen to my iPod the most while traveling.

—*PARISA BASTANI*
UNIVERSITY OF PENNSYLVANIA, SENIOR

. . . .

AN IPOD OR COMPUTER SPEAKERS ARE A MUST for a dorm room. It is really nice to get back and be able to just sit and listen to some music before going to bed or to be able to provide a bit of background music when hanging out with friends.

—*ANDREW ALCORTA*
HARVARD UNIVERSITY, FRESHMAN

. . . .

MY IPOD IS NOT ONLY FOR EXERCISING, but for getting involved in music life in the dorms! My campus is probably just one of many with music file-sharing programs so that you can connect to the music libraries of other people who live nearby. This means you can LEGALLY listen to tons of music for free any time of the day. I ended up vastly expanding my song collection based on what I heard at school.

—*MOLLY*
BROWN UNIVERSITY, SOPHOMORE

Estimated number of bicycles in use on campus at Stanford University— 15,000.

MY STEREO SYSTEM. I got to have beats. You can drown someone out if you have to; just get into your own little zone.

—*KENTON*
UNIVERSITY OF VIRGINIA, SENIOR

• • • • • • • •

A JOURNAL. It's kind of a manic-depressive time, freshman year. There are really big highs and really big lows. During the lows it helps to write it out.

—*ANONYMOUS*
YALE UNIVERSITY, SOPHOMORE

• • • • • • • •

❝Get an alarm clock radio. If you go out late the night before, it's got to be real loud so you actually get up.❞

—*KEVIN WALSH*
GEORGETOWN UNIVERSITY, SOPHOMORE

• • • • • • • •

BRING EXTRA LIGHTING for your dorm room, an air mattress in case a friend comes over, and a fake ID.

—*JESSICA*
BARNARD COLLEGE, JUNIOR

• • • • • • • •

A KAYAK: I am an introvert and I love spending time alone.

—*DENALI*
PRINCETON UNIVERSITY, JUNIOR

A NICE WATERPROOF BOOK BAG. If it rains, your books get wet and there's not a lot you can do to fix them. It hurts the sell-back value, too.

> —*B.M.*
> *UNIVERSITY OF MARYLAND, JUNIOR*

• • • • • • • •

A MECHANICAL PENCIL WITH A BIG ERASER. If you're like me and you'd rather pay attention in class than do a bunch of reading, a good mechanical pencil is great for taking clean, concise notes.

> —*J.S.*
> *UNIVERSITY OF GEORGIA, GRADUATE*

• • • • • • • •

EARPLUGS. There's a lot of noise in the dorm.

> —*RICK SHILLING*
> *PENNSYLVANIA STATE UNIVERSITY, GRADUATE*

• • • • • • • •

IF I COULD BRING ONE THING to college, it would be maturity. But I suppose that's what college is all about . . . living and learning!

> —*ANONYMOUS*
> *INDIANA UNIVERSITY, GRADUATE*

• • • • • • • •

MY LAPTOP AND MY FAVORITE MOVIE. While I used my laptop for almost all my work, it was especially important to me for sending and receiving instant messages with my friends. And whenever I had a bad day, I would pop my favorite movie in the VCR and begin to feel better within minutes. I must have watched *When Harry Met Sally* 100 times during my freshman year. It was an emotional lifesaver.

> —*DANIELLE FRIEDMAN*
> *DUKE UNIVERSITY, SENIOR*

Bring your wallet and a lot of money.

> —*COLIN O'CONNOR*
> *GEORGETOWN UNIVERSITY, JUNIOR*

A BOX FAN of reasonable torque and a bath towel, preferably damp. The fan directed out the dorm window was to create an exhaust vacuum effect while the damp towel, covering the gap at the foot of the door, prevented the escape of any extraneous, ahem, smoke.

—*A.D.*
UNIVERSITY OF NEW HAMPSHIRE

* * * * * * * *

A CELL PHONE. Since you're out so much, if people want to get in touch with you—your parents, your friends from high school, your friends here—it makes it much easier.

—*EAMONN MORAN*
GEORGETOWN UNIVERSITY, JUNIOR

* * * * * * * *

PATIENCE: Having to deal with financial aid and the registrar can be very trying at times.

—*ADAM*
FLORIDA AGRICULTURAL AND MECHANICAL UNIVERSITY
GRADUATE

* * * * * * * *

ORANGE-FLAVORED GATORADE. More Gatorade is consumed to relieve hangovers than while playing any sport. And stay with orange, because red can stain when it comes back up.

—*ANONYMOUS*
UNIVERSITY OF FLORIDA, GRADUATE

* * * * * * * *

BRING AN UMBRELLA. Yes, it rains at college, too.

—*PHIL*
UNIVERSITY OF VIRGINIA, SENIOR

* * * * * * * *

I WOULD BRING SLEEP IN A BOTTLE.

—*COLLEEN*
PRINCETON UNIVERSITY, JUNIOR

Stuffed animals. . . I brought mine!

—*CATHERINE G.*
BARRETT
BRYN MAWR
COLLEGE
SOPHOMORE

A GEORGE FOREMAN GRILL. Those grills are so fast and easy, and everything is pretty good, from steak to grilled cheese. No college kid should be without one.

> —JEFF
> BOWLING GREEN STATE UNIVERSITY, GRADUATE

A BIBLE IS AUTOMATIC. It's something aesthetic you can bring from home. If you want to look at it every day, you can. I remember, after September 11, everyone was in the middle of my hall, praying. So it always helps.

> —JERI D. HILT
> HOWARD UNIVERSITY, SENIOR

UNDERWEAR.

> —WALTER
> UNIVERSITY OF MARYLAND–COLLEGE PARK, SOPHOMORE

EVERYONE SHOULD BRING one book that they really enjoy reading and re-reading. I brought *Ender's Game* by Orson Scott Card, and whenever I was having a really stressful week or just needed a break from the required reading for classes, I read my comfort book.

> —SARAH
> WELLESLEY COLLEGE, SOPHOMORE

A FEW CANDLES, a pack of cigarettes, and some good poetry.

> —ANONYMOUS
> CALVIN COLLEGE, GRADUATE

Bring your mom's credit card.

> —J.G.
> GEORGE WASHINGTON UNIVERSITY, SENIOR

WHAT *NOT* TO BRING

DO NOT BRING A COMPUTER. I've never used IM and I get by. Here's how it works: Because I don't have a computer in my room, I'm never in my room. Since I'm never in my room, I'm always outside in the quad. Since I'm always in the quad, I see my friends. Since I'm always seeing my friends out here, I don't need to see them on IM. The reason you need IM is because you're always in your room with your computer. It creates its own problem and solves its own problem. Get rid of the computer and you won't need IM. And you can spend that $1,500 on beer and food and spring break trips.

> —*RICH MURPHY*
> *GEORGETOWN UNIVERSITY, JUNIOR*

• • • • • • • •

I JUST DIDN'T KNOW WHAT TO BRING, so I kept packing every little thing I might need or want to have with me. I would have brought my bathroom and bed, too! When I got to school I had no place to put anything. I ended up bringing back as much stuff as I could each time I went home. After break, I came back up with only the things I really needed.

> —*ILANA COOPERSMITH*
> *RUTGERS UNIVERSITY, GRADUATE*

• • • • • • • •

THERE'S NOT ENOUGH SPACE to keep your stuff, so don't bring a lot of stuff.

> —*MARINNA FADOR*
> *BOSTON COLLEGE, FRESHMAN*

I CAME HERE WITH MY DAD'S STATION WAGON and a minivan filled with my stuff. About a week ago, my parents came back and we packed the station wagon back up and sent stuff back home. It was too much. I brought my notes from my classes in high school. I brought my books from home. I didn't even want to look at a book or notes unless it was from a current class.

—*H.D. BALLARD*
UNIVERSITY OF VIRGINIA, FRESHMAN

• • • • • • • • •

YOU CAN GET BY WITHOUT A COMPUTER and a printer: It's not that difficult. I don't have a cell phone, and I've never had one. You don't really need books because you can go to the library and get the books. You don't need anything, really. You can sleep on someone's floor. You can borrow people's shampoo or soap. You could borrow someone's deodorant. You don't really need anything.

—*MARTIN*
GEORGETOWN UNIVERSITY, SOPHOMORE

• • • • • • • • •

DON'T BE THE ONLY PERSON IN YOUR DORM with a car, and if you are, don't let other people borrow it. If you do, there will be trouble.

—*HANNAH*
EMORY UNIVERSITY, JUNIOR

TOP FIVE THINGS *NOT* TO BRING

1. **Ice hockey gear:** You'll be home again before it gets cold enough to use it. And if your goal is to impress potential dates, hang a medal on the wall or put up a photo of you and your team with a trophy—packs the same punch but takes up much less space.

2. **Your jewelry collection:** You don't need it all, and you definitely don't need the stress of making sure it doesn't get stolen. And you don't have the space.

3. **Your favorite books:** If you have them lying around, you may end up reading when you should be out meeting people.

4. **Romantic candles (or any other kind):** They're against the rules. Don't go down in history as "that *@#%& freshman who burned down our dorm." Besides, you can buy electric candles nowadays for those special occasions when mood lighting is in order.

5. **Inspirational posters of any kind:** If you need a reminder to "Hang in there," put it in your planner—not on your wall, where it'll hang your social life.

A GUITAR. It's something that relaxes me, and it helps socially. You can always pull out your guitar and play on the lawn or wherever, and other people will come up and talk.

—LEAH PRICE
GEORGETOWN UNIVERSITY, SOPHOMORE

I WOULD BRING MY PILLOW—it smells like my sleep.

—ANONYMOUS
UNIVERSITY OF RHODE ISLAND, SOPHOMORE

A CLIP-ON READING LAMP. Or just a light you can shut off from your bed.

—AMANDA
WELLESLEY COLLEGE, SENIOR

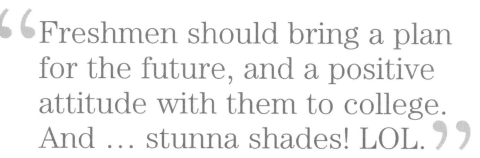

"Freshmen should bring a plan for the future, and a positive attitude with them to college. And … stunna shades! LOL."

—SHAQUEENA LE'SHAYE LEWIS
UNIVERSITY OF MIAMI, GRADUATE

FAKE IDS ARE A GOOD IDEA. My sister said I wouldn't need one until spring semester. That is not true. That is bad advice. If your friends decide to go to a bar, you can go with them. If you don't have an ID, you simply can't go.

—BAYLESS PARSLEY
UNIVERSITY OF VIRGINIA, FRESHMAN

THE MOST IMPORTANT THING any incoming freshman should take with them to college is an identity as a strong individual. Having great organizational skills and a weekly to-do list will cut down on the stress.

—*QUONIAS*
UNIVERSITY OF WEST GEORGIA, SENIOR

• • • • • • • •

BRING THE ABILITY TO FOCUS. Focus on your academics and remember why you're going to college in the first place.

—*J.M.G.*
DUKE UNIVERSITY, GRADUATE

• • • • • • • •

AIR FRESHENERS; you can make your dingy room smell like apples and cinnamon. When I got to my dorm room it smelled like sweat and smelly socks. Most first-year dorms don't have air conditioning, so be prepared and bring something that smells good.

—*Y.H.*
UNIVERSITY OF VIRGINIA, JUNIOR

• • • • • • • •

A GROUNDED SENSE OF SELF and an open mind. These two things will keep you optimistic and prepared for the new and exciting journey ahead. You will have a greater confidence and will be able to stay true to yourself in trying situations. These are the best years of your life, so enjoy every minute of them!

—*HAYLEY MASON*
HOWARD UNIVERSITY, SOPHOMORE

Get Set: Leaving Home

Leaving home can be scary, exciting, stressful, joyful, time-consuming, hilarious, tragic, and tough. Rest assured, almost no one manages to get from home to college with perfect dignity and grace. You may think you're just fine with going away (until the moment arrives, that is.) Or, you may fear the event for weeks in advance. Either way, you're probably in for a surprise; departing for school is never as bad, nor as easy, as you think.

Here's some advice on getting mentally set to go: Stay busy, spending plenty of time with friends and family; make sure absolutely everyone has your cell phone number and mailing address at school; and swap worrying about the future for enjoying the present.

Getting dropped off was like nothing else. My parents were crying, so I felt pretty awkward. I wasn't crying, but I was moved, for lack of a better word.

—*R.J.*
University of Delaware
Sophomore

I thought I'd be the most homesick person on this campus, but it wasn't that bad. You just have to make it quick.

—*C.H.*
University of Virginia
Freshman

LEAVING FAMILY IS A BIG ADJUSTMENT. I got lonely my first year and my parents were pretty strict about keeping me at school until I got over it. It was very hard but I grew from it. When I joined the football team, they came up for games, which was great. But the way I fought it mostly was by keeping busy; that's the best way. It's still hard.

—*Ryan Smith*
Carnegie Mellon University, Junior

• • • • • • • •

DON'T BE AFRAID TO LEAVE HOME, no matter what. When it was time for me to start college, leaving my mom while she was fighting breast cancer was one of the hardest things I ever had to do. But if I had stayed home, I wouldn't have met my husband, whom I am still gaga over after six years of courtship and three years of marriage. And Mom was the prettiest breast cancer survivor and mother of the bride ever.

—*Erica Lange-Hennesey*
Texas State University, Senior

• • • • • • • •

LEAVING HOME IS ALL ABOUT you and your parents each having more sex, more frequently and more easily. C'mon—the 'rents act all weepy to see their little chick flying the coop, when in reality they can't wait to turn their bedroom into a steamy den of *coitus parentalis*. And you feign maturity, eager to take on the responsibilities of living on your own and furthering your education, when in reality you are ecstatic that at the end of a night, instead of having to do it in the back of your car in the school parking lot, you can finally take a special someone home to the (relative) privacy of your dorm room.

—*John*
University of Wisconsin at Madison, Graduate

WHEN MY PARENTS MOVED me to college, the dorm didn't have elevators, so they helped me carry my stuff up four floors. After that, we went back to the hotel where they were staying and I burst into tears. I said, "Please take me with you. I want to go home. I'll go to school there." My dad looked at me and said, "I would take you, but I just moved all of your stuff up four flights of stairs. Stay a semester and then see what you think." That was great advice.

—*ERIN*
CENTRAL BIBLE COLLEGE, GRADUATE

" I was sadder to leave my friends than my parents. I'll see my parents again and they won't change. But leaving all my high school friends . . . everyone's going to be different, because they all went to different schools. "

—*BAYLESS PARSLEY*
UNIVERSITY OF VIRGINIA, FRESHMAN

BE SURE TO GET THERE EARLY on the first day. When I got to school, it took us over four hours to get everything moved in. My room was on the 14th floor, so we couldn't just walk stuff up the stairs. It took forever to wait for the elevator.

—*SARAH TIPPY*
WESTERN ILLINOIS UNIVERSITY, SENIOR

HEAD**LINES**
Best Advice and Top Tips

- Leaving home is harder than you think.
- Say goodbye to your parents quickly—it will be easier on all of you.
- Once you adjust to the shock of being away from home, you'll have a great time.
- It can be harder to leave your friends than your family—you know you'll see your family again.

A LOT OF WHAT COLLEGE IS ABOUT is getting past a lot of preconceived notions. Be prepared for change.

> —*MICHAEL A. FEKULA*
> *UNIVERSITY OF MARYLAND, GRADUATE*

I WENT TO COLLEGE IN THE SAME AREA I grew up in. I didn't think it would be that great; I'd have my mom breathing down my neck all the time. But actually it's really nice. I forgot to bring some stuff and I just went home and got it. And I can go home anytime and take a bath.

> —*LUCY LINDSEY*
> *HARVARD UNIVERSITY, FRESHMAN*

SAY GOODBYE, KISS THEM, AND MAKE THEM DRIVE AWAY QUICKLY.

—*C.H.*
UNIVERSITY OF VIRGINIA, FRESHMAN

I REMEMBER WHEN MY MOM LEFT me in the dorm to go back home, it was very quiet and pretty scary . . . not only because I was in a strange place, but because I was totally alone. Things may seem hard at first, but it only gets better. You'll see later that your college days are your best!

> —*ANONYMOUS*
> *INDIANA UNIVERSITY, GRADUATE*

My family lives in Oman, so it was hard for my mom: when she dropped me off, she knew I wouldn't be back for Thanksgiving. It's hard to leave your parents: You're used to the family environment so much more.

—*Natasha Pirzada*
Georgetown University, Sophomore

• • • • • • • •

"It's better going to a college far, far away, because when you need something done, or you miss your family, you have to stick through it. When you're at a college close by, it's hard because your parents still think you're in high school and want to see you every day."

—*Katie Holden*
Rutgers University, Freshman

• • • • • • • •

I had a really good time after I committed myself. I think it's all a matter of making the decision that you want to be there and you want to be doing what you're doing. People spent a lot of time choosing the college they want to go to. It makes a big difference if you're excited about where you end up.

—*Anne*
George Washington University, Senior

WHAT'S IN A NAME?

It makes little difference when you're an upperclassman (Ah! That sounds nice) but when you're just starting out, wouldn't it be nice to be addressed with some respect? Go ahead and set the standard by calling yourself what you'd like others to call you.

- **Freshman:** classic, traditional. Also somewhat sexist.

- **Frosh:** short, convenient, and gender-neutral; unfortunately, ugly.

- **First Year or First-Year Student:** also gender-neutral, but sounds a lot better.

I WAS EXPECTING MY MOM to be sadder. She was like, "All right, see ya." I was like, "Is that it? That's all I get?" But I was the third one to get dropped off. They were sad the first time.
—*M.A.S.*
UNIVERSITY OF VIRGINIA, GRADUATE

• • • • • • • •

I THOUGHT I WAS GOING TO HATE COLLEGE. My parents dropped me off my first day and were leaving me there, and I looked at them and said, "I don't think this is going to work out. Can I just come back to the hotel with you guys?" They were just like, "Nope, sorry." My mom got in the car and started crying. And my dad was like, "She'll figure it out." I stayed and I ended up having a great time in school.

—*J. DEVEREUX*
GEORGETOWN UNIVERSITY, GRADUATE

Go: Starting Out

You're coping with all the emotions that go along with leaving home. You're attempting to cope with all your hopes and fears about college. You have a to-do list three pages long, and your college's orientation program will have you busy from 7 a.m. till midnight for what seems like the next month. And in the midst of all this chaos, people keep telling you that these are the best years of your life! You really hope they're wrong.

Would it help to know that fun and adventure will eventually worm their way in through the insanity? They will. Would it help to know that your college years *can* be some of the best years of your life, but that they can also serve to open doors to even greater experiences? They can.

So take a deep breath, hold onto your to-do list, and jump in. And read on to hear how other students successfully swam to the other side.

The teachers are going to try to scare you the first week or two and you'll feel overwhelmed. But just keep on track.

—*GREG*
JAMES MADISON
UNIVERSITY, JUNIOR

THE HARDEST THING ABOUT LEAVING HOME was getting used to the freedom. I went from a setting where everything was controlled by my parents to one where I could do whatever I wanted. You have to balance things; have fun, but don't go crazy!

—*CANDACE LA PAN*
UNIVERSITY OF NORTH CAROLINA AT GREENSBORO
SOPHOMORE

- - - - - - - -

DON'T TRY TO FIND A GROUP OF FRIENDS. First, meet as many people as possible and wait until later to find your group.

—*JENNIFER A. SICKLICK*
GEORGE WASHINGTON UNIVERSITY, FRESHMAN

- - - - - - - -

THE FIRST DAY, MOST FRESHMEN HAD NO IDEA how to get from their dorm rooms to their classes. They were pitifully obvious, standing around the bus stops, trying to read the bus route maps inconspicuously. The worst cases were the poor geeks tracing the routes with their fingers. So arrive on campus early. The week before classes start, just get on the main bus route near your dorm. Ride the entire route—learn where it goes. Then do the same for each of the other routes. That way, when classes start you won't be late, lost, or an obvious neophyte.

—*TONYA SMITH*
UNIVERSITY OF GEORGIA, GRADUATE

- - - - - - - -

WHEN YOU MOVE INTO YOUR NEW ROOM, choose the bed where people will see you when the door is open. While you are moving in, people will walk by and see you setting up your room and will stop and say hi.

—*B.K.*
CORNELL UNIVERSITY, GRADUATE

DON'T EVEN THINK ABOUT IT

DO NOT show up with mono and bronchitis. When you arrive at school all you'll want to do is smoke tons of dope and kiss the ladies, both of which are contraindicated treatments for your affliction.

DO NOT think that the type of mono and bronchitis you have won't be contracted by the young lady with whom you spend your first few days at school kissing and smoking dope.

DO NOT think that it's perfectly acceptable to kiss the roommate of the young lady you've been kissing, just because it's late and you and the roommate have been drinking in a dark room alone, smoking tons of dope, and her breasts seem oh so lovely.

DO NOT think that either one of the roommates will accept your proposals to go on kissing both of them behind the back of the other roommate.

DO NOT think that the roommates will not share stories and commiserate and call you a philandering bastard behind your back, especially once they figure out they both have mono.

DO NOT think that it's just fine to smoke even a tiny bit of dope at this point.

And when you're in the hospital with double viral pneumonia for two weeks, **DO NOT** expect that either of the roommates will come visit you.

—*Lee Klein*
Oberlin College, Graduate

HEADLINES
Best Advice and Top Tips

- Arrive on campus early to learn the layout of the campus before classes start.
- Freshmen tend to travel in packs; try to walk with just one or two other people.
- The first few days can be overwhelming, but the adjustment comes quickly.
- Be outgoing, meet as many people as you can those first few weeks of school.

THE LIVING IS COMPLETELY DIFFERENT. At home, my parents took care of everything. It's a big adjustment: doing laundry, cleaning dishes, going out and getting food. I get back to school from a vacation and I forget—I'm kind of expecting my friends to be making food.

> —MATT MONACO
> GEORGE WASHINGTON UNIVERSITY, FRESHMAN

. . . .

I MADE MOST OF MY FRIENDS IN THE BEGINNING. You start off hanging out in a big group and then you realize whom you relate to, and those are the people you spend your time with.

> —ANDREW KARELITZ
> UNIVERSITY OF PENNSYLVANIA, FRESHMAN

. . . .

THAT FIRST DAY OF COLLEGE felt like a grown-up version of summer camp. Some of us hadn't realized that kids really did grow up in these far-away places. It was not odd to hear, "No really, c'mon; Iowa?" or, "Kalamazoo is a *real* place?!"

> —MICHAEL
> GRADUATE

Smile. it helps.

—CASEY
GEORGETOWN
UNIVERSITY, SENIOR

I **REMEMBER WALKING** into my first lecture hall and saying, "Wow!" There were 700 people in one room and I was shocked. Then the kid behind me whispered, "Aww, freshman." It only took one class for me to get used to the atmosphere. It wasn't so bad!

—*ORLY COBLENS*
UNIVERSITY OF MICHIGAN, FRESHMAN

• • • • • • • •

IT'S **NOT WORTH TRYING TO SAVE TIME** by buying your books early. My friend and I were told that the first days of college are really crazy, and the advice was to "buy all your books right away to avoid lines!" We bought $400 worth of books (each), including a hardcover dictionary. We realized we had done it all wrong the next day, when we looked at our schedule, which needed some revisions. Make sure your classes are totally lined up before buying your books.

—*JANNA HAROWITZ*
MCGILL UNIVERSITY, GRADUATE

• • • • • • • • •

COLLEGE **WAS AT FIRST** a horrific and strange experience for me because the world was larger than I thought it was. But everyone has to start somewhere. Don't feel scared or inferior, because everyone around you had to start out where you are!

—*K. HARMA*
WESTERN WASHINGTON UNIVERSITY, GRADUATE

• • • • • • • • •

DON'T **TRAVEL IN HERDS THE FIRST WEEK.** For example, when attending the obligatory frat parties and keggers, don't travel to and from with your entire dorm. Everyone will know you are a freshman. Choose a couple of people to go with and try to blend in.

—*ANONYMOUS*

Don't be afraid to go up to people and introduce yourself.

—*MANI*
UNIVERSITY OF MARYLAND FRESHMAN

Don't be too shy to ask for help. A lot of people are confused, but if you're lost together, there's more chance of getting it right.

—*Alfie Williams*
Georgia Institute
of Technology
Sophomore

Before you start, talk to a current student or recent grad and ask for advice. It may be worthless, but it may help you avoid some pitfalls.

> —*Anonymous*
> *Union College*

• • • • • • • •

I skipped all the orientations. My sister told me I didn't have to go to them if I didn't want to. So I took that as, "Go to the bar instead." But that's not the best advice. That way, all you meet are bar people. I never knew the other three-quarters of our class that didn't go to bars.

> —*Casey*
> *Georgetown University, Senior*

• • • • • • • •

Before classes start, take a walk through campus and get acquainted with the buildings. That way, you can recognize some of the buildings and sites later, through the chaos. On my first day, there were so many people running around that it was fairly intimidating for me, and it was difficult to find my classes.

> —*Michael Albert Paoli*
> *University of Toronto, Graduate*

• • • • • • • •

One of the biggest challenges I've encountered is finding time to eat at the dining hall. The first week I was here, I hardly ate at all because I didn't know when to go and didn't have enough people to go with. I hate going there alone. You walk in and you don't know which table to sit at. You can sit with anyone and they'll probably be nice about it. But you feel like you have to go with someone, just for security.

> —*C.H.*
> *University of Virginia, Freshman*

CAN YOU HANDLE THIS?

At Knox College, they figure your body is nice and relaxed after a summer off. So the college invented a little tradition known as the Pump Handle: Everyone forms a greeting line, and the president of the college shakes hands with each of the hundreds of students, faculty and staff. No problem, right? Except that when he's done, every last one of those hundreds of students, faculty and staff has to shake hands with every other person, too.

THE FIRST DAYS OF COLLEGE ARE THE BEST: For a few brief drunken moments, there are no cliques, no caste, no class, and no classes. It's a big, egalitarian, drunken orgy. At least, that's the way I partially remember it; I could be wrong.

> —JOHN
> UNIVERSITY OF WISCONSIN AT MADISON, GRADUATE

. . . .

THE FIRST FEW DAYS OF COLLEGE ARE WEIRD; you're bombarded by cheesy campus groups and pressured to commit to a thousand things that aren't even cool. Take time to relax. Don't worry about jumping into anything too soon.

> —KATIE MCAFEE
> BAYLOR UNIVERSITY, JUNIOR

. . . .

THE FIRST FEW MONTHS WERE EASIER than I thought they would be. But everyone I knew hit a patch right before they went home, after they'd been here for a couple of months. It was easy to come here, but after a couple of months you start to miss the security of home. Especially when the tests start.

> —D.F.
> NEW YORK UNIVERSITY, SENIOR

STARTING OUT, EVERYBODY IS BASICALLY LOST. You might look around and think you're the only one who is lost. But everyone is going through the same thing.

—*JOHNNY*
GEORGETOWN UNIVERSITY, JUNIOR

• • • • • • • •

TRY TO BE AS OUTGOING AS YOU CAN. All the people that I'm friends with now I met the first two or three weeks. You end up being closest with the people that you meet early on—because you're all in the same situation, going through the same thing. You're all in a new school, no one knows anyone.

—*CHIP JONES*
HAMILTON COLLEGE, JUNIOR

• • • • • • • •

"Find a campus map. The weekend before classes begin, figure out where all your classes are. You'll feel much more at ease on the first day."

—*WENDY W.*
UNIVERSITY OF GEORGIA, GRADUATE

• • • • • • • •

I JUST HAVE TO GO UP TO PEOPLE I don't know and try to make friends. It's a lot different from high school, where everyone knows you, and you're friends with everybody.

—*KEVIN BUSHEY*
GEORGIA STATE UNIVERSITY, FRESHMAN

CAN I GET SOME CREDIT HERE?

You may be starting college with a few credits already under your belt. Don't forget to follow these steps to make that credit official!

- **Advanced Placement:** If you took any AP exams, check to see whether your college will give you academic credit for them. Most colleges have a handy chart indicating exactly how many credits and which course requirements you can get based on your score. Hint: this chart can usually be found on the Admissions Web site. Last but not least, don't forget to have your scores sent to your college!

- **International Baccalaureate:** Many colleges are now willing to award credit for IB work as well. It's not as common as Advanced Placement, but it's on the rise. Alas, handy charts are rare when it comes to IB; IB credit is usually evaluated by an expert on campus. Ask at Admissions or consult your academic advisor.

- **A-Levels:** If you're coming from an international school run on the British system, you may have A-Level credits. These can make you eligible for more advanced coursework. Before you register for classes, check in with an academic advisor.

- **Prior College Credit:** Be sure to have your official transcripts sent from the Registrar's Office of your previous college to your new college. If you think your credit might affect your course choices for your first semester, be sure to review an unofficial copy of your transcript with an academic advisor.

THINGS WON'T BE PERFECT AT THE BEGINNING.
You're going to have a couple of rough months
when you're trying to find your niche and
remember why on earth you came to college. But
give yourself time to integrate, to decide how you
want to spend your time, who you want to spend
your time with, and what kind of people will
complement those objectives. You can drive
yourself crazy trying to do everything with all
sorts of people or you can try to figure out what
makes you happy and whom you're comfortable
with. But that won't happen immediately. It takes
at least a year, maybe a little longer.

> —*ANONYMOUS*
> *UNIVERSITY OF VIRGINIA, SENIOR*

**Keep your
Social Security
number handy
for the first
several days.**

—*BRIAN TURNER*
*UNIVERSITY OF
GEORGIA, GRADUATE*

• • • • • • • •

JUST GIVE IT TIME. At first, I would call or
IM some of my old buddies from high
school, talking with old friends. It was good to
have some close friends as a sounding board for
the things I was going through.

> —*WONNIE RYU*
> *EMORY UNIVERSITY, SENIOR*

• • • • • • • •

THE FIRST FEW WEEKS, freshmen move around
in packs. Try to make friends with some
upperclassmen. You're more likely to get into
parties without a herd of freshmen around you.

> —*KEVIN WALSH*
> *GEORGETOWN UNIVERSITY, SOPHOMORE*

Expectations: College Dreams & Campus Reality

C omplete these two sentences: *"The best thing that could happen to me this semester would be ..."*; and (you guessed it), *"The worst thing that could happen to me this semester would be ..."*!

Now compare your answers with your classmates: the odds are good that you'll share the same, or similar, hopes and fears. Is the work too hard (or too easy)? The dorm crowd too crazy (or not crazy enough)? The food inedible (or only unidentifiable)? One thing you can be sure of is that you are certainly ready to deal with whatever happens. If your nightmare scenario actually occurs, you'll be able turn it around. And if you're having trouble, the university has professionals who have seen it all before—and can help.

My biggest worry when I was a freshman was that I would be broke all of the time … and I was.

—*Cecilie*
Parsons School
of Design, Junior

My biggest misconception about college was that I would be one-hundred-percent free of parents, and I definitely wasn't. I had to force myself to become more independent by getting a job and not calling home every day.

—*Chidimma Uche Eto*
Duke University, Graduate

• • • • • • • •

Everyone talks about how college is an opportunity to start over … but no one ever mentions how to recover from horrendous first impressions. What if I came off as completely socially inept? How could I recover from that? I felt a little "off" in terms of language. I'd been used to speaking a mixture of Chinese and English—Chinglish, if you will—so suddenly switching to pure English was an adjustment. I'd often be talking and have to wave my hands around trying to translate a word into English. I don't think my fears ever turned into reality, since I have a fair amount of friends now. Chalk that one up to worrying way too much about a new, unknown situation.

—*Mel*
University of Virginia, Sophomore

• • • • • • • •

I'm not too big on the drug/alcohol thing: in fact, I abstain from both altogether. My biggest fear for college was that I wouldn't fit in: that people would find me "lame"; that I wouldn't make friends, being an abstainer and all. However, I found that other kids were really not as shallow as I thought. I had no problem making friends. Drinkers, non-drinkers, math nerds, ice-climbers, Trekkies … you name 'em, I befriended 'em. As clichéd as it sounds, people liked me for who I was.

—*Drew Hill*
Colby College, Junior

GETTING THE MOST OUT OF YOUR MENTOR

Peer mentor programs are a hot trend at colleges and university administrators think it's a wonderful idea to match up freshmen with older, wiser students who can show you the ropes and make you feel at home. Unfortunately, too many initial meetings between peer mentors and mentees go like this:

"Okay, so do you have any questions?"
"Uh, not right now."
"Oh, okay."
(Mentor and mentee sit in awkward silence.)

If you are at risk for mentor meeting discomfort, don't just sit there—memorize these useful questions, and you'll be all set! Your mentor will feel wise and helpful, and you may actually learn something.

- What was the most helpful thing anyone ever told you about college?

- What scared you the most about starting college? How did you cope?

- What's the best way to make close friends?

- Did you make any big mistakes your freshman year? What would you do differently?

- What was the best thing that happened to you freshman year?

HEAD**LINES**
Best Advice and Top Tips

- Sometimes it takes a while to find your group of friends. Be patient.
- The constant need to define yourself can be very stressful.
- If you feel like transferring, or if you just feel 'out of it,' hang on. Try harder to join groups and meet more people before making any big decisions.
- Lots of students worry about adapting to a very different culture when going to a school in a different region of the country, not to mention a different country altogether.

MY BIGGEST FEAR about college was that on the first day, I wouldn't be able to get to any of my classes on time.

—*KEVISHA ITSON*
NORTHERN ILLINOIS UNIVERSITY, FRESHMAN

• • • • • • • • •

I WAS CONCERNED ABOUT adapting to a southern school and its culture, since I came from San Francisco, but I soon realized the culture might be preppy and southern, but the minds of the students are more progressive. Professors are also just as open, so I felt more at ease as my freshman year went by. At first you might feel alienated, judging by the cliques around the students and the huge presence of Greek life. Regardless of your personality, you'll find your own group of friends who share the same interests.

—*ANONYMOUS*
UNIVERSITY OF VIRGINIA, JUNIOR

IN THE BEGINNING

THE MOST DIFFICULT THING freshman year was the constant need to define yourself in every conversation, in every new person you meet, and in every class you attend. You're in a totally new environment and no one knows who you are. That was kind of unnerving. It took me a while to embrace it, but I found my best friends in the middle of my first semester, and that helped me. I found them when I was rappelling off the football stadium. I found my niche. Here I get to be the crazy hippy outdoorsy rock-climbing adventure-racing person, which is really great.

> —*DENALI*
> *PRINCETON UNIVERSITY, JUNIOR*

THE BEST PART ABOUT FRESHMAN YEAR was having the independence away from home and getting to choose my classes and what I was going to do with my time.

> —*ELIZABETH ROTH*
> *UNIVERSITY OF PENNSYLVANIA, SENIOR*

IT'S FUNNY; I think if I'm not in class I must be late for something or missing something. I'm so used to being in school eight hours a day!

> —*TOBIAS*
> *HARVARD UNIVERSITY, FRESHMAN*

IN THE BEGINNING OF FRESHMAN YEAR, everybody is looking for the party and making friends as fast and easily as possible. You get sucked into doing things that you might not want to do, like, you're hanging out with a crowd during orientation and they want to go to some frat party, and you might not really want to do that. You have to not be afraid to stand apart and not participate in something that you don't really want to do. That way, you find the friends who are really like you. The people who are not doing the things that you don't want to be doing are waiting to meet people just like you.

> —*MOLLY*
> *BROWN UNIVERSITY, SOPHOMORE*

THE OTHER SIDE OF THE DESK: THE CASE OF THE MISSING FRESHMAN

Colleges measure success in many ways, but one of the most important is retention: how many students who start out at the college actually stay, persist, and eventually graduate. In order to make retention numbers as high as possible, college administrators are always looking at what helps students stay and what causes students to leave. We know that the students who aren't connected to anyone—peers, resident advisors, faculty, student life, staff—are more likely to struggle academically and socially, which can lead to dropping out or being expelled. As a result, when college administrators get together for meetings we often talk about the "disconnected" freshmen: the students who aren't showing up for class, who don't come to dorm meetings, who sit alone in the dining hall, who don't make eye contact when they're walking across campus. Those students may *feel* invisible, but they aren't. College staff and faculty usually notice if a student is isolated from others, and we do want to help.

ONE PARTICULAR FEAR that I had coming into Rice was that I would no longer stand out in the classroom or in extracurricular, since practically everyone who comes to Rice was a standout in her high school. I thought everyone might be really competitive in classes or cutthroat about getting leadership positions. My first few years I applied for jobs, internships, and leadership positions and was rejected for practically all of them. Rather than get discouraged and give up, I just kept trying and continued to develop good relationships with supportive members of the faculty.

—*EMILIA*
RICE UNIVERSITY, JUNIOR

I **THOUGHT THAT COLLEGE** would be what you learn in the classroom. But the real wealth of information is not from your professors: It's from the other people you meet and the experiences you have.

> —*RENE*
> *DUKE UNIVERSITY, GRADUATE*

• • • • • • • •

MY NUMBER ONE WORRY was being away from my mom. Luckily, my school was only an hour and 45 minutes away, so I went home every weekend. We also had a really good mobile-to-mobile plan where we could talk as much as we wanted to for free.

> —*QUONIAS*
> *UNIVERSITY OF WEST GEORGIA, SENIOR*

ASK THE ADVISOR

College just started, but I really don't like it here. Should I transfer?

Lots of students have a tough first week, month, or even semester, but that doesn't necessarily mean that things won't get better. In fact, if you stick around, you may find out that this college is the right one for you after all.

So why do you feel so out of place now? Starting college is a huge adjustment, and it's rare for that adjustment to go 100-percent smoothly. If you give up now and stop trying to make friends, enjoy your classes, and get involved on campus, you'll never know what might have been.

MY BIGGEST FEAR before starting school was moving to another city, especially one like Atlanta. I thought I was going to be living in the Deep South and I was afraid of being completely bored with Atlanta. I coped with this by concentrating my time on finding the good in moving and seeing the move as an opportunity to explore a completely new place. I ended up enjoying what Atlanta has to offer.

—*ALEX*
EMORY UNIVERSITY, SOPHOMORE

A MAJOR CONCERN was that I was obviously out of touch with American pop culture, having lived overseas all my life. I wasn't quite sure how important it was to be "in the know," and stressed about that a lot. I even wondered if I should start studying up on entertainment blogs. I decided it was a waste of time to try to get excited about people I've never heard of and decided to just stay out of touch with American pop culture instead.

—*MEL*
UNIVERSITY OF VIRGINIA, SOPHOMORE

MY NUMBER ONE WORRY was gaining the "freshman 15." So I went to the gym three times a week, I joined the dance team, and I became a vegetarian. That's a lot of stuff, but it worked.

—*M.T.*
GEORGIA STATE UNIVERSITY, SENIOR

Dorms: The Good Life?

Your parents tell you that your dorm is a hundred times fancier than the dorms they had when they were college students—you just wish they could see what your hall looks like on Sunday mornings. And even at the very best of times, five minutes after the custodial staff tunneled their way through, there are still plenty of interpersonal adventures to face. There's the neighbor who steams broccoli every single night at 6:45. And the neighbor who stays in shape by kicking a soccer ball against the wall for hours. And then there's you—wanting to have fun and hang out, but sometimes craving just one moment of peace and privacy. Read on to see what else you might be in for—and what to do about it!

If you put a thousand freshmen into a building, anything can and will happen.

—*B.*
GEORGE WASHINGTON
UNIVERSITY, SENIOR

MAKE FRIENDS WITH PEOPLE who are not on your hall. That way, when you need a break from your dorm or your roommate, you can call those people and say, "I need to get out of here, I'm coming over!" I would usually completely leave my dorm during the day. I wouldn't return to my room until the evening. That way my life didn't revolve around my hall. Find something to do by yourself outside your dorm, like biking, running, or singing; whatever it is that will get you out.

　　　　—*SUMMER J.*
　　　　UNIVERSITY OF VIRGINIA, SENIOR

• • • • • • • • •

IF YOU'RE GOING TO LIVE IN THE DORM, I hope you like noise. Dorms are what they are advertised to be: a place to meet people and have lots of fun. Some of my best friends to this day are people I met and bonded with while trying to survive dorm life. So, if you opt for living in the dorms, expect a lot of fun and interesting experiences; just don't count on getting a lot of studying or sleep.

　　　　—*K. HARMA*
　　　　WESTERN WASHINGTON UNIVERSITY, GRADUATE

• • • • • • • • •

I WISH I'D BEEN MORE SOCIABLE. I wish I'd met more people, because now I don't really know that many people, except for my close friends. Now that everyone has gone their separate ways I don't really know any casual acquaintances or anything on campus. You form bonds in your freshman dorm and when everyone moves out and goes to other dorms, you can go see them and visit and that kind of stuff. It's kind of like a network that you can use throughout your college career. And I don't really do that.

　　　　—*T.*
　　　　STANFORD UNIVERSITY, SENIOR

WHENEVER YOU LEAVE YOUR DORM ROOM, bring your key with you. My friend woke up late one day and half-unconsciously took a shower in the dorm bathrooms. He only had a towel on, and flip-flops. After his shower he returned to his dorm room to find it locked; he was locked out. Everyone was in class, even his RA. He had to run to the other side of campus in his towel to our friend's laundry room to borrow some clothes so that he could go to lunch and to class.

—*E.F.*
CLAREMONT MCKENNA COLLEGE, SOPHOMORE

• • • • • • • • •

LIVE IN THE DORMS WITH FRESHMEN in small ratty rooms. It doesn't sound right, I know, but it's what I wish I had done. My school had a variety of dorms that ran from old, predominantly freshman dorms with tiny, two-person rooms, to newly renovated, upper classman dorms that were like six-person apartments. I chose the middle of the road; a mostly upper-classman dorm with large rooms. Big mistake. These types of dorms aren't conducive to meeting lots of people, which is what freshman year is all about.

Through a classmate in one of the older dorms with tiny rooms, I discovered a social wonderland. Everyone in the building was a freshman, everyone kept their doors open, and everyone wandered around meeting and greeting. There was pretty much a family or little town atmosphere; everyone hung out and did lots of stuff together. This is what the freshman experience was supposed to be.

—*JEFF*
BOWLING GREEN STATE UNIVERSITY, GRADUATE

Dorm life
is an essential
experience.

—*MELISSA K. BYRNES*
AMHERST COLLEGE
GRADUATE

HEADLINES
Best Advice and Top Tips

- Find out how big your dorm room is before you arrive so you don't pack too much stuff.
- Be respectful of your roommates and clean up after yourself.
- Set a monthly cleaning schedule with your roommates, and stick to it.
- Try to meet all the people on your floor—it makes sharing a bathroom easier.
- Living in the freshman dorms is the best way to meet other students.
- Dorm life means adjusting to living with a lot of other people in a small space.

Dorms are a good place if you can deal with living in a box with another person.

—*K.M.*
  NORTHWESTERN UNIVERSITY GRADUATE

I LIVED IN DORMS FOR THE FIRST TWO YEARS. I lived in an all-girl dorm, and for the first two weeks, everyone was happy. But then we all started getting our periods at the same time, and everyone became bitchy all together. It was terrible. And the dorm was filthy. You'd think an all-girl dorm would be clean, but girls are definitely dirtier than guys. Our bathroom was disgusting. And the end of the year was ridiculous—we had garbage cans spilling into the hallways. Living off campus now is like a slice of heaven.

—*SUSAN LIPPERT*
  EMORY UNIVERSITY, JUNIOR

OFF-CAMPUS FOLLIES

I thought living in a dorm would be stifling and stupid, so, I got an apartment next to campus with three other roommates. Now *that* was stupid. Friends from the dorms—and their friends—considered our place Party Central, since they had no other place to go and were too young to get into bars. There was a parade of people in and out of the place almost 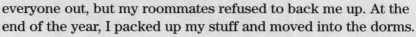 every night—not to mention an abundance of alcohol and drugs. The police came four different times, warning us to quiet down. Regulars included the entire trumpet section of the marching band, a five-piece rock band of bare-chested guys, a torch-juggling pharmacy student, and a cross-dresser named Phil. The apartment was trashed and I was always afraid of getting in big legal trouble. I tried to kick everyone out, but my roommates refused to back me up. At the end of the year, I packed up my stuff and moved into the dorms.

—W.
UNIVERSITY OF GEORGIA, GRADUATE

ADVICE FROM A FORMER R.A.

- **MAKE FRIENDS WITH YOUR RESIDENT ASSISTANTS.** They know most of the professors and staff on campus and can put you in touch with people a lot more easily than if you had to just walk in or cold-call an office.

- **IF YOU HAVE ROOMMATE PROBLEMS,** handle them right away. If you wait, you might get stuck with someone who already had a roommate move out, so you'll probably end up with a worse roommate.

- **IF YOU DRINK UNDERAGE,** use cans, not bottles, and be quiet. You're far less likely to get caught if you're quiet.

- **IF YOU SMOKE POT,** don't do it in your room. It is very easily smelled and tracked down.

- **IF YOU DAMAGE YOUR ROOM,** report it immediately. The staff likes students who are up-front and appear apologetic. If we find it when you move out, you will definitely get a bigger bill, and your parents will be mad.

- **FIND OUT THE DORM RULES UP FRONT.** Some schools can call your parents for offenses, some schools can revoke your housing for getting in trouble, and so on. You don't want to have to explain to your parents mid-semester that you got kicked out for playing your stereo too loud.

- **DO ANYTHING YOU CAN TO MOVE IN EARLY.** Moving in with everyone else is a nightmare.

- **YOUR RESIDENCE DIRECTOR CAN ALSO BE A GOOD RESOURCE** to talk about classes, professors, what to take and what to avoid, and other campus tips. Many students avoid the hall staff, but if you drop by on occasion, they will go out of their way to give you good information and help you.

—*MELISSA*
GRADUATE

I MET MY FIRST TRUE COLLEGE FRIEND when my best friend from high school came up to visit me on Welcome Weekend. We sat with my bedroom door open and played our guitars. A girl who played guitar heard us and came by to talk. She became my first college friend.

—*AMY FORBES*
MISSISSIPPI STATE UNIVERSITY, GRADUATE

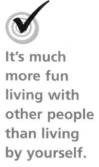

It's much more fun living with other people than living by yourself.

—*MATT LACKNER*
PRINCETON UNIVERSITY GRADUATE

• • • • • • • •

DON'T PICK COED DORMS. The guys on our floor were doing illegal drugs and I didn't like that. I didn't get along with them, and I didn't get to bond with other girls. If I could do it over I would choose an all-girl dorm; I think I would make more friends that way.

—*TYLER MARIE FREEBERG*
UNIVERISTY OF CALIFORNIA AT SANTA BARBARA, JUNIOR

• • • • • • • •

LIVING AT HOME AND GOING TO SCHOOL isn't bad at all. It's fine with me; I mean, college rooms are pretty small, and I wake up early enough to beat the traffic.

—*ERIC CABRERA*
GEORGIA STATE UNIVERSITY, FRESHMAN

• • • • • • • •

I'M AN ONLY CHILD and I lived with three girls in one big room. It was a pretty big adjustment the first semester. I remember being kind of miserable. You don't get much sleep and there's a lot of work to do. But you get through it.

—*ANNE*
GEORGE WASHINGTON UNIVERSITY, SENIOR

• • • • • • • •

TRY TO GET PLACED IN THE FRESHMAN DORMS. Even though the long elevator wait and community bathrooms seem horrible—and they are—you won't meet anyone if you live in the smaller, nicer dorms.

—*ASHLEY LEAVELL*
BOSTON UNIVERSITY, SENIOR

WE HAD MICE. We had a sewer pipe break in our building, and all these little mice were running around. So we set traps. Our hall worked together to catch them; it was teamwork.

—*LAUREN WEBSTER*
BARNARD COLLEGE, JUNIOR

LIVE IN A DORM and get the freshman experience. You don't have the amenities that you have in an apartment, but you have the experience; sharing the hall, sharing space with roommates.

—*JESSICA*
UNIVERSITY OF PENNSYLVANIA, JUNIOR

❝No matter how nice your R.A. is, don't date him. It always turns out to be a bad thing.❞

—*KYM*
SAN JOSE STATE UNIVERSITY, SOPHOMORE

I LIVED IN A CO-OP MY FIRST YEAR, so I wasn't pampered by the dorms. It's chaos 100 percent of the time, but it's worth it. It's about self-sufficiency. We don't go to the army after high school, like they do in Israel. Here we go to college, so here is where we need to learn independence, develop a thick skin, and learn how to balance life.

—*KATE LEFKOWITZ*
UNIVERSITY OF CALIFORNIA AT BERKELEY, JUNIOR

IF YOUR PARENTS LIVE LOCALLY, resist the temptation and the savings to live at home. I lived at home and it was a big mistake. There are two reasons. First is the commute: I missed an important quiz one day because I missed my bus, and it really cost me. It is a hassle to schlep back and forth. The second reason is the bonding: Most kids make their best friendships with kids who live in or around their dorm or frat. I missed that bonding and never made it up.

—*NAYEMA*
CARNEGIE MELLON UNIVERSITY, SOPHOMORE

. . . .

LEARNING TO LIVE WITH PEOPLE—even people you don't like—is an important skill to have.

—*MELISSA K. BYRNES*
AMHERST COLLEGE, GRADUATE

. . . .

I MADE MY CORE GROUP OF FRIENDS by living in the dorm freshman year. Relationships are based more on physical proximity than anything else, so most of your friends are probably going to come from your dorm.

—*CAITLIN BERBERICH*
UNIVERSITY OF GEORGIA, GRADUATE

. . . .

MY FRESHMAN YEAR WAS THE BEST YEAR of my life. Within two days of arriving I had made some of the best friends I've ever had. I lived in a freshman dorm, which I recommend very highly. Everyone is going through the same things you are, and they're all looking to make friends, so it makes for a tight-knit community. In the mixed dorms there are a lot of people who already have their friends, so they just aren't as outgoing.

—*T.P.*
STANFORD UNIVERSITY, SENIOR

Make sure you have good music coming out of your room since that's a good conversation starter.

—*B.K.*
CORNELL UNIVERSITY GRADUATE

Top 5
Best Dorms

Based on students' ranking of dorm comfort:

1. Loyola College in Maryland

2. Franklin W. Olin College of Engineering

3. Smith College

4. Scripps College

5. Bryn Mawr College

MAKE IT A POINT to get to know everyone on your floor at the dorm. Invite everyone to a weekly pre-dinner cocktail party. Play some icebreaker games so that everyone gets to know everyone else. Without their old high school cliques and social circles to fall back on, most people are truly eager to meet new people and make new connections. My dorm years were phenomenal, thanks to all my fantastic floor mates.

> —*LAURA WOLTER*
> *UNIVERSITY OF TEXAS AT AUSTIN, GRADUATE*

• • • • • • • •

DORM ROOMS AREN'T BAD—I mean, you just need to know how to organize your stuff. I don't have any problems, really. All my roommates get along, and there's no conflict. You know how guys are—we just go with the flow, there's nothing we need to agree on.

> —*JESSE SAFO*
> *GEORGIA STATE UNIVERSITY, FRESHMAN*

• • • • • • • •

ONE OF THE MOST IMPORTANT THINGS about surviving freshman year is that if you live in coed dorms like I did, you're going to see people in all states of life. You're going to see them on the can, you're going to see them before they've painted their face on, and you're going to have to get over the shock.

I've met long-term friends in the dorms. Everyone bonds in a totally different way when you live there. People go through difficult times—separation from family, separation from friends—and you all have that in common.

> —*ZACH FRIEND*
> *UNIVERSITY OF CALIFORNIA AT SANTA CRUZ, GRADUATE*

GIVE YOURSELF UP to the cabin fever that sometimes comes with dorm life. Never again will you have the opportunity to run around in your pajamas, darting into the open doors that line the halls. Once, when it was snowing, my roommate and I opened our door, blasted music, ran to every one of our friends' rooms, did a little dance, then moved on to the next. It's one of the goofiest memories I have of my freshman year.

—*ALLISON GRECO*
MONTCLAIR STATE UNIVERSITY, GRADUATE

• • • • • • • • •

WE WOULD ALWAYS play jokes on each other. We had a suite mate who had really bad vision. One time, my roommate took her glasses off when she was washing her face and she couldn't find them. She was panicking. But we got my roommate back by taking all her clothes and towels while she took a shower. And when she came out, we were waiting outside with a camera. She was pissed! She was not a good sport about it.

—*S.R.I.*
CORNELL UNIVERSITY, GRADUATE

• • • • • • • • •

DORM LIFE CAN HAVE A BAD REPUTATION, but don't knock it. Everyone should have the experience. We had a blast in the freshman dorms—we had a grill on the patio, so we'd barbecue at night sometimes, especially if the cafeteria food was creepy. It's a great way to meet people—and after this year you have the rest of your life to pay your own electric bill.

—*J.I.*
SONOMA STATE UNIVERSITY, JUNIOR

Bottom 5 Worst Dorms

Based on students' ranking of dorm comfort:

1. **United States Coast Guard Academy**

2. **University of Hawaii - Manoa**

3. **University of New Orleans**

4. **United States Merchant Marine Academy**

5. **University of Oregon**

Seek out the people on your floor who have installed bars in the bedrooms. They will be fun to hang out with.

—*AMY FORBES*
MISSISSIPPI STATE
UNIVERSITY
GRADUATE

ONE OF MY FRIENDS LIVED above a group of guys who would blare music until one or two in the morning. She would go down in her pajamas and ask them to turn the music down, but they never did. So one morning when she got up at six, she opened up her windows and blared country music until she could hear them stirring and cursing.

—*ANONYMOUS*
WESTERN WASHINGTON UNIVERSITY, GRADUATE

REACH OUT IMMEDIATELY to people living on your floor. It didn't thrill me to know that I would have to share a bathroom with 40 other girls. But I ended up having the most fun. Bonding with my roommates and floor mates, going to floor events, and even playing pranks were all memories to be cherished.

—*RAE LYNN RUCKER*
BIOLA UNIVERSITY, GRADUATE

TO BATTLE HOMESICKNESS:

1. Keep busy. Go to campus events.

2. Decorate your dorm room; that can definitely make it feel more homey. A comfy bed with lots of padding and sheets will be your best friend.

3. Call home. It's OK to call multiple times a day, especially when you just want to hear Mom or Dad's voice. I still do it as a sophomore.

By second semester, you'll be calling the dorms your home.

—*SHEILA CRAWFORD*
NORTH CAROLINA STATE UNIVERSITY, SOPHOMORE

FIVE REASONS WHY YOU SHOULD JOIN YOUR DORM COUNCIL

1. It's the fastest way to learn the names of everyone in your dorm.

2. You'll always have an excuse to talk to the cutie down the hall... "As your dorm representative, I just wanted to see if you had any requests or concerns concerning dorm life? Any requests at all?"

3. You can put it on your résumé.

4. Actually make dorm living conditions better!

5. It's one of the very few organized student activities you can participate in without putting on shoes.

GET A ROOM NEAR THE SHOWERS. My dorm was always so cold in the mornings, especially in the winter. I hated that long walk down the hall while I was practically naked.

—ANONYMOUS
YOUNGSTOWN STATE UNIVERSITY, SENIOR

KNOW YOUR SPACE before you pack up and arrive. One family came with a U-Haul full of stuff—a bed, desk, everything—and saw there was no room for any of it. They turned around and drove it right back home.

—*TOM SABRAM*
CARNEGIE MELLON UNIVERSITY, SOPHOMORE

• • • • • • • •

"You have to be conscious of everyone around you. And also, living in the dorm, everyone knows about everyone else. If you do something dumb, everyone knows about it."

—*MAUREEN SULLIVAN*
GEORGETOWN UNIVERSITY, SOPHOMORE

• • • • • • • •

RESPECT YOUR ROOMMATE and don't leave pizza in the room for a week. It's not your roommate's job to throw it out. The room stinks; it's not livable. People don't want to come in your room because it stinks. And don't try to blame the bad smell on the fact that your roommate's clothes are on the floor. That is not what's causing the nasty, rotten smell in your room. That would be the pizza box that you left there for a week.

—*ANONYMOUS*
UNIVERSITY OF VIRGINIA, SOPHOMORE

SET MONTHLY CLEANUP TIMES and stick to them. Failure to do so might result in an infestation of dust bunnies.

> —*KHALIL SULLIVAN*
> *PRINCETON UNIVERSITY, JUNIOR*

• • • • • • • • •

I LIVED IN A MIXED DORM my freshman year. I was sad because I wanted to live in an all-freshman dorm, but there were these two senior guys on my hall whom I became close with. It's wonderful because they graduated and they stayed in the Bay Area; if I ever have problems or want to talk about something, they're in the real world and have a little more perspective. They influenced what classes I took as a freshman and what major I picked. I think it's important to take advantage of those resources and not be afraid to seek them out and talk to them about classes and stuff. As a freshman I thought, "Oh my gosh, they're so much older than I am." I was so intimidated. But now, as I'm going into my senior year, I see it from the other side and I want people to come talk to me; if I could help somebody the way I was helped in my freshman year by upperclassmen, that would be awesome.

> —*JULIE TORRES*
> *STANFORD UNIVERSITY, SENIOR*

Don't be shy. Go up to people in your building and introduce yourself.

> —*KELLI*
> *UNIVERSITY OF DELAWARE SOPHOMORE*

UNUSUAL HOUSING OPTIONS

- Schiller International University (Florida) has university-owned and -operated hotels.
- Springfield College (Massachusetts) has an 81-acre "campground and outdoor adventure area".
- Southern Vermont College boasts a 27-room Edwardian mansion.
- Taylor University (Indiana) has a "NASA-approved clean room" for the neat freaks.

DECORATING TIPS: A WORLD OF INTERIORS

MAKE SURE TO TALK TO YOUR ROOMMATE to see what you need to bring and what you don't. I talked to my roommate before I moved in but we did not discuss everything and ended up having two phones, two answering machines, and then there were many things we forgot to bring so we had to go out and buy them. And, get a rug—it's a good investment for a dorm. The floors are usually dirty and a rug at least looks cleaner.

> —*E.M.G.*
> *University of South Florida, Junior*

• • • • • • • • •

GUYS, KEEP YOUR ROOMS CLEAN, because there will be girls in your room and they'll be turned off if you have disgusting rooms.

> —*Reid Attaway*
> *James Madison University, Sophomore*

IF YOU'RE GOING TO STEAL FURNITURE for your dorm room, steal it from the lounge. They won't find it until they spray for bugs over spring break—then you only have a few weeks of classes left anyway.

—*J.G.*
FLORIDA STATE UNIVERSITY, GRADUATE

. . . .

GO NUTS ON THE DECORATING. Be tacky, be shocking. This is the only time in your life you can get away with hanging a beer sign in your window or assembling a Buddha shrine in your bathroom. I actually had an Elvis shrine in my bathroom.

—*WENDY W.*
UNIVERSITY OF GEORGIA, GRADUATE

. . . .

SPEND TIME MAKING YOUR ROOM a place you would want to hang out in and study in. If you don't feel comfortable in your room, which is basically your college home, where are you going to feel comfortable?

—*JULIE*
PRINCETON UNIVERSITY, SOPHOMORE

MY DORM ROOM WAS WRECKED. It was an absolute mess. I chose a dorm room where we had our own bathroom; that was a huge mistake. It got destroyed. You have a roommate and you think, "Well, maybe I'll wait for him to clean it up." But it never happens. By the end of the year, I didn't even go in there.

—*JOHNNY*
GEORGETOWN UNIVERSITY, JUNIOR

• • • • • • • • •

WHEN I CAME TO SCHOOL, I KNEW NO ONE. I entered an all-male dorm and everyone thought we were dirty, stinky guys—and we were. With no girls around, there was no need to really focus on hygiene. But because we were so isolated, we bonded super tight and have great friendships for life. We have the last laugh: Now we can bathe, but the other folks don't have our strong friendships. All-male dorms are a good idea.

—*JUSTIN PEABODY*
CARNEGIE MELLON UNIVERSITY, JUNIOR

• • • • • • • • •

LEAVE THE DOOR OPEN to your dorm room. Prop it open with a chair if it won't stay open on its own. People will wander by, and if you're doing something fun—like watching a movie, playing a video game, or eating candy—they'll stop to see what's up. I met a lot of people this way.

—*LAUREN TAYLOR*
UNIVERSITY OF GEORGIA, GRADUATE

Talking to Strangers: Your Roommate & You

The gods smile upon you and you score a single dorm room. Privacy! Space! Peace and quiet! You're so lucky—or are you? Hear all that laughter and great music coming from the triple down the hall? That's where the fun is. That's where you're not.

And that's the roommate dilemma: On the one hand, cheek-by-jowl (or worse) with a total stranger (or worse); on the other hand, a passport to adventure! A best friend for life! With luck, sensitivity, and some negotiating, you can achieve that precious middle ground. And if not, well, just knock on the door of that triple down the hall; the party's still going on.

Some people make great friends, and some people make great roommates.

—YALDA A.
UNIVERSITY OF
CALIFORNIA AT
BERKELEY
GRADUATE

DON'T WORRY IF YOUR ROOMMATE is from a different world. I moved in with a gal from small-town Ontario, Canada, who had never met a Jewish person. When she found out I was Jewish, she asked me all sorts of funny questions. On one occasion, when I explained that Lay's potato chips were kosher, she worried that she'd be converting to Judaism by eating a bag! We never became close friends, but she was a perfect roommate for me. We kept the place clean, were respectful of each other's stuff, and had a perfectly nice relationship.

—A.S.
QUEENS UNIVERSITY, GRADUATE

• • • • • • • •

I'M IN A TRIPLE. What happens in a triple is that two people combine and go off together. And that's what happened with me; I'm the odd one out. But I don't feel bad about it because they're not my kind of people.

—AMY HOFFBERG
UNIVERSITY OF DELAWARE, FRESHMAN

• • • • • • • •

MAKING FRIENDS WAS MY NUMBER ONE worry before going to college. I'm incredibly shy; during orientation week, I didn't go to half the planned activities for my dorm. Before I knew it, everyone had settled into their own groups. One day I was talking to my mom about a bench-painting event going on at my dorm; she encouraged me to just go outside. So I did; by the end of the day, I had a dinner date with the girl who is now my closest friend. Talk to random people because you'll find something you have in common to bond over. With my friend Carrie it was a love for Cosmic Cantina chicken burritos.

—SAMANTHA STACH
DUKE UNIVERSITY, JUNIOR

DURING MY FRESHMAN YEAR I lived with an Orthodox Jew, a practicing Seventh-Day Adventist, and an atheist/agnostic. We survived— in a room made for two people, with four beds and four alarm clocks—by learning to leave G-d out of it!

> —BRIAN ROSEN
> PRINCETON UNIVERSITY, GRADUATE

Feel free to avoid your roommate if you need to.

> —JOHN BENTLEY
> TRINITY UNIVERSITY
> GRADUATE

• • • • • • • •

DON'T BE ROOMMATES with your old high-school friends because then you just bond together and you don't meet other people. But if you live with a new person she'll introduce you to a whole bunch of other aspects of life. She'll open you up to a whole world you wouldn't have expected. It worked for me. It was a good experience with my roommate and I learned a lot.

> —KYM
> SAN JOSE STATE UNIVERSITY, SOPHOMORE

• • • • • • • • •

YOUR ROOMMATE IS THE FIRST PERSON you really get to know. After going to bed, my roommate and I would talk for about 45 minutes about the most random things. It's the person you meet first and know the best first. You branch out from there and get to know the whole floor.

> —BRYAN
> GEORGETOWN UNIVERSITY, SOPHOMORE

• • • • • • • • •

I LOVE MY ROOMMATE. She's my closest friend here. We talked the day after we got the rooming information and we clicked on the phone. Don't come on too strong with your roommate, and don't think you have to be friends right away. But if you do, that's great.

> —M.D.
> BOSTON COLLEGE, FRESHMAN

HEADLINES
Best Advice and Top Tips

- Be honest on your roommate form or you may end up with someone you don't get along with.
- Don't live with your high school friends if you're at the same school; meet new people.
- If you and your roommate are at odds, don't be afraid to request a room change.
- Having a roommate you click with can be the best part of college life.

IF YOU HAVE A ROOMMATE WHO'S PSYCHO, don't be afraid to leave. Just go to the R.A. and get reassigned. It's a hassle, but it's better than living with a psycho.

—*S.G.*
COLUMBIA UNIVERSITY, SENIOR

• • • • • • • •

YOU CAN BE INDIFFERENT TO PEOPLE you pass on your walks around campus, but if you're indifferent to your roommate, silence turns into coldness, and coldness turns into animosity, which might turn into hatred. So continue to cultivate your relationship with your roommates. Also, if you know that you are a naturally introverted person, go for a single. Many upperclassmen choose to have singles, so they must know something.

—*SEAN CAMERON*
PRINCETON UNIVERSITY, SOPHOMORE

BE REALLY HONEST ON YOUR ROOMMATE FORM or you might end up with somebody you don't get along with. It's hard to share your personal space with someone else. The space tends to be really small.

—*RUTH FEINBLUM*
BRYN MAWR COLLEGE, JUNIOR

• • • • • • • •

FRESHMAN YEAR WAS CRAZY. It was tough to get adjusted to school life; there was a lot of partying and a lot of girls. Just say no—to everything. And if your roommate can't say no, change roommates. My roommate couldn't say no, and I couldn't say no; we just played off each other. It wasn't good.

—*KENTON*
UNIVERSITY OF VIRGINIA, SENIOR

• • • • • • • •

MY FIRST ROOMMATE HAD MADE OTHER PLANS. But I got a new roommate, and it was a great experience. Sometimes you click and get along with someone. We didn't argue, and we had a lot of fun. We each had our own separate lives; our boyfriends got along. It was a great roommate setup. The lesson: If your first roommate doesn't work out for whatever reason, there's probably someone else out there who will become one of your best friends.

—*GINGER M. BRODTMAN*
SPRING HILL COLLEGE, GRADUATE

• • • • • • • •

CHECK UNDER YOUR ROOMMATE'S BED for old, moldy food. For two weeks our room completely stunk. People were avoiding my room and I was wondering, "What's going on?" I never thought to look under my roommate's bed. When I did I found an old can of salsa and moldy bread.

—*SIERRA*
CAL POLY SAN LUIS OBISPO, JUNIOR

When in doubt, put on a movie and watch it with your roommates. It promotes bonding and seems to make any problems fade away.

—*RAE LYNN RUCKER*
BIOLA UNIVERSITY
GRADUATE

TRUE TO FORM

Hope for the best, but expect the worst. When I moved into the dorms, I was expecting that the college would pair me up with someone who shared my interests, and who would become my new best friend. Boy, was I in for a surprise! I had *five* other roommates:

- A slightly overweight girl from San Diego who was some kind of singer. She would sing constantly . . . and I mean *constantly*. She was extremely bossy, annoying, and required a lot of attention.

- A Goth lesbian. She would sit on the patio, smoke a pack of cigarettes an hour, and cry about how some girl had screwed her over.

- A girl who wore black lipstick and drawn-in eyebrows. We only saw her when she answered the door for her homeys (who all looked like they belonged on the streets of L.A.), and then they would lock themselves in her room and smoke pot for days on end.

- An Asian girl who told her father she was living in the dorms, but was actually living with her boyfriend. I think I saw her six times in the whole year (one of those times, she asked to borrow a pair of my underwear!).

- And Julia. She was the roommate I needed. She was like me and she became my best friend.

Ultimately, I learned to accept people for who they are; you will find that there is something to love about each of them. My roommates opened my eyes (and heart) to diversity.

—HEATHER POLLOCK
CALIFORNIA STATE UNIVERSITY, GRADUATE

I LIVED WITH MY BEST FRIEND and it was the worst thing I did my freshman year. We didn't speak for a year after that. It was like a competition, rather than a partnership, always seeing who could make plans to do something cool, seeing how high the dishes could stack up. At first, we did everything together, but then learned we didn't like each other's company that much and almost never talked. That's not easy when you live with someone. When the year was finally over, it was a relief. We'd had enough of each other; there was no reason to hang out.

—*IRVING BURNS RAMSOWER III*
UNIVERSITY OF FLORIDA, GRADUATE

* * * * * * * *

"If your roommate is not good— for instance, if the person steals your food, throws dirty laundry on your bed, etc.—get out as soon as possible because your life will be hell. And it's easy to do that, too; just go to your R.A."

—*K.*
NORTHWESTERN UNIVERSITY, GRADUATE

* * * * * * * *

THE WORST THING THAT HAPPENED with my roommate: She decided to tap dance at 7 a.m. to get back at me because I kept her up at night.

—*MELANIE*
PENNSYLVANIA STATE UNIVERSITY, SOPHOMORE

THE ROOMMATE-SELECTION SURVEYS never ask questions that are meaningful enough to give you insight into how it's really going to be like to live with someone. So just expect the unexpected and get ready to be flexible. According to the survey, my freshman-year roommate appeared to be a conservative who liked country music. She turned out to be a very dynamic and wild gal who kept me laughing throughout the year.

—*K. HARMA*
WESTERN WASHINGTON UNIVERSITY, GRADUATE

I HAD A ROOMMATE who had sex in the room while I was sleeping. I thought they were just lying there; I would hear whispering and I thought they were just talking. Nope, they were porking. They told me later, when they were drunk. That's all right though, I'm OK with that.

—*SEIJI YAMAMOTO*
STANFORD UNIVERSITY, GRADUATE

DON'T LET PEOPLE'S FLAWS get to you so hard. Everyone has flaws. If your roommate is messy, discuss it. One friend's roommate was a total slob. She would make macaroni and cheese, eat half of it, and let the other half sit for a week. I saw lemon juice curdle in her room. It was gross!

—*KEISHA*
EMORY UNIVERSITY, SENIOR

MY ROOMMATE THINKS I'm messy and I think she's too neat. We argue over that. And we have a division going down the middle of the room; her stuff on one side and mine on the other.

—*WHITNEY*
YALE UNIVERSITY, FRESHMAN

I HAD A ROOMMATE WHO SNORED and I had to go to the study lounge to sleep. I would take my blanket and comforter and sleep on a couch or chair at two in the morning. I got out the second semester. I didn't have the heart to tell him. Other than the snoring, we got along great.

—RICK SHILLING
PENNSYLVANIA STATE UNIVERSITY, GRADUATE

- - - - - - - -

"Set up ground rules with your roommate. I walked in on my roommate and her boyfriend having sex in the middle of our floor. Another time, they did it in the room when they thought I was asleep. Not cool!"

—CHAVON MITCHELL
XAVIER UNIVERSITY, GRADUATE

- - - - - - - -

I WOULD ARGUE with my roommate. She would tell me that I'm an obsessive-compulsive and she couldn't deal with it anymore. And I would be like, "What are you talking about, you psycho." So, I spent a lot of time in the library, which is a good thing.

—S.
UNIVERSITY OF VIRGINIA, SOPHOMORE

ASK THE ADVISOR

I'm having a few problems, and not just with my classes. It's not like I can't handle it, but it would be nice to just talk to someone and not have them tell me all the things I should be doing differently.

The staff at the counseling center are trained to listen, and not to tell you what to do. You are an adult, and can make your own decisions, but sometimes it helps to talk through your experiences with someone objective. Counseling sessions are confidential, so you can be upfront and honest about whatever's on your mind without worrying about it getting back to your professors, your friends, or your family.

IN ORDER TO DEAL WITH MY ROOMMATE and the guy with whom she was cheating on her boyfriend, I found ways to vent my frustration, like blow-drying my hair in the middle of the room at 8 a.m. while they were still asleep, or coming back to the room unexpectedly to catch them at awkward times. These things were pretty harmless but they made me feel somewhat better.

—*ALLISON GRECO*
MONTCLAIR STATE UNIVERSITY, GRADUATE

THE SCHOOL ASSIGNED ME A ROOMMATE, and we didn't get along at all. She was completely my opposite—she smoked, she swore, she was messy. It was very uncomfortable anytime we were in the room together. Eventually we avoided that situation, except to sleep. As soon as the semester was over she asked for a transfer, and I was never happier.

> —*JENNY PRISUTA*
> *YOUNGSTOWN STATE UNIVERSITY, SENIOR*

• • • • • • • •

SCHEDULE MONTHLY OUTINGS with all of your roommates. And if you pay the bill, that really messy roommate might make an effort to clean up after himself every now and then.

> —*KHALIL SULLIVAN*
> *PRINCETON UNIVERSITY, JUNIOR*

• • • • • • • •

DON'T BRING ANY preconceived notions about what your roommate will be like. You might be disappointed, or you might go into the situation not being as open as you could when you realize the person is completely different than you imagined.

> —*DANIELLE*
> *DUKE UNIVERSITY, GRADUATE*

• • • • • • • •

MY ROOMMATE AND I TALKED via e-mail before we came to school. We realized we had a lot in common. We both play guitar and we were both bringing acoustic guitars. Then we got here and we realized we both have completely different tastes in music. But we get along really well. We compromise really well. If it's time to clean the room, we don't fight about it. One of us volunteers and it gets done.

> —*REID ATTAWAY*
> *JAMES MADISON UNIVERSITY, FRESHMAN*

I have a terrible roommate. He plays video games all the time. He stays up until six in the morning. Needless to say, I lose a lot of sleep.

—*ANONYMOUS*
ST. JOHN'S UNIVERSITY FRESHMAN

IN ORDER TO SURVIVE YOUR ROOMMATES, you have to be friendly and considerate. If you are nice, you will get treated the same way (and if you don't, then you have a reason to be treated like a jerk). Some people like living alone in singles, but I enjoy a crowd. Sure, it makes hooking up tricky (and hilarious) sometimes, but it also expands your social circle, and gives you lifelong friends—or enemies! It all depends on what kind of person you are.

—*PETE*
PRINCETON UNIVERSITY, SOPHOMORE

• • • • • • • •

“ “I talked to my roommate on the phone and I was totally convinced that I wasn't going to like her. She sounded like a person who was very different from me, but now she's one of my best friends. ” ”

—*LAUREN*
GEORGETOWN UNIVERSITY, SOPHOMORE

• • • • • • • •

MY ROOMMATE AND I have a big difference in music tastes. I listen to rock and alternative, and she listens to this really bad R&B all the time. Whoever gets to the room first gets to choose the radio; sometimes it's a dash from class back to the room.

—*ANONYMOUS*
YALE UNIVERSITY, SOPHOMORE

I WALKED INTO MY ROOM for the first time freshman year to see that my roommate had decorated my side of the room with posters, a hanging thing over my bed, and the quote "G-d is dead" on the eraser board. That night I took everything down because I wanted to put up my own stuff. That was the start of our amazing roommate relationship. Oh, and the fact that her boyfriend lived in my room. My survival was pledging a sorority, so I was never there.

—*M.*
AMERICAN UNIVERSITY, FRESHMAN

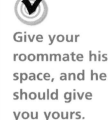

Give your roommate his space, and he should give you yours.

—*DANIEL RUSK*
UNIVERSITY OF MARYLAND
SOPHOMORE

FIVE THINGS NOT TO SAY TO YOUR ROOMMATE

1. "I just know we're going to be best friends." (Pressure!)

2. "Sure, I don't mind if your boyfriend/girlfriend sleeps here." (You'll regret it later.)

3. "We're so alike ... do you mind if I tell people we're twins?" (Creepy!)

4. "Borrow whatever you want." (Don't say it if you don't really mean it.)

5. "You want to major in WHAT?"

I WOULDN'T WANT TO GO BACK to the living conditions I was in freshman year. You can learn a lot, but it's aggravating when you have to deal with someone who doesn't blend with your personality. For instance, I'm not real neat, but my roommate freshman year was a real neat freak. We had our problems there. Don't bend over backwards for your roommate, but there are sacrifices you have to make. When you say "compromise," it sounds like you have to lose something to make the other person happy. Instead, you find a way to make it a win-win situation.

> —BRIAN
> JAMES MADISON UNIVERSITY, JUNIOR

WHEN I STARTED COLLEGE, I was under the impression that a roommate was a temporary assignment, much like weeklong summer camps. However, after a few weeks of living with the most miserable person ever imagined, I came to realize that he didn't seem to be going away. In college it's important to be comfortable with your living arrangements: If you're unhappy, tell someone.

> —ANONYMOUS

I'VE ALWAYS BEEN SOMETHING OF A MAMA'S BOY. She was always great about picking up after me and everything. By the end of my fall quarter, my room looked like a hurricane had come through and then came through again. It was God-awful; it was a nasty pigsty. My roommate was a neat freak, but he was pretty cool with it.

> —F.
> STANFORD UNIVERSITY, SOPHOMORE

NEAT NERDS WELCOME

My roommate smoked Dunhills all day. There were piles of ashes under his bed; it was disgusting. He left stuff strewn about, so I was always kicking stuff back to his side of the room. At first appearance he seemed cool, like someone I would get along with. He was a wrestler, really into writing, but he was a dud and really unmotivated to do well—or do anything—in school. I tried not to confront him, but there were times when he'd be up late—making noise or smoking—and I was the one who would be getting up for class in the morning. I do recall one run-in, where there was a little pushing involved. Beware of kids who taunt you and don't respect your privacy. You may not appreciate it on day one, but you'll be happy with a soft-spoken, class-attending roommate. It's tough to find someone in sync with you. You may think you want to room with someone who on paper appears to be like you, but it could be misery living with him or her.

—J.
COLUMBIA UNIVERSITY, GRADUATE

USE YOUR INGENUITY to get a good roommate. When you are listing what you are like in the application for roommates, be honest. I know a guy who pretended to be a "stay in and study" kind of guy, and he got stuck with a roomie who never left the room and had a sleeping disorder. If he had been honest and said he liked to party, this would not have happened. If you get a bad roommate, get out of it before it gets worse. The longer you wait, the harder it is.

—*JUDSON KROH*
CARNEGIE MELLON UNIVERSITY, JUNIOR

• • • • • • • •

I WAS TOLD I would have just one roommate my freshman year. Little did I know I'd have a permanent visitor: my roommate's boyfriend. He was like "the guy on the couch"; he would stay Friday to Wednesday, always on the couch, on my computer, or even on my bed when I came home from class. Although I was open to guests, I had to tell my roommate I was sick of having a dude in my space all the time. It didn't go down well. Soon she moved down the hall into a single; she set up her very own love nest.

—*LISA G.*
NEW YORK UNIVERSITY, JUNIOR

• • • • • • • •

THE OTHER DAY, my roommate asked me to leave the room. I asked why. He said, "You know." He wanted to be alone, if you know what I mean. So I left, for like an hour. That's one of the things you have to put up with when you have a roommate.

—*C.*
COLUMBIA UNIVERSITY, JUNIOR

DON'T LET THINGS THAT BOTHER YOU linger too long. My friend went out with a guy that I had been seeing. That hurt my feelings. Instead of resolving the problem immediately, I waited until I was too angry to discuss it like a rational adult. I learned later that she honestly never intended to hurt me. But since I waited until I was furious, her feelings got hurt and she never got over it. Our friendship never fully recovered.

—*ERIN*
CENTRAL BIBLE COLLEGE, GRADUATE

• • • • • • • •

MY ROOMMATE IS MY TWIN SISTER. I get along with her. We know how to live together; my sister does the laundry and I clean the room.

—*MANI*
UNIVERSITY OF MARYLAND, FRESHMAN

Freshmen, realize that you're going to spend enough time with your roommates anyway, so it's not necessary that they come with you wherever you go.

—*ANONYMOUS*
UNIVERSITY OF VIRGINIA SOPHOMORE

LESSON: TALK ABOUT IT

My roommate was a very sweet girl, but she had the most bizarre sleep schedule and work schedule ever. We lived in a one-room double, and she liked to go to bed at 5 a.m. and then wake up at 8 a.m. and do more work. Then she would go to class until 3 p.m. and then sleep in our room until 9 p.m. I felt like I could never enter the room without disturbing her. I let it bother me for a lot longer than I should have: I didn't say to her, early on, "Can you do your work somewhere else at four in the morning?" As soon as I did talk to her about it she was really understanding.

—*MACKENZIE LUZZI*
PRINCETON UNIVERSITY, SOPHOMORE

Become good friends with your R.A. He or she could be nice, and may one day help you lock your horrible roommate into the room with pennies.

—ANONYMOUS
MICHIGAN
TECHNOLOGICAL
UNIVERSITY
GRADUATE

MY ROOMMATES WERE ALL from the deep South. One of them was the daughter of an Episcopalian minister. We got into some clashes. She told me that I was going to hell, in all seriousness. She was concerned for my soul. So, I didn't have anyone to talk to about that. But other than that it was fine. I had some friends who went to a bigger college nearby, and I would drive an hour and a half to hang out with them there.

—HANNAH SMITH
HARVARD UNIVERSITY, JUNIOR

• • • • • • • •

MY ROOMMATE CAME with one bag to school, he didn't have any sheets for his bed, and he had this long beard that he used to cut in the sink and it got everywhere. He was a wreck. He couldn't be more different from me and the other guys in our suite. I tried to be friends with him, but it became clear that we were opposite personalities. So we agreed to disagree. He wasn't so bad that I couldn't live there, but I spent a lot of time out with my friends and every once in a while showed up there to sleep.

—JOHN BENTLEY
TRINITY UNIVERSITY, GRADUATE

• • • • • • • •

I HAD ARRANGED TO BE ROOMMATES with a high school friend—and the adage that you don't know someone until you live with them really applies. They may do things that you find bothersome, and if you weren't living with them, these characteristics may not have been revealed. So I recommend not rooming with someone you've known previously.

—YALDA A.
UNIVERSITY OF CALIFORNIA AT BERKELEY, GRADUATE

SOME PEOPLE THINK IT'S BETTER to live with someone who's just like them. But I learned that's not always the case. During my freshman year, I was paired with someone who was like me: a "clean freak." We got along fine, but surprisingly enough, we never became close friends. After she moved out at the end of the first semester, I moved in with Veronica. I knew she was a little more cluttered and messy than I was, but we became best friends. She is easy to talk to, and living together was a blessing.

—*EMILY TUCK*
CALIFORNIA STATE UNIVERSITY, GRADUATE

ONE OF MY ROOMMATES was very conservative, very traditional. The other was this vegan lesbian. They were both wonderful people, but it was interesting to be occasionally mediating between the two.

—*MELISSA K. BYRNES*
AMHERST COLLEGE, GRADUATE

FIND OUT WHO YOUR ROOMMATE IS before you come—and check him out. If he is not a good fit, get out of it. If you complain loud enough, they will swap him for you. This is great advice.

—*DEREK LI*
CARNEGIE MELLON UNIVERSITY, JUNIOR

IT'S HARD BEING SICK WITH A ROOMMATE. You have to share this really small space. I once had this health-nut roommate who was a germophobe. That was really bad. Every time I got sick, she would open doors with a Kleenex. What was I supposed to do? I couldn't go home.

—*KAIT DUNTON*
UNIVERSITY OF VIRGINIA, JUNIOR

DON'T GET "SEX-ILED"; set ground rules with your roommate right away. One month into freshman year, my roommate's 26-year-old boyfriend moved in, and I found myself sex-iled for an entire week. When I tried to get into my room to get some books, it was locked. These kinds of situations can be avoided by talking about the possibility in advance.

　　　　　—LAURA TRUBIANO
　　　　　　HAMILTON COLLEGE, JUNIOR

I WENT FROM NEVER HAVING TO SHARE anything in my whole life, including my bedroom, to moving into a triple with two girls who were my complete opposite. How did I manage to survive? Flexibility and compromise.

　　　　　—RAE LYNN RUCKER
　　　　　　BIOLA UNIVERSITY, GRADUATE

LEARN HOW TO SLEEP THROUGH ALARMS. My roommate got up every morning at five o'clock to go to basketball practice. Her alarm woke me every morning for a good two months. Get some sort of system, where you put a pillow over your head, and then you take the pillow off after your roommate leaves so you can hear your own alarm.

　　　　　—CATE
　　　　　　BROWN UNIVERSITY, JUNIOR

WE HAD A BAD ROOMMATE THE FIRST YEAR. He was really unstable; he would go from loving us one minute to hating us the next. He was really inconsiderate to our neighbors and friends. After a couple of months, we had to go to the building director and have him thrown out.

　　　　　—PAUL HEITHOFF
　　　　　　GEORGE WASHINGTON UNIVERSITY, SOPHOMORE

My Face, Our Space: Social Networking & Online Communities

As the students in this chapter will tell you, *MySpace* and *Facebook* are great—in moderation. They're powerful tools for fun and making positive connections, especially if they lead to real-world interaction and don't replace it entirely. (You'll know you've gone too far if you forget what to do when you meet that cute sophomore in the bookstore line, or if "dinner with friends" starts to mean carrying takeout food to your computer desk.) After all, a tool is only as good as its user. As Sir Roger L'Estrange said so poetically: "It is with our passions as it is with fire and water; they are good servants, but bad masters." Sure, this was three centuries before the Internet, but Sir Roger really knew his stuff. Read on for some 21st-century wisdom.

I USE FACEBOOK to see how high school friends are doing during the year and how college friends are doing during the summer. I look at people's pictures and walls most often. I'm happy enough with that; it can be a huge time sink, so I don't spend more than an hour or two a week on it.

—AMANDA
WELLESLEY COLLEGE, SENIOR

• • • • • • • •

" Facebook has become as much a part of the college experience as beer and books. Heck, people probably spend more time with Facebook than they do with the other two combined. "

—ANONYMOUS
WASHINGTON AND LEE UNIVERSITY, JUNIOR

• • • • • • • •

THE BEST BENEFIT ABOUT FACEBOOK is being able to reconnect with people you haven't seen in a long time. But I would tell freshmen to think about where they want to be ten years from now and try to evaluate what you put up on your Facebook profile based on that. If you are trying to go into law or politics, and you have a scandalous picture up, someone could copy it, paste it, and save it for later.

—J.M.G.
DUKE UNIVERSITY, GRADUATE

Oh, Facebook: It's like globalization on the college level.

—MEREDITH
BROWN UNIVERSITY
SOPHOMORE

FACEBOOK 101

This sounds kind of weird, but I think being able to "friend" people on Facebook and learn a little bit about them gave me more confidence to approach them in person and hang out. When I first got my college e-mail address before my freshman year, I was able to register for Facebook and see who some of my future classmates would be. I felt kind of timid at first, but soon I got friended by a few people and I started friending some myself. Once we got to campus, I was able to meet some of them and start non-awkward conversations ("Hi, um ... you're in this class?"). I think Facebook is an excellent networking tool for freshmen, especially those who are worried that they won't know anyone when they arrive. I'd encourage incoming freshmen to not be afraid to friend (but not stalk) other incoming freshmen, if they can find even one thing in common with them—for instance, the same residential college, or the same prospective major. The worst that can happen is that the friend request will be denied. In that case, they can always try again once they meet that person face-to-face.

—EMILIA
RICE UNIVERSITY, JUNIOR

IT'S EASY TO GO ON FACEBOOK and start looking at pictures and writing on walls. I just make it a policy not to do it while involved with academic work. And you can have it set up so that you get an e-mail every time your Facebook page changes—every time someone posts a picture of you, someone writes on your wall, or sends you a message—and I took all those options off.

—JOSH
PRINCETON UNIVERSITY, SENIOR

HEADLINES
Best Advice and Top Tips

- Facebook and MySpace can be a great way to begin to meet people, but follow up soon with person-to-person encounters.

- Don't post information about yourself that could be viewed negatively, even though you have some control over who will see your photos and details.

- It's easy to misjudge people when all you have to go by are their Facebook or MySpace pages.

Try to have a variety of pictures rather than one where you look exactly the same in 300 different poses.
—RON Y. KAGAN
CUNY/MACAULAY
HONORS COLLEGE
SENIOR

YOU DON'T NEED TO put all of your contact information on your Facebook page. There are people who put their phone numbers, addresses, e-mail address and IMs. Your phone number and your address is way too much information. Your friends know where they can find you.
—ANONYMOUS
DUKE UNIVERSITY, GRADUATE

COMPARED TO MY FRIENDS, I am not a Facebook addict. Some people are on it 24/7. I use it to keep in touch with old friends. I also notice that you get a lot of random Facebook invitations from random people. I don't recommend sending random invitations to people unless you're willing to get to know them.
—MORGAN
COLUMBIA UNIVERSITY, FRESHMAN

TOP FIVE IMAGES/ ACTIVITIES *NOT* TO SHOWCASE IN YOUR PROFILE

1. Drugs

2. Alcohol, even if you're 21

3. Destroying or "improving" university property

4. Anything naked, sexual, or both

5. Yourself with half your face in light and the other half in darkness—it's not illegal or against school rules, but you'll look just like the other 10 million people doing the same dumb thing.

SOMETIMES YOU MEET A PERSON, talk with him online, and become good friends; then you meet in person and you wished you'd kept it online. The awkwardness factor is pretty big when you meet people through sites like Facebook. I don't usually interact with people online unless they had some other real-world connection to me already.

—*TERRY*
DUKE UNIVERSITY, SOPHOMORE

Use your privacy settings.

—*MICHAEL*
　NORTHWESTERN
　UNIVERSITY
　SOPHOMORE

A LOT OF PEOPLE THINK that "untagging" themselves in pictures will ensure that people won't see those pictures and connect them to whatever they're doing in them. But actually they have a lot more control over who sees the picture if they allow themselves to be tagged and just adjust the viewer settings on it. Many people are worried about future employers seeing certain pictures, but it's a better idea to claim the picture and exercise control over it.

—*SARAH*
　WELLESLEY COLLEGE, SOPHOMORE

• • • • • • • •

66 It's good to avoid half-naked pictures and full body shots. Generally, a nice close-up of your beautiful face is best! 99

—*STEPHANIE LEIGH DOCKERY*
　WILLIAMS COLLEGE, GRADUATE

• • • • • • • •

THE IDEA THAT A RELATIONSHIP is "official" when it's listed on Facebook is totally ridiculous. It's led to a fight with my last girlfriend and a confrontation with the friends of a girl before that. It's totally ridiculous but its part of college life; it's unavoidable. My friend who is just starting college couldn't find his new roommate on Facebook and now is worried that the guy's a social recluse, just because he's not on a Web site.

—*ANONYMOUS*
　WASHINGTON AND LEE UNIVERSITY, JUNIOR

AVOID PUTTING UP ANY PICTURES that you would not want your grandmother to see. Freshmen should do their best to untag pictures that portray possibly incriminating activities, such as underage drinking. You never know who can look at your profile.

—*KAMALI BENT*
CORNELL UNIVERSITY, GRADUATE

· · · · · · · ·

"Putting your telephone number, your address, your relationship status, pics of yourself with cups in your hand (or 150 pictures of yourself, in general) is *way* too much information to put on Facebook."

—*DANIELLE*
DUKE UNIVERSITY, GRADUATE

· · · · · · · ·

THE KEY TO BEING POPULAR on Facebook is having lots of friends who are on the site, and also remaining active yourself. If you're posting on ten "walls" each day, you're bound to receive lots of wall posts yourself. It goes the same for messages and pokes.

—*GERALDINE SARAH COWPER*
CUNY/MACAULAY HONORS COLLEGE, SENIOR

FACEBOOK AND MYSPACE are great tools for meeting new people and learning about different organizations. However, it is a tool that is provided through the Internet, and should therefore be utilized with caution. Avoid pictures that put your character in question. Many university administrators and outside companies have Facebook and MySpace accounts. Such pictures can prevent you from getting a job or becoming part of a certain organization of interest at school.

> —SIMORE EDWANNA AFAMEFUNA
> UNIVERSITY OF MIAMI, JUNIOR

• • • • • • • •

WHEN I FIRST GOT INTO COLLEGE and found out who my roommate was, I looked him up on Facebook. All of his pictures were sketchy; I didn't know what his deal was. He was always wearing some sort of flower crown and frolicking with girls. I thought, "This will make for an interesting year." I definitely judged him, which probably wasn't the best thing to do, because he ended up being nothing like his Facebook pictures. He's now one of my best friends. I wouldn't judge anybody by their Facebook pictures, because a lot of people don't put enough thought into them to give a good first impression.

> —DAN AMERMAN
> YALE UNIVERSITY, SOPHOMORE

• • • • • • • •

I DO NOT USE ANY OTHER social networking site besides Facebook. When I was in a band we used MySpace to promote our music, which was useful, but that was it.

> —JACOB
> UNIVERSITY OF MARYLAND
> SOPHOMORE

Extracurriculars: Clubs,Organizations & More

So many clubs, so little time! Most college graduates will tell you they wish they'd done more extracurriculars during their four years. Those years will go by in a flash, so if you see a group you want to join, don't wait till next semester. Think big, think broad, think quirky: There's Dumbledore's Army for Harry Potter fanatics, a fencing team, singing groups, community service clubs—one of these groups is just waiting to give you the best experience and best friends of your college years. Sign up for everything. If, later on, you find yourself with too many things to do, you can always cut back.

EVERYONE HAS TO FIND SOMETHING: it can be just watching a movie on a Tuesday night, hanging out in the hall with friends at 2 a.m., a weekly yoga class, or just reading a book for fun. But you need something outside of schoolwork and the party scene or else you just run out of steam before each semester ends.

—SAMANTHA STACH
DUKE UNIVERSITY, JUNIOR

• • • • • • • •

I TOOK A DIFFERENT APPROACH to extracurricular activities and decided to intern instead. I started interning freshman year. But I found it better to spend my time with a few activities that are very important to me, rather than spread myself thin trying to build my résumé.

—GERALDINE SARAH COWPER
CUNY/MACAULAY HONORS COLLEGE, SENIOR

Go meet new people; they won't bite!

—JANELLE
UNIVERSITY OF
GEORGIA, JUNIOR

• • • • • • • •

WHEN I WAS IN HIGH SCHOOL, I was involved in everything. College is at a high level so you have to narrow it down. My favorite things in high school were theater and singing, so I just concentrated on those two things when I came to college. Pick what you enjoy and put your all into it.

—DAN AMERMAN
YALE UNIVERSITY, SOPHOMORE

• • • • • • • •

ONE GREAT THING about joining everything freshman year—I still get random e-mails from, say, the Korean Society or the Indian Students Organization, inviting me to their open houses. So I can go and have all sorts of wonderful free dinners. I have a friend who managed to spend only $14 on food for a whole week!

—DENALI
PRINCETON UNIVERSITY, JUNIOR

ASK THE ADVISOR

I hear people talking about extracurricular activities, and other people talking about co-curriculars. What's the difference?

Guess what — there is no difference! A few years ago, we student-affairs advisors started using the term "co-curricular activities" instead of "extracurricular activities" in order to underscore the importance of the learning you do *outside* the classroom. The prefix "extra" means that something is, well, extra: not equal; more. Although your classes are of vital importance, editing your college newspaper or running a tutoring program for local school children may be just as important in developing your intellect and professional skills.

I WAS PART OF MY SCHOOL'S Sustainable Food Initiative, which was building an urban garden. During my second semester at school, I spent a lot of time hauling rocks out of dirt. Those less masochistically inclined will probably find that there are lots of easier ways to become involved in environmental issues on campus.

—*MOLLY*
BROWN UNIVERSITY, SOPHOMORE

HEADLINES
Best Advice and Top Tips

- Clubs are a great way to network with other people.
- Extracurriculars are also a good way to try out something new.
- Organizations in your area of academic interest may even offer scholarships.
- It's your free time, so make sure you're having fun.

THE RIGHT CLUB for each freshman depends on the student and his/her interests. For me, and for many other African American students at the University of Miami, the best organization to join was United Black Students. At other colleges, the organization may be referred to as the Black Student Union. It is one of largest student organizations on campus. In addition, despite its name, it is open to all students of different races. Other great organizations include the Inspirational Concert Choir, Yellow Rose (a service organization for women) and BOND (the male version of the previous). All of these organizations can be an asset to freshmen adjusting to campus life.

—*SIMORE EDWANNA AFAMEFUNA*
UNIVERSITY OF MIAMI, JUNIOR

• • • • • • • •

BECAUSE I'M JEWISH I joined Hillel House. I love the activities that they do, such as visiting soup kitchens and organizing meetings where they bring in a speaker. I am going to join them on their trip to New Orleans for Habitat for Humanities.

—*CAROL*
HUNTER COLLEGE, FRESHMAN

I'M GAY. My college has a queer student union; their meetings take place every week, with typically 30 in attendance. Another organization, Queer Allied and Activism, discusses LGBT issues, and we try to implement actions to try and improve our community. This is definitely the more political organization, whereas the first is geared more towards social mixing, where hooking up is quite common. Some others prefer the "hooking up" scene.

—*ANONYMOUS*
UNIVERSITY OF VIRGINIA, JUNIOR

▪ ▪ ▪ ▪ ▪ ▪ ▪ ▪

" There is a Howling at the Moon Club at Mt. Holyoke; when it is a full moon, you can hear them all over campus. "

—*RUTHANN*
MOUNT HOLYOKE COLLEGE, GRADUATE

▪ ▪ ▪ ▪ ▪ ▪ ▪ ▪

MY FRESHMAN YEAR at George Washington was a lonely experience. I didn't really know anyone on my first floor. But the more I talked to other freshmen, the more I realized there was opportunity to network with other people. I got involved with a bible group on campus; it was an amazing time of sharing the bible, meeting people who cared, and singing songs. It was a beautiful experience.

—*MICHAEL CHOE*
GEORGE WASHINGTON UNIVERSITY, GRADUATE

CHANGING THE WORLD

I'M EXTREMELY CONCERNED with Americans' sense of sustainability. I fear that older generations have completely failed us by creating a society where a $10 gallon of gas will crush the economy. Living in Atlanta is a study on how not to plan a city with the future in mind. Americans need to reevaluate their desires to ensure that our society remains sustainable. Hopefully my college education will not only enable me to live a sustainable lifestyle, but also allow me to influence others to do the same.

—*ALEX*
EMORY UNIVERSITY, SOPHOMORE

· · · · · · · · ·

THE BEST CLUBS AND ORGANIZATIONS to join on campus (outside of Greek life) are those that involve volunteering. It is a way to help others and to get to know your community at the same time. Sometimes it's easy to forget that your college/university does not exist in its own bubble. There are people, places and spaces that exist outside your classroom and dorm walls. Go out and explore. It will make you a more in-tune person in the end.

—*A.F.K.*
DUKE UNIVERSITY, GRADUATE

· · · · · · · · ·

I HAVE ALWAYS TRIED TO LIVE by the quote by Gandhi, "Be the change you wish to see in the world." At this point in my life I am still unsure about what to do or what my main purpose is. In fact, I am now doing my ninth internship since beginning college and still have no idea. All I can do at this moment is live in a polite, friendly manner and be compassionate towards my peers in life. I really do think it is the little things that count.

—*GERALDINE SARAH COWPER*
CUNY/MACAULAY HONORS COLLEGE, SENIOR

I WANT TO CHANGE THE WORLD by learning self-defense techniques, and teaching other students and people what the art of self-defense is all about. It's a great way of increasing one's energy and knowing how to act in certain situations.

—*MICHAEL CHOE*
GEORGE WASHINGTON UNIVERSITY, GRADUATE

• • • • • • • •

AT SCHOOL, I JOINED AN ORGANIZATION called p3. P3 stood for Paraprofessionals Promoting Peer*fection. We welcomed all the new freshmen in and were the first faces they saw at orientation. Along the way we pretty much gave them a heads-up on what to expect, and at the end we served as their mentors throughout the year if they chose to have one. You didn't get any compensation for being a p3; just the gratification and rewarding feeling when one of your mentees tells you that they don't think they could've made it through their freshman year without you.

—*BRITTANY*
ALBANY STATE UNIVERSITY, GRADUATE

• • • • • • • •

WE HAVE A VOLUNTEER PROGRAM at the university called Madison House. They arrange all different kinds of activities to get involved in the community; helping out in classrooms, teaching English as a second language, and volunteering for hospital duties, among others. It's really heartening to see the school make an impact in the community and to know that the students truly care enough to wait in line just to volunteer.

—*JO*
UNIVERSITY OF VIRGINIA, SENIOR

COLLEGE IS DEFINITELY a time to become an activist. There are many terrible things in this world that could and should be changed, but we can only do so much, so it's important to find a cause that is meaningful to you. For me, this cause is climate change.

—*DREW HILL*
COLBY COLLEGE, JUNIOR

• • • • • • • •

COMMUNITY SERVICE organizations such as the Red Cross and Project Giveback not only help the community but they make you feel good about yourself, knowing that you made a difference is someone else's life. If you have free time, and you need something to do, helping others is the perfect way.

—*HAYLEY MASON*
HOWARD UNIVERSITY, SOPHOMORE

• • • • • • • •

I DON'T WANT TO change the world; I just want to make individual lives better.

—*TIFFANY*
STANFORD UNIVERSITY, SENIOR

I FOUND MY FRIENDS through a huge variety of different activities, including the rugby team, the residential college council, an a cappella group, Outdoor Action Leaders, not to mention people that lived right by me. My best friends come from activities; otherwise I would have never met them.

—*DENALI*
PRINCETON UNIVERSITY, JUNIOR

- - - - - - - -

"When you hear something that you don't agree with, stand up and say something."

—*TRICIA-NOEL BURKE*
HAMPTON UNIVERSITY, GRADUATE

- - - - - - - -

EXTRACURRICULARS ARE WHAT COLLEGE IS ABOUT; creating your own niche. If you're an academic, start a publication. If you're an actor, launch a theater. I started a debate team that competed against the Ivy League schools. Now I'm creating a theatre program located at Lincoln Center, with master teachers from Yale, Julliard, and NYU. At this great space, students and professional New York creatives will be working to produce plays together.

—*RON Y. KAGAN*
CUNY/MACAULAY HONORS COLLEGE, SENIOR

ON DIVERSITY

ONE OF MY BEST FRIENDS here is from Nepal. Conversations with him have opened my horizons. I learned a lot about different cultures and how women are treated in Nepal. I was talking about visiting and he was like, "These are things you can expect." It's refreshing. Be prepared to ask questions when you don't understand things, and be open to new ideas and people.

—*MEREDITH*
BROWN UNIVERSITY, SOPHOMORE

• • • • • • • •

I AM CAUCASIAN and am definitely a minority at my school. I have embraced this and been able to immerse myself into a vast array of cultures and people. I know that most of my friends went to homogenous, "white" schools and have not been able to face racial or discrimination issues up front. Hunter College enables students to interact with people from all over the world. This diversity has kept me open-minded and aware of the issues surrounding race. I am thankful that I have been able to attend West African dance classes and taste Islamic food during the Dean's Hours.

—*GERALDINE SARAH COWPER*
CUNY/MACAULAY HONORS COLLEGE, SENIOR

BE A PART OF SOMETHING that you sincerely enjoy because it's your free time. Upon my arrival on campus, I decided to dedicate my time and efforts to Duke Africa. It served as a space where I could celebrate my Nigerian culture, learn about other African cultures, and become informed about issues and causes affecting Africa socially, economically and politically.

> —D.A.
> DUKE UNIVERSITY, SENIOR

• • • • • • • • •

I'M IN THE YALE ALLEY CATS. I spend a lot of time singing and hanging out with everyone in the group. We travel around the world. It has given me a solid group of friends. It's one thing to rely on roommates. But you have friends that you share so much in common with—be it singing, traveling, or performing. That common ground brings people together.

> —DAN AMERMAN
> YALE UNIVERSITY, SOPHOMORE

• • • • • • • • •

MY FRESHMAN YEAR, I joined an "a capella" group. This gave me an instant set of friends. My sophomore year, I joined the mountaineering club. Their weekend excursions and the boulder time at the rock wall helped me to counterbalance the burden of intense classes and blow off some steam. I met a lot of cool people in this club and strengthened my relationships with previous friends.

> —DREW HILL
> COLBY COLLEGE, JUNIOR

• • • • • • • • •

CLUB SPORTS ARE FUN, non-threatening ways to get your exercise in, as well as a way to meet a variety of people. Most people who join club sports are a grab bag of personalities.

> —STEPHANIE LEIGH DOCKERY
> WILLIAMS COLLEGE, GRADUATE

I'm in a dance company on campus. It's student-run; we choreograph all of our own pieces, we set the lighting and the music. We rehearsed last night from 11 p.m. to 1 a.m. It's a lot of work, and I'm sleep-deprived because of it, but I love it.

—COLLEEN
PRINCETON
UNIVERSITY, JUNIOR

PLANET COLLEGE

BECAUSE OF A VARSITY SPORT AND A MUSIC GROUP, I personally have not had the time to commit to any environmental organizations. That being said, I have found I can still make a substantial difference just in my own dorm. A lot of kids on campus will leave windows cracked in the winter, leave lights on, and throw away recyclables. These things take very little effort to do but make a huge difference when hundreds of students are doing them together. You don't have to join an environmental group to avoid being wasteful.

> —*ANDREW ALCORTA*
> *HARVARD UNIVERSITY, FRESHMAN*

• • • • • • • • •

I DO NOT THINK THAT EVERY STUDENT HAS AN OBLIGATION to become actively involved in an environmental organization. University provides every student with many opportunities to become civically engaged. I do think that every student has an obligation to act responsibly towards the environment, from thinking about how many pages they print to how often they turn off the lights before exiting a room. Simple steps like this can create an environmentally conscious person.

> —*JOSH*
> *PRINCETON UNIVERSITY, SENIOR*

• • • • • • • • •

MY SCHOOL IS VERY ENVIRONMENTALLY CONSCIOUS, with recycling bins everywhere and an emphasis on recycled goods. Take shorter showers, don't use styrofoam if at all possible, and be aware that your actions almost always affect the environment.

> —*JACOB*
> *UNIVERSITY OF MARYLAND, SOPHOMORE*

IT IS A COLLEGE STUDENT'S RESPONSIBILITY to educate himself or herself on the climate change issue. Saving the environment and taking on global warming isn't for everyone, but if a student feels passionate about the cause it is a worthwhile pursuit, just like any interest.

—*PARISA BASTANI*
UNIVERSITY OF PENNSYLVANIA, SENIOR

• • • • • • • •

THERE ARE TONS OF WAYS TO LEND SUPPORT. One group here sponsored a meal where students were encouraged to bring their own bowls and utensils to cut down on wasted water needed to wash dishes. Even if you don't want to become a member of a group, I think it's important to listen to and cooperate with the environmental groups' programs. They are doing them to make the campus a better, cleaner place. It's so easy to take part in a program and give them the support they need. It's easy to try to change little things, like drink water out of the bubblers instead of bottled water, actually put your cans in the recycling, and turn out the lights in your room. Starting sustainable patterns of living at college will prepare you to continue them for the rest of your life. It's every student's responsibility to put in the effort.

—*TOBIAS*
HARVARD UNIVERSITY, FRESHMAN

THE OTHER SIDE OF THE DESK: STARTING YOUR OWN CLUB

Every September, at least five of my freshman advisees stop by my office to ask me how they would go about starting their own club. They're full to the brim with energy and enthusiasm—they want to be entrepreneurs, pioneers, leaders, captains, or presidents. In almost every case, they haven't actually checked the club list of the college to see if someone already had that bright idea for a board-game club, ultimate Frisbee team, or *Heroes* discussion group. Most of the time, someone has.

If you're interested in starting your own club, congratulations you on your creativity and initiative. But before you get too attached to the idea, consider some of the benefits of joining an *established* club:

- The hassle of getting the club approved and registered has already been take care of by somebody else.

- You'll become part of a group—a group of people with whom you have at least one thing in common.

- The club may already have a presence and reputation on campus; when you join, you'll be able to build on that social capital.

- You can work your way up to a leadership position, learning good stuff along the way, so that you'll be ready when the time comes.

But if the club you want doesn't exist, and there's no other club even remotely similar, and you're ready for the energy- and time-consuming task of promoting your idea, getting other people to buy in, and working with the administration to get things off the ground, *and* you think your college just has to have such a club … go for it!

ONE THING THAT REALLY HELPED was that I played soccer my freshman year. The soccer team was more than just a team. It wasn't like it was from 4-6 p.m. on weekdays and then a game on Saturdays. It was a whole community. You saw people on campus; you yelled. We had a participation ceremony my freshman year, and I still remember the song we sang during the a cappella jam. We wore capes and magic wands and we were "super soccer firsties." It was more than just soccer; we were really part of the college community.

—*RUTHANN*
MOUNT HOLYOKE COLLEGE, GRADUATE

• • • • • • • • •

FRESHMEN SHOULD JOIN CLUBS that fit their majors. This allows you to meet and get to know the people who will be taking the same type of courses as you, which is a good thing to know if you are ever sick and miss class or have a question about a course or professor. This also helps you form a bond with people you are likely to see years down the road, in your profession.

—*H.N.F.*
PENNSYLVANIA STATE UNIVERSITY, GRADUATE

• • • • • • • • •

THE BEST CLUBS to join are the ones that incorporate your major. Many offer scholarships, field trips, invite guest speakers, and can give you a bit of background on what you need to do to succeed. They also provide community service, which is a great experience for anyone. Many of these clubs also connect you with professionals whom you can shadow and get internships with.

—*WHITNEY*
VALDOSTA STATE UNIVERSITY, JUNIOR

Join different clubs from the ones that your roommate or friends are in. It's good to branch out of your comfort zone and connect with a variety of people.

—*E.S.*
DUKE UNIVERSITY GRADUATE

WHEN I WAS A FRESHMAN, I joined a Chinese club, because I was majoring in Chinese and it really helped me network. I still had that common network when I left Duke. I would advise freshmen to join an ethnic or religious club; I found that those were the clubs that kept people grounded.

—*SHEVON*
DUKE UNIVERSITY, GRADUATE

• • • • • • • •

THERE'S AN ACTIVITY FAIR that takes place the first two weeks you're on campus. The gym is filled with tables for all the different groups—a cappella groups, dance groups, religious organizations, community-service organizations—and you put your name down on the lists of all the ones you might want to be involved with. The first two weeks of classes, you get e-mails from 20-25 organizations, but then you slowly whittle down to the ones you can see yourself actually dedicating your time to. It's difficult. Choose two or three organizations and just go with those. I try to be involved with something that keeps me active physically, along with something that keeps me involved with the community.

—*JOSH*
PRINCETON UNIVERSITY, SENIOR

Filling the Daytime Hours: Choosing Classes

I t's OK to admit it: *every semester when the new class schedule comes out, you get a little adrenaline surge. Even if some of your new courses might be boring or hard, there's always a chance that others will be amazing. You might even find out what you want to do with your life! But there are also the questions. What requirements should you do first? What if you're interested in everything and it won't all fit in your schedule? And how do you sniff out those life-changing professors among the cranky, the mediocre, and the just-ok? Read on for answers!*

Ask people what the best class they've ever taken is.

—*Summer J.*
University of
Virginia, Senior

ALL THE GOOD STUFF YOU DO ACADEMICALLY, you do in your junior and senior years. So, try to do all the crap in your freshman and sophomore years. Get it out of the way so you can enjoy your last two years.

—*Anonymous*
Johns Hopkins University, Junior

• • • • • • •

IF PROFESSORS GIVE OUT E-MAIL ADDRESSES, use them! Don't send anything raunchy, even if you are in love with your English professor. Use it to communicate about class work. E-mail them if you happen to have skipped class and want to know what you have missed. This is a sure way to win points with them. By humanizing them, you make them a friend. I have done this a few times and they seem to like it when you are involved in school, even when you are not.

—*Edie Sherman*
Kingsborough Community College, Senior

• • • • • • •

I WENT TO A JEWISH PRIVATE HIGH SCHOOL and we were in classes from morning until night. We still had a lot of work, but not like college. In college, we have classes a couple of hours a day and the same amount of work. Freshman year, I felt like I was falling off the cliff with all the work. But I got used to it.

—*Chana Weiner*
Barnard College, Sophomore

• • • • • • •

LEARN A LANGUAGE. If you've taken a language in high school, take more of the same and become fluent. If not, learn a new language, but think about one you might actually use. Even if you aren't thinking about a term abroad, pick a language and go for it.

—*Anonymous*
Union College

GO FOR THE GOOD TEACHERS and the bad times instead of the good times and bad teachers. I took calculus the first semester at 8 a.m. and that time just sucked. But I had a good teacher and I got an A. Second semester, I took a class at 1 p.m. and it was a hard teacher, and I got a C.

—*AMY SCEVIOUR*
GEORGIA INSTITUTE OF TECHNOLOGY, SOPHOMORE

Make your own path and find your own teachers.

—*EBELE ONYEMA*
GEORGETOWN
UNIVERSITY, SENIOR

"Never sign up for a 7 a.m. class. Yes, you did it in high school, but Mom was always there to keep waking you up, and if by some miracle you do make it to an early class, you will sleep through the lecture when you get there."

—*J.T.*
UNIVERSITY OF FLORIDA, GRADUATE

FALL IN LOVE with someone in your class right away; student, T.A., professor, whomever. You'll be hard-pressed to skip class. If there is no one in your class to love, then pick someone to hate and show up every day to make his or her life a living hell.

—*S.P.*
UNIVERSITY OF GEORGIA, GRADUATE

HEAD**LINES**
Best Advice and Top Tips

- Avoid early-morning classes if you don't want to sleep through lectures.
- Experiment—take a class or two outside your desired major.
- If you think the first class of the semester is boring, drop the course—it won't improve.
- Talk to students who already took the class you're interested in to see if the professor is any good.

KNOW WHICH CLASSES TO SKIP, and which classes not to skip. This is really a key point, because some professors don't care one way or another if you show up for class. All they care about is your test and homework performance. There are other professors who are sticklers for attendance, and even if you are an A student you can end up with a C, because of poor attendance.

—*TONYA BANKS*
MIAMI UNIVERSITY, GRADUATE

• • • • • • • •

I WOULD RECOMMEND that during your first year, you take a class that is outside what you think you want to do. You'll meet other people, and freshman year is a really good time to meet a lot of people. Take the P.E. classes; it's something active. If you're in a very academic school, go out and have something active in your life. It's a good release. I did martial arts—Tae Kwon Do. That was really fun and you meet a lot of different people there. And kick some ass.

—*JASPER*
UNIVERSITY OF CALIFORNIA AT BERKELEY, JUNIOR

DON'T BELIEVE PEOPLE when they tell you a professor is really good. They're probably wrong. I've taken about three classes because someone told me the professor was so cool and so good, and those are the three classes I hated the most. Then I hated the people that recommended the classes to me. Find the classes that interest you, and you'll be fine.

> —*EBELE ONYEMA*
> *GEORGETOWN UNIVERSITY, SENIOR*

THE THING THAT STANDS OUT THE MOST about my freshman year is the fact that I was completely responsible for my learning. No one cared if I came to class or not; no one cared if I took notes or studied for a test. I remember thinking that it was wonderful to have so much freedom, and if the professors didn't care, why should I? I took full advantage of having no attendance phone calls, no conduct grades, no authoritarian instructors. By the time I figured out that I was wasting my time (and my parents' money) and that I had to take responsibility for my education, it wasn't too late, but my GPA never fully recovered.

> —*S.A.S.*
> *UNIVERSITY OF SOUTH FLORIDA, GRADUATE*

JUST BECAUSE SOME PEOPLE don't go to class and still get A's doesn't mean you can skip class and still get A's. You can try it, but I wouldn't recommend it.

> —*J.D.*
> *EMORY UNIVERSITY, SENIOR*

Take the most interesting and easiest classes you can find, have a good time, and try not to flunk out.

> —*JUAN GONZALEZ*
> *CLEMSON UNIVERSITY, GRADUATE*

THE CHILI PEPPER AND YOU

Everyone looks at professors' ratings before signing up for classes. But can you trust those anonymous scorecards? Do they tell you everything you need to know? Do you really care whether your professor got the chili pepper (the indication of personal attractiveness)? How can you get the most benefit out of ratemyprofessors.com?

Ratemyprofessors.com uses five measures:

1. Easiness
2. Helpfulness
3. Clarity
4. Hotness
5. Overall Quality

These categories will probably help you if you're looking for a fun elective or an easy 'gut' course. But if you're looking for a strong course in your major, you may need to ask yourself a few extra questions before you follow the advice you'll find on this site:

- Does the reviewer use foul language? This usually indicates a student is disgruntled over a grade, which means that he or she is not exactly objective.

- Is the reviewer's spelling and/or grammar on the pathetic side? Be suspicious if the low ratings are in the Easiness and Clarity categories; the issue was probably the student, not the professor.

- Are there enough reviews posted for you to make an informed decision? If there are just one or two, you probably want to find out more before you decide whether to register.

DON'T OVERLOAD; don't take too many classes. I took too many classes. I was staying up to five and six o'clock in the morning, missing classes that morning. That's not fun.

> —*ALBERT SO*
> *GEORGIA INSTITUTE OF TECHNOLOGY, SOPHOMORE*

• • • • • • • •

FROM AN ACADEMIC PERSPECTIVE, I would advise freshmen to use that first year as your sandbox year. It's really important. It's OK to screw off. It's OK to go out and experiment.

> —*W.J.F.*
> *GEORGETOWN UNIVERSITY, JUNIOR*

• • • • • • • •

IF YOU PLAN TO WORK for Goldman Sachs in four years, your entire future seems to rest on whether you secure a seat in Accounting 101. But this is a misguided approach. You should use your first few semesters to take the courses most dissimilar to your goals. If you plan to major in business, take a course in French New Wave Cinema or British Lit. If you think you're a chemist, take physics. If you want to speak Hebrew, take Arabic.

> —*DOUG*
> *WAKE FOREST UNIVERSITY, GRADUATE*

• • • • • • • •

MOST PEOPLE JUST DO SCHOOL—you don't see a lot of students doing research, playing sports, doing extracurricular activities—and one can sense the monotony. I suggest you take the perspective that grades don't count and take classes with professors who are passionate about what they're teaching. Learn, don't just take classes that you think will yield a higher grade.

> —*YALDA A.*
> *UNIVERSITY OF CALIFORNIA AT BERKELEY, GRADUATE*

Share your school supplies with fellow classmates. Believe me, there's going to be a time when you forget something in the future, so volunteer your extras.

> —*J.S.*
> *UNIVERSITY OF GEORGIA GRADUATE*

When studying Far East religions, don't confuse a llama with the Dalai Lama, the spiritual leader of Tibet.

—*LYNN LAMOUSIN*
LOUISIANA STATE UNIVERSITY
GRADUATE

IF YOU KNOW SOME PEOPLE who are already at your college, talk to them and see which professors are good and which ones suck.

—*ANDREW OUZTS*
GEORGIA INSTITUTE OF TECHNOLOGY, SOPHOMORE

• • • • • • • •

ACADEMICALLY, TRY TO GET TO KNOW PROFESSORS. He's not some guy in the Emerald City hiding behind the curtain. Your professor is just a person.

—*PHIL*
UNIVERSITY OF VIRGINIA, SENIOR

• • • • • • • •

GO TO EVERY CLASS; that's half the battle. If you do, you'll pass. I went to the majority of classes freshman year, but I would've done so much better if I had gone to all of them.

—*KRISTIN THOMAS*
JAMES MADISON UNIVERSITY, JUNIOR

• • • • • • • •

EVERYBODY'S SMART IN COLLEGE. At least give yourself a semester before you dive into the hard classes. I was in the top 10 percent of my high school class and I felt real good about myself. But it took me the first year of college to realize I had to work real hard to make good grades.

—*JONATHAN COHEN*
EMORY UNIVERSITY, SENIOR

• • • • • • • •

STAY LATE AFTER CLASS and ask questions. It's good to be known by your professors; later on you'll need recommendations from them. It's important that you did more than just get a good grade, that your professor remembers you.

—*JAWAN AYER-COLE, M.D.*
FLORIDA A&M UNIVERSITY, GRADUATE

SLAVE OF APHRODITE

At the beginning of my freshman year, I was hit by Cupid's arrow. It was a direct hit—for the entire semester I was in love with my Introduction to Classical Studies professor.

Professor, whom I referred to reverently as "the 13th Olympian Goddess," taught an auditorium full of undergraduates about the follies, jealousies, battles, and—most prominently—the sex lives of Greek gods and mortals alike. I had always loved Greek mythology, but this class brought excitement and legitimacy to my obsessive hobby. I had read Catullus in my Latin class in high school, so I thought I was fully prepared for the unique and bizarre proclivities covered in my professor's 101 class, but those depraved Greeks and Romans surprised me time and time again! I think I was most surprised that this racy curriculum was discussed and taught in public! Can she talk about what seems clear to be the origins of NAMBLA at the podium?

Not all of Classical Studies was NC-17; I figure that a taste now and then kept the coeds awake and returning each week. But I loved all of it: the philosophy, the art, the architecture, the myths and poetry. Sappho, Euripides, Ovid, and Herodotus. I was hooked, to the class and to the deity who posed as our teacher. Vivid memories of hiding behind kiosks and trees while watching her every move attest to my naiveté and somewhat unhealthy fixation.

Once the semester ended, I pored over the class listings, hoping to fill my schedule with more classics and more chances to listen and catch glimpses of my professor. Alas, she was only teaching graduate classes, so my first encounter with the 13th Olympian Goddess turned out to be my last. However, I remained smitten with the subject and decided to join the Classics Department.

—PHIL CARMEL
UNIVERSITY COLLEGE–SALFORD (ENGLAND), GRADUATE

TAKE A WIDE VARIETY OF CLASSES. You may find that you are interested in a subject you hadn't previously considered. Plus, freshman year is the best time to experiment with that sort of thing. And before you decide to take a certain class, make sure you know something about the professor teaching it. Ask around, search the Web; anything. A good or bad professor can genuinely make or break a class.

—*DANIELLE FRIEDMAN*
DUKE UNIVERSITY, SENIOR

"Figure out the social scene of your school before you make any schedules. It's no fun going to class hungover on Friday mornings!"

—*ERIN*
SUFFOLK UNIVERSITY, GRADUATE

I'M USUALLY THE TYPE OF PERSON who does all his work, but now, I actually have to think. The workload isn't harder, but it's different. I take a lot more notes now. I'm in a study skills class and they suggest a system for taking notes—dividing the page into three sections, writing notes in one part, cues for main ideas in another, and summaries in the other. I don't like that system, but it helps to try different things.

—*DUSTIN CAMAC*
UNIVERSITY OF DELAWARE, FRESHMAN

MANY FRESHMAN CLASSES ARE HUGE, so it might be hard to let the professor know that you exist. To counter this, follow the advice everyone tells you: don't be late, and take notes. Someone gave me advice about note taking and said that if you hate it, then just bring in a tape recorder and tape the lecture. So I did, and yes, it was easy, but I never listened to the tapes; or if I did, it was always a crappy recording.

In some classes they don't take attendance, which might make you feel more like not going. But it feels good if you go anyway, and you never know if you'll miss a day with a pop quiz or extra credit. As you get more focused on your major, the classes get smaller. Be involved and know your professors; ask them for advice and talk to them.

—*LESLIE M.*
UNIVERSITY OF FLORIDA, GRADUATE

. . . .

GET TO KNOW YOUR TEACHERS, because when it comes down to getting a better final grade you might need a little help. And if your professors know you, they might be willing to help you.

—*MATT BURLESON*
UNIVERSITY OF TENNESSEE AT MARTIN, GRADUATE

FOUR PHRASES THAT TAME BUREAUCRACY

1. "I'm so sorry to bother you ..."
2. "I read all the information on your website and I just have one more small question ..."
3. "Hello, how are you today?" (So obvious, yet so rarely used!)
4. "My RA said you were a good person to talk to about ..."

AND THE MORAL OF THE STORY IS . . .

There was one class I had when I gave a big speech to the whole class, while hung over. That was a bad idea. I had an economics professor who picked out a few people to give speeches; to teach his class, basically. The night before, I got pretty drunk. The speech was on Milton Friedman's theory on something or other. I was so hung over when I tried to give the speech, I couldn't talk; I just mumbled. The professor asked me questions: "Do you mean this means that?" I said, "Yeah, yeah, that. Yes, of course." And so we got through the whole thing, and afterwards he pulled me aside and said, "Wow, I've been teaching this class for 20 years, and that is the worst description I've ever heard." And yet, I passed the class. I talked to the professor. I realized I screwed up, and I made up for it. So the moral is, if you screw up, talk your way through it. Don't let it lie. People understand.

—*Anonymous*
University of Texas, Graduate

Make your professors think you care about their class. Get to know them one-on-one. Stay after, go to their office hours; even if you don't give a rat's ass about their class, make them think that you care.

—*Brett Strickland*
Georgia State University, Sophomore

IF THE FIRST CLASS of the semester is boring, drop it! If a professor can't make the first twenty minutes of the first class exciting, it is going to be a long semester. Go into add/drop week with a list of possible classes to take. Go to seven or eight classes in a week, or more. Then choose the best of those. It makes for a hectic week, but it will make the semester so much better.

> —SUMMER J.
> UNIVERSITY OF VIRGINIA, SENIOR

• • • • • • • •

WHEN LOOKING FOR AN EASY ELECTIVE, ask a few athletes. As a former student-athlete who usually had taxing courses for my major, I was pretty good at finding less taxing electives, GPA boosters, blow-off classes, etc. This allowed me to keep my sanity. Also, ask around to find out if your chosen elective is as interesting as it sounds. I almost signed up for "Costumes Through the Ages." It sounded like it might be a good elective to take. After asking around, I found out the class is boring and difficult.

> —HASSAN
> UNIVERSITY OF TULSA, GRADUATE

• • • • • • • •

GEOLOGY (AKA "ROCKS AND JOCKS") is much harder than the course description would lead you to believe.

> —LYNN LAMOUSIN
> LOUISIANA STATE UNIVERSITY, GRADUATE

• • • • • • • •

IT'S ESSENTIAL THAT YOU BUILD up a grade cushion in your first year. That way when you're a junior or a senior and things get tough, you don't have to worry as much about your GPA.

> —YAP
> NEW YORK UNIVERSITY, JUNIOR

When it comes to choosing professors, always check the Web site ratemyprofessor.com

> —JESSIE
> VILLA JULIE
> COLLEGE, JUNIOR

Take the opportunity to participate in class. Never again in your life will you be confronted with such an open forum for sharing ideas; this is the time to develop your skills to make a persuasive point.

—*SCOTT WOELFEL*
UNIVERSITY OF MISSOURI
GRADUATE

DON'T TAKE MORE THAN ONE CLASS that has a lot of reading. I picked some classes that had too much reading, so I am always reading. I average four hours a day, maybe longer. I go to class, take a break, go to dinner, and then go to the library. I'll be in the library until 1 a.m.

—*BAYLESS PARSLEY*
UNIVERSITY OF VIRGINIA, FRESHMAN

. . . .

I TOOK COURSES THAT WERE HARDER, not what normal freshmen took. I ended up not doing as well as I should have. There's no harm taking a class you've taken already in high school. Because freshman year is about getting used to your environment, and if you're studying all the time, it's harder to do that.

—*NATASHA PIRZADA*
GEORGETOWN UNIVERSITY, SOPHOMORE

. . . .

BE WARY OF CLASS TITLES like "Frodo's Epic Nightmare," "American Humor," and "Introduction to Comparative Politics." They might sound interesting, but the professors could be dry and boring.

—*JACKIE*
STATE UNIVERSITY OF NEW YORK AT BINGHAMTON
GRADUATE

. . . .

TAKE CLASSES THAT YOU ACTUALLY LIKE, that you're actually interested in. Everyone I know is taking all these intense classes in subjects that they're not interested in, and they're miserable. But I'm having a great time.

—*LUCY LINDSEY*
HARVARD UNIVERSITY, FRESHMAN

I TOOK INTRODUCTION TO BUSINESS. We had routine, online quizzes on the *Wall Street Journal*. They were weekly and worth 10 points each. I got seven out of 10 on the first quiz and I panicked and did not know what to do. One of my friends said to go to the T.A.'s office hours. She said this because it was a huge class and the professor didn't know who you were. My friend also suggested I sit in the front row of the class. I then went to the T.A.'s office hours and she said, "Sarah, don't worry about it. I am happy that you are showing dedication by coming to my hours." A few minutes later, the professor walked in and said to my T.A., "How are your students in the section?" She said, "They're fine, and by the way this is Sarah Fass; she was concerned about her quizzes." My professor said, "Oh, I know who she is. She sits in the front of my class. And by the way, don't worry about the quiz, just keep sitting in the front row."

—*SARAH FASS*
AMERICAN UNIVERSITY, FRESHMAN

ON THE DOUBLE 101

At the United States Coast Guard Academy, before you begin your studies, you have to survive Swab Summer, a seven-week "traditional military indoctrination... designed to help young civilian students transition into the Academy 'lifestyle.'" The training process includes general military skills, physical conditioning, seamanship, swimming, and—oh yes—academics. And forget about sleeping in after a tough day: morning formations are at that oh-so-friendly 6:20 hour.

ONE OF MY STRANGEST MEMORIES is attending a class taught by a dead man. One of the freshman-level psychology courses consisted of videotaped lectures from a professor who died in the 1960s. I don't remember his full name but his first name was Fred, so everyone called him—you guessed it—Dead Fred. I wish I had a picture of 500 students all staring at small monitors streaming a flickering, grainy, black-and-white, talking head three times a week. Maybe it was all just one big psychology experiment.

—*SCOTT WOELFEL*
UNIVERSITY OF MISSOURI, GRADUATE

• • • • • • • • •

"Do not take an easy teacher who's boring. I'm in one of those classes this semester. I find it so much better if you like the teacher and it's a tough class than if you dislike the teacher and it's easy."

—*M.M.*
BOSTON COLLEGE, JUNIOR

• • • • • • • • •

ALWAYS TALK TO STUDENTS who took the classes in the past to find out whether the class or professor is hard or easy, good or bad, nice or mean.

—*HASSAN*
UNIVERSITY OF TULSA, GRADUATE

YOU. WILL. TEACH. ME.

One thing I learned my freshman year is that teachers don't have to have their Master's degree to teach; they just need to have one in progress. That's good for them because the school usually pays for it, but bad for the students because it means the professor doesn't already know everything he's going to be teaching you and will often be distracted by his own studies.

It's important to make sure your teacher actually knows more than you. Be brutal. Ask a million questions. I can't tell you how frustrating it is to be paying over $300 a class and hear, "I'll have to look that one up," in response to a question you already know the answer to. Don't be afraid to be very, very mean to your teacher. Bad teachers waste your time and should not be there. You have to believe they have no feelings and drive them the hell out.

Don't let your teacher be a slacker and don't let him forget things. This should be dealt with according to the size of the college and the amount of students. For the love of sweet Jesus, my class was the only one my teacher taught, and he'd sometimes forget his notes!

By the way, the best teachers don't use notes.

—STEVEN COY
SAN DIEGO STATE UNIVERSITY, SOPHOMORE

MAKING DA VINCI LOOK EASY: CRACKING THE ACADEMIC CURRICULUM

Choose one course from Category 3A. Pick two courses from different academic departments in Category 2E. If both 2E courses are taken on campus, and not satisfied by Advanced Placement, students may apply them toward Requirement PD/C or PD/D, but not both. The same course may be used to satisfy 3A and PD/A, but if the course is worth fewer than three credits it must be repeated for PD/A.

This applies only to students matriculating before Fall 2007. All other students should consult the 2008-2011 Bulletin. We apologize for the delay in printing the 2008-2011 Bulletin. It should be available within six months. In the meantime, questions may be directed to the Dean of Arts and Sciences. Although this position is currently vacant, the new Dean should be selected ... in around six months.

Are they kidding???

Navigating the general education requirements of your college can be as mind-twistingly complicated as filing taxes for the average multinational corporation or filling out your driver's license application. But don't despair; help is here.

- Does your college offer an online degree audit system? Use it! But whatever you do, don't be fooled into thinking that requirements are just a series of boxes to fill in, or annoying tasks to "get out of the way" so that you can go on to the good stuff. Your Gen. Ed. courses might turn out to *be* the good stuff you've been waiting for all these years.

- All those confusing letters, numbers, and symbols actually represent something: the range of skills and knowledge that the faculty of your college think every student ought to have. If you take half an hour to read up on the purpose and design of the general education curriculum, you'll start to see at least some method to all the madness. (Hint: try the front section of your course catalog and the Mission Statement online.)

- Still stumped? Go see your academic advisor or favorite faculty member. They will be happy to let you in on the secrets cleverly concealed behind the baffling charts and lists.

Choose your classes based on the professor, instead of the class description.

—*ROBIN JALEEL*
   EMORY UNIVERSITY
   GRADUATE

BEFORE SIGNING UP FOR ANY CLASS, find out who is teaching it, and go talk to them. At the beginning of the year, most professors are just sitting around waiting for students to drop in. You can learn way more about a class, and the professor teaching it, by spending 10 minutes with the professor, one-on-one. You'll get a sense of what will be required and how much of a hard-ass the teacher is going to be.

    —*DON WAZZENEGER*
       YOUNGSTOWN STATE UNIVERSITY, SENIOR

• • • • • • •

I WISH I'D HAD A BETTER IDEA of the classes I wanted to take. When you get here it's a bit of a scramble; you have so many options. You have a course book that's 3,000 pages and you have to flip through it and find stuff.

    —*TOBIAS*
       HARVARD UNIVERSITY, FRESHMAN

Studying: Why, When & How

As if getting into college weren't hard enough, now you have to get through it! Everyone told you that the readings would be denser, the papers longer, and the exams tougher, but you were hoping none of that would actually happen in your case. But here you are, and it's happening. Just remember, those college admissions officers let you in because they knew you would be able to do the work. This chapter will help.

Buy beaten-up, used books that have been highlighted and have notes in the margins: Instant Cliff's Notes!

—*Jen*
  University of Georgia Graduate

ONE OF THE LESS POSITIVE MEMORIES from my freshman year occurred during final exams of first semester. I had stayed up until 4 a.m. studying material for my art history final, and was extremely confident that I would perform well and get the A that I had expected based on my 96 average going into it. I awoke the next morning to the horrifying realization that my alarm clock had not gone off and I had already missed the entire exam. I was so disappointed and angry at myself. The zero score averaged into my grade brought it down to a B-, which brought my GPA down almost half a point. To avoid this disappointment in the future, I make sure to set a backup alarm, and sometimes even a backup-backup alarm, on important test days.

—*Maxwell Hockstad*
  State University of New York at Albany, Sophomore

• • • • • • • •

THE MAP IS NOT THE JOURNEY and the notes are not the course. Take notes but don't try to be a stenographer. Use class notes to enhance your understanding of the course; for example, flagging areas for follow-up in text or with the instructor.

—*Scott Woelfel*
  University of Missouri, Graduate

• • • • • • • •

THE HARDEST PART IS KEEPING A SCHEDULE; having to do your work and putting that ahead of fun, because you can do whatever you want in college. But that will catch up to you. I went out the night before my Calculus 1 final; I ended up almost failing it.

—*Theodore Schimenti*
  Columbia University, Freshman

DON'T READ IN YOUR BED; you'll fall asleep. I would read in my bed and I would, obviously, fall asleep. When you're in your bed, that's what you do. And then you start to associate reading with sleeping, so anytime you try to read anywhere, you fall asleep. So, don't read in your bed.

—*BETHANY*
JAMES MADISON UNIVERSITY, SENIOR

66Leave your room when you study. With all the computers and stereos and TVs nowadays, it's so hard to get work done when you're sitting there.99

—*TAYLOR*
UNIVERSITY OF MARYLAND, SOPHOMORE

THE PROBLEM I HAD WAS THE PRIORITIZATION. You have a lot more free time in college than in high school. But you think you have more free time than you actually have. And by November of freshman year, you're behind. I don't know any-one who wasn't behind. You tend to forget to study when you first get here. You have parties, freedom from parents—you almost forget that you're in school. Freshman year, people would go to 60 to 70 percent of classes, at best, because they would stay up late and then miss morning classes. You almost forget how important educa-tion is. You worked for 12 years to get here, but just because you're here, the work doesn't stop.

—*ZAK AMCHISLAVSKY*
GEORGETOWN UNIVERSITY, SENIOR

Sleep a lot. And always go to class.

—*SARAH*
GEORGIA INSTITUTE OF TECHNOLOGY GRADUATE

HEADLINES
Best Advice and Top Tips

- Find a place where you can study without interruption—most likely not your room.
- Don't skip classes—it makes the work that much harder.
- Self-discipline is the key to academic success.
- Don't wait until the last minute to get your work done—you'll only regret it.

DO HOMEWORK RIGHT AFTER CLASS. Study for a test the whole night before. Other students will understand why you look like hell.
—*RICHARD*
GEORGIA SOUTHERN UNIVERSITY, GRADUATE

• • • • • • • •

FRESHMEN COME IN AND EXPECT TO GET AN A. But then you realize you were a big fish in a small pond in high school, and in college there's a bunch of other big fish and you've got to step it up a notch.
—*K.K.*
NORTHWESTERN UNIVERSITY, GRADUATE

• • • • • • • •

ONE THING THAT IS DIFFERENT between college and high school is homework. College professors expect you to do the homework for your own benefit—which means for no credit. There is no homework given out to pad your grade. That's why it's important not to miss lectures.
—*JAMESE JAMES*
UNIVERSITY OF TULSA, GRADUATE

KNOW HOW TO ACCESS all the teachers' information. Most professors expect you to be able to download syllabi, assignments, labs, things to write up. Your grades are online. It's more difficult if you can't do these things. It's not impossible, but it's more difficult.

You need to study as much as you can during the day, between classes, rather than wait until the evening when it's more distracting, with TV and friends and social things.

—*LEAH PRICE*
GEORGETOWN UNIVERSITY, SOPHOMORE

* * * * * * * *

"Study individually 70% of the time, in groups 20% of the time, and seek the professor's or teaching assistant's help 10% of the time. Divide your time up like this and you're golden."

—*SEAN CAMERON*
PRINCETON UNIVERSITY, SOPHOMORE

* * * * * * * *

DON'T MISS ANY CLASS, even if you think what the teacher is doing that day isn't significant. You never know what they could say that might affect the school year.

—*K.M.*
HOWARD UNIVERSITY, SOPHOMORE

IF YOU'RE QUESTIONING whether or not to go to a party, you better not go to that party, you know what I'm saying? Kids in college don't have good judgment. That's how you learn responsibility, learning how to listen to yourself. Some kids are like, "You think I should go to that party? Because I've got a midterm." It's like, "Keep your ass inside and study. You just answered your question." Learning how to answer your own questions; that's a big part of college.

> —ANONYMOUS
> BROWN UNIVERSITY, SOPHOMORE

The self-discipline is the toughest thing. You have to set up time to study.

—*Z.S.*
GEORGE
WASHINGTON
UNIVERSITY
FRESHMAN

FIRST SEMESTER IS KEY; this is what you need to prepare for. From there it is downhill. Get ready to work really hard and then establish a foundation. From there you will be able to just maintain. To do well you have to work hard and the time to begin is freshman year, first semester. So, enjoy your summer and come ready to work hard.

> —INSU CHANG
> CARNEGIE MELLON UNIVERSITY, JUNIOR

DO NOT RELY ON the school's computing facilities. I suggest getting a laptop, and I also suggest getting a laptop lock. I've heard stories where people get up from their computer for a minute—to go to the bathroom or get a drink—and a minute later their computer is stolen.

> —DIANA SHU
> UNIVERSITY OF CALIFORNIA AT BERKELEY, SOPHOMORE

FLIRT WITH THE PROFESSORS. It comes in handy when you need to be late on your term paper because you partied all weekend.

> —ANONYMOUS
> UNIVERSITY OF GEORGIA, GRADUATE

FRESHMAN YEAR IS A CRITICAL TIME to motivate yourself academically. Talk to your academic counselor. If you mess up in your first year, you get in a psychological track and will continue to spiral down. Then your self-esteem goes down and everything else breaks down. Then you drop out.

> —*M.N.M.*
> *COLLEGE OF SAN MATEO, SENIOR*

DON'T BE AFRAID TO STAND OUT. Speak up in your classes; free your mind in your application essays; go against the grain; say something outlandish that will make them remember you over the others in the bubble gum craze.

> —*HILLARY*
> *BOWLING GREEN STATE UNIVERSITY, GRADUATE*

AFTER THE HONEYMOON

The first month of freshman year is often a happy blur of parties, new friends, and leisurely lessons. Often heard on the grassy quad or amongst the votive candles of the campus coffee shop:

> *"I can't believe classes are so easy."*
> *"I learned all this stuff in AP Bio."*
> *"4.0, no problem."*

But beware—the honeymoon doesn't last forever. About a month into the semester, the *review* will be over. Your professors will start covering *new* material, fast.

Be ready!

AVOID PUTTING STUDYING OFF until the last minute. After a lecture, I would always go back and go through my notes and rewrite them. If the professor says something more than once, that is a strong clue that it is important. In high school, I could get away with cramming the night before; that changes in college.

—SARAH TIPPY
WESTERN ILLINOIS UNIVERSITY, SENIOR

GO TO OFFICE HOURS. Professors will tell you what to expect, and what you need to improve. I've gone to office hours and actually had T.A.'s change my grade because they read the paper again and realized that they graded it too harshly. I had it happen twice. I showed them that I did know the material, even if it didn't come out in the paper.

—EVELIN OCAMPO
UNIVERSITY OF CALIFORNIA AT SANTA BARBARA, JUNIOR

COLLEGE ISN'T LIKE HIGH SCHOOL; you have to actually try to get good grades. When I was a freshman I would write a paper with no thesis and think that I would still get an A on it (which happened in high school). Then you get the paper back and you get a B-minus and it says, "You don't have a thesis." It's hard to slip things by professors; they know the tricks, especially in freshman classes. You have to try that extra bit harder.

—KIM KAPLAN
STANFORD UNIVERSITY, SENIOR

WAKE UP EARLY AND STUDY. Even if you're not a morning person, make yourself one. It's the quietest time in the dorm and you'll be so productive.

—SEAN CAMERON
PRINCETON UNIVERSITY, SOPHOMORE

PUT IN YOUR TIME IN CLASSES first, then bother with clubs and other activities after.

> —*BRANDON HOGAN*
> *HOWARD UNIVERSITY, SENIOR*

• • • • • • • •

DON'T WAIT TO WRITE EXTREMELY LONG PAPERS until the night before they're due. Writing under pressure is one thing; writing under extreme, debilitating pressure is something else entirely.

> —*DANIELLE FRIEDMAN*
> *DUKE UNIVERSITY, SENIOR*

• • • • • • • •

I'M AN OVERACHIEVER, so I spent too much time studying my freshman year. My main advice is to make sure you balance studying with having fun. When you have fun, it's a lot easier to sit down and study.

> —*KIRSTEN GIBBS*
> *GEORGIA INSTITUTE OF TECHNOLOGY, JUNIOR*

REALITY BITES (BUT YOU STILL NEED TO BE HONEST WITH YOURSELF)

Don't kid yourself thinking that you are going to work on a project or do any studying at all on weekends; it ain't gonna happen. I used to think like this: OK, test Tuesday. Today is Thursday. That means I have five days to prepare. But it never worked out like that. What really happened is that Friday was Friday (party day) and on the weekend the party continued. Monday was for recovery. You have to factor reality into your planning.

> —*KEN KEEL*
> *UNIVERSITY OF VIRGINIA, SENIOR*

I HAVE TO DO MY WORK RIGHT when it's assigned, otherwise I can't do it.

—*JENNIFER A. SICKLICK*
GEORGE WASHINGTON UNIVERSITY, FRESHMAN

• • • • • • • •

COLLEGE IS NOT HIGH SCHOOL; it requires you to think in very different ways than one is used to. Find one place on campus where you can study without being interrupted, and designate a portion of your time for that purpose. When reading, read for content, and know what you are reading (it makes skimming that much more effective). If you must cram, going to bed earlier and waking up at 6 a.m. to force a few more hours in is more effective, because at least you are awake for the test. But then again, that's just me.

—*AMY*
PRINCETON UNIVERSITY, FRESHMAN

• • • • • • • •

BUCKLE DOWN EARLY. Do your work early. The temptation gets greater the later in the year it gets.

—*LAURA GZYZEWSKI*
DESALES UNIVERSITY, JUNIOR

• • • • • • • •

THE KEY TO SURVIVING AND HAVING FREE TIME is to know what the teacher wants you to know and just study that. Skip everything else if it's not necessary to get a good grade in the course.

—*ANONYMOUS*
UNITED STATES MILITARY ACADEMY AT WEST POINT
JUNIOR

• • • • • • • •

NEVER, EVER GO TO THE LIBRARY ON SATURDAY, unless it's during finals. Take a break one day a week and have fun.

—*STEVE DAVIS*
FLORIDA STATE UNIVERSITY, GRADUATE

Get some friends who can edit a paper. They'll come in handy. And for every hour you study, do 15 minutes of fun stuff. It helps keep a balance.

—*CONOR MCNEIL*
EMORY UNIVERSITY
SOPHOMORE

IN COLLEGE, YOU HAVE these one- and two-hour chunks in the day with nothing to do. A lot of people spend that time taking a nap or watching TV or checking e-mail or putzing around. It's a good habit to keep a homework assignment on hand, so when you have a spare moment you can pull it out and start reading it. It helps you keep up with it all.

—*CATE*
BROWN UNIVERSITY, JUNIOR

> "I study about three or four hours every night. For tests, you really can't cram it in, but I do about six hours before tests."

—*R.J.*
UNIVERSITY OF DELAWARE, SOPHOMORE

I STUDY AT NIGHT WHEN IT'S QUIETER; 10 p.m. to 4 a.m. Then I sleep all day. My roommate studies then, too. It's hard to find people you get along with who have the same patterns of sleep.

—*WALTER*
UNIVERSITY OF MARYLAND–COLLEGE PARK, SOPHOMORE

IF YOU GET A B OR A C, DON'T WORRY. When you're going into the job world after graduating, there's no company that's going to say, "Well, you didn't do well in Western Civilization."

—*RHIANNON GULICK*
GEORGETOWN UNIVERSITY, SENIOR

An hour of class is worth more than five hours of poring over notes.

—*Dan*
Miami University
Freshman

No matter how sick you might be during finals week, do not take any cough medicine. And read the labels on any cold medication you take for any reference that the medicine will make you drowsy. I was sick as a dog my first finals week, but I made the mistake of taking medication that made me so tired I couldn't stay up to cram. And no amount of caffeine can overcome the depressants in that medication. Just put up with the runny nose and drink coffee.

—*Anonymous*
Youngstown State University, Senior

• • • • • • • •

You can't procrastinate as much as you do in high school. You get behind, and you get behind, and you get behind, and then you get further and further behind, and you don't know what to do about it. I had a 4.0 in high school, when I could have slept through every class, and now I'm struggling. I have to pick up my study habits.

—*Kevin Bushey*
Georgia State University, Freshman

• • • • • • • •

Don't miss even one day of homework. If you fall behind, it's so much harder to catch up.

—*Natasha Pirzada*
Georgetown University, Sophomore

• • • • • • • •

This is something my dad told me: You should look at college like a nine-to-five job. You wake up and you do all your work nine to five so that you're not stuck doing your work at 3 a.m., like I always am. Then you're tired and you end up sleeping through your first class, like I always do. So, get your work done early and then you have time to socialize.

—*Jenna*
Boston College, Freshman

GO OUT TO PARTY ON THURSDAYS, Fridays and Saturdays, but stay at home on the other days. I don't have classes on Friday; you should try to schedule that. And I don't study on Sundays; that's for watching football. During the week, I go to class and then study about two hours a night.

> —*FRED*
> *UNIVERSITY OF RHODE ISLAND, JUNIOR*

• • • • • • • •

SOME OF MY MOST PRODUCTIVE STUDY SESSIONS were studying in groups. Find a classroom that's empty in the evening, write notes and questions on the chalkboard, quiz each other, and have fun with it.

> —*K. HARMA*
> *WESTERN WASHINGTON UNIVERSITY, GRADUATE*

• • • • • • • •

I GO TO SCHOOL IN A BIG CITY, and there's always the temptation to go out and do something. You can't escape it. You have to realize, when night-time comes, you're going to want to go out. So you have to do your work in the day; otherwise, your work won't get done.

> —*CATHY*
> *COLUMBIA UNIVERSITY, SENIOR*

• • • • • • • •

IN ENGLISH LITERATURE, don't watch the movie instead of reading the book. I didn't read all of *A Clockwork Orange* and I had an exam on it, so I watched the movie. I didn't know how obvious it would be that I substituted the book with the film. Never rely on the movie rendition or, for that matter, what you find online! Your professor makes you read the book for a reason.

> —*VERONICA*
> *QUEENS UNIVERSITY, GRADUATE*

Be careful when buying used books. The person who had the highlighter before you may have been an idiot.

> —*J.T.*
> *UNIVERSITY OF FLORIDA GRADUATE*

Watching the sun come up while studying is not a good thing.

—*JAMESE JAMES*
UNIVERSITY OF
TULSA, GRADUATE

I HAD TO GET USED TO READING A LOT. For my business class, I have about 40 pages to read after every class. For Latin American studies, there's a chapter for that, too. As soon as I get out of classes I do my homework. Then I do more homework at night.

—*S.E.*
UNIVERSITY OF MARYLAND, FRESHMAN

• • • • • • • •

IN HIGH SCHOOL, I NEVER REALLY DID ANY WORK during the day. Here, it's essential to do some work during the day because I find myself easily distracted at night. There's so much freedom and you have so much time in your day, it's tough to balance it all.

—*MOLLY DERINGER*
BROWN UNIVERSITY, FRESHMAN

• • • • • • • •

DON'T STUDY IN YOUR ROOM; you won't ever get to it. Your phone and neighbors will be too enticing. I would suggest a quiet cube at the library, if you really need to get something done.

—*J.S.*
UNIVERSITY OF GEORGIA, GRADUATE

• • • • • • • •

I DON'T CRAM FOR EXAMS. I have trouble studying and focusing. I just assume that I know the material. Instead of cramming, I go over the notes I've taken in class and I go over what I highlighted in my book, and by that point, I probably know everything that I need to know. I take good notes; in an hour-and-a-half class, I write four pages. But I don't study until it's time for the test. I just review it. I never pull an all-nighter.

—*EDITH ZIMMERMAN*
WESLEYAN UNIVERSITY, SOPHOMORE

DON'T PARTY TOO MUCH and then cram. I did, which resulted in my very low GPA my freshman year. As a result, I had to work very hard to make up for it.

—*JESSICA TAYLOR*
STATE UNIVERSITY OF NEW YORK AT GENESEO, GRADUATE

" **It's good to go to class every day, at least to make an impression that you care.** "

—*LUKE MOUGHON*
GEORGIA INSTITUTE OF TECHNOLOGY, SOPHOMORE

I PULLED AN ALL-NIGHTER LAST NIGHT. I get an adrenaline rush from the fact that it's the last second, and I can stay up late without a problem. But I don't recommend doing it, if you can avoid it.

—*M.M.*
NEW YORK UNIVERSITY, SENIOR

MOUNTAIN DEW AND CAFFEINE PILLS HELP you get through all-nighters.

—*ANONYMOUS*
UNIVERSITY OF RHODE ISLAND, SOPHOMORE

GET INVOLVED WITH PEOPLE who are taking classes with you. When you have friends who are doing the same thing with the same goals, it's easy to work together, and you can build off each other, rather than trying to do everything by yourself.

—*COURTNEY WOLFE*
GEORGIA STATE UNIVERSITY, JUNIOR

I ONCE STAYED UP THREE NIGHTS back-to-back. It was fairly intense. I drank coffee, but it was mostly adrenaline; you do what you've got to do. Also, I used to eat chocolate-covered espresso beans. They taste good and it gives you a little boost.

—*B.*
MASSACHUSETTS INSTITUTE OF TECHNOLOGY, GRADUATE

* * * * * * * *

THERE'S LESS DAY-TO-DAY WORK than you have in high school, so you think that you don't have that much and you continue not doing that much. Then it hits you. It all piles up. That's not good.

—*LUCY LINDSEY*
HARVARD UNIVERSITY, FRESHMAN

* * * * * * * *

❝Get old tests from previous semesters; old tests and note-books. There's a code name for this at most schools; find this out the first week of school.❞

—*SEBASTIAN*
GEORGIA INSTITUTE OF TECHNOLOGY, GRADUATE

* * * * * * * *

YOU GET ADDICTED TO IM. Don't get addicted. You'll be writing a paper and you think, "I'm bored." So you start chatting on IM and a one-hour paper turns into like five hours. Take your Internet cable and have someone hide it when you're writing your paper, so you don't get distracted.

—*ASHLEY*
GEORGETOWN UNIVERSITY, SOPHOMORE

I'M TAKING BIOLOGY and you have to read every night to keep up. Two or three days before our exam, I decided I would study for the test. I read eight chapters in three days. That's how I studied.

—*PATRICK*
UNIVERSITY OF RHODE ISLAND, FRESHMAN

• • • • • • • •

DON'T GET TOO DOWN ON YOURSELF if your grades are not as good as they were in high school. You have to get used to each professor and how they grade. I was pretty much an A/B student in high school, but my first semester in college was B/C. Some of my friends went through the same thing and really got down about it and started partying more. I went the other way and started working harder. It really paid off.

—*JENNY PRISUTA*
YOUNGSTOWN STATE UNIVERSITY, SENIOR

• • • • • • • •

That the workload in college is like shoveling snow. If you do a little bit every day, you'll get by. If you wait until everything piles up, it becomes an impossible task.

—*NICHOLAS BONAWITZ UNIVERSITY OF ROCHESTER GRADUATE*

GOT A MAC? DON'T ASK, DON'T TELL

Do not bring your iMac with you to the Citadel. The military academy in Charleston, South Carolina, provides technical support only for the Microsoft Windows operating systems. But the University of Indiana has a policy that it will offer total tech support to any and all computers belonging to students.

YOU CAN BALANCE IT. If there's a choice between doing work and going to a party, I would probably go to the party. I would go to the party before I try to do my paper, but you should try to do your paper before you go to the party.

—*SWEETS*
GEORGIA STATE UNIVERSITY, JUNIOR

• • • • • • • • •

I'VE LEARNED TO LISTEN TO THE PROFESSOR and what he's saying— not just scribble down every-thing that he says—and then try to summarize his thoughts on my notes. Not word-for-word, but the main points.

—*JOSH*
PRINCETON UNIVERSITY, SENIOR

• • • • • • • • •

DON'T TRY TO STUDY ON A FRIDAY NIGHT. You're trying to study in the dorms and people keep coming in. Don't even try.

—*NOURA BAKKOUR*
GEORGETOWN UNIVERSITY, SENIOR

WHAT IF I'M NOT AS SMART AS I THOUGHT I WAS?

Here are the top three ways to be a better student, fast:

1. Sit in the front of every class. Now you'll stay awake.

2. Buy a different notebook or set up a separate binder section for each class—and use it! Now you'll keep up with the material.

3. Reread (or read for the first time, as the case may be!) all your class syllabi. Now the semester holds no unpleasant surprises.

REWARD YOURSELF FOR TASKS COMPLETED by participating in an extracurricular activity or hobby.

—*DAVID*
ANDERSON UNIVERSITY, SENIOR

• • • • • • • •

"Set aside a time every day when you study. No matter what else you do that day, when that time comes, you sit down and study. It can be 45 minutes to an hour. If you do it every day, you'll do better in school."

—*JAKE MALAWAY*
UNIVERSITY OF ILLINOIS, GRADUATE

• • • • • • • •

THE FIRST WEEK HERE, I stayed in my room and studied too much. My second week, I realized I'd missed out on social life, so I stayed up really late socializing in the dorms and did my work only on the weekend. Neither of these methods worked very well. Then I started making a schedule for myself at the beginning of the week, writing down an outline of what I would have to do. I set a reasonable bedtime for myself. Now, I stick to that schedule and I really enjoy myself.

—*CAROL*
HUNTER COLLEGE, FRESHMAN

YOU HAVE TO KEEP WEIRD HOURS. Sometimes at 3 a.m. you're doing your work. But it's just what you have to do.

—*T.O.*
HOWARD UNIVERSITY, SOPHOMORE

• • • • • • • • •

I PULLED MY FIRST ALL-NIGHTER LAST WEEK. I did two nights in a row. I was up from 5 a.m. on Tuesday morning to 3 p.m. on Thursday afternoon. It was tough. I went to class to turn in my second paper on Thursday; I got there, sat down, and hit the desk. I fell asleep and someone woke me up at the end of class and I turned in my paper. Diet Coke with lemon pulled me through.

—*WHITNEY*
YALE UNIVERSITY, FRESHMAN

Money for Your Life: Working & Finances

N o matter what else you learn this year, you'll learn that nothing is free—especially in college, where they definitely know how to pile up the fees and surcharges. In this chapter, you'll see how other students managed to keep their costs down and even get some money coming in. Read on to find out why working (especially on campus) isn't so bad, particularly if you get a job where you can eat for free, bond with the dean, study while working, meet cute fellow students, or maybe even exercise a tiny amount of power. As a freshman, you basically have zero power—so why not become that kid in the campus post office who controls the date stamp? Or the one in the cafeteria who decides which classmate will receive that extra dollop of Jell-O? Take control of your finances and live that dream!

DON'T THINK THAT WHEN YOU GO to the ATM machine and do a "current balance" check, the figure it spits out is really your current balance. I thought it was. I amassed probably $500 in bounced check fees my first semester. No one ever taught me how to balance a checkbook. Get your parents to teach you that before you go, and then make sure you do it when you're at school.

—*K.E.R.*
FLORIDA STATE UNIVERSITY, GRADUATE

FRESHMAN FACTOID

How students cover the cost of college:

• Financial aid and scholarships (37%)

• Pay for it themselves (9%)

• Parents pay (13%)

• Some combination of the above (41%)

IF I WERE WRITING A BOOK about the things they don't tell you when you enter college, the first chapter would cover the hidden costs of living away from home—travel, long distance telephone, and school supplies, for example. However, the most shocking expense is food: the midnight pizzas, the birthday dinners, the celebration dinners, and the random exoduses from campus when you just can't take it anymore, add up in a hurry.

—*ADAM*
ELON UNIVERSITY, SOPHOMORE

I HAVE AN ON-CAMPUS JOB in the women's studies department and in the dance department. Also, they have a bartending agency here and you get paid $20 an hour. I took the course so I can do that when I want to. I don't think all colleges have a bartending course, but usually there's a babysitting agency. Working on campus doesn't pay as much, but it's so much easier. There's nothing to do; I get paid for doing my homework.

—*LAUREN WEBSTER*
BARNARD COLLEGE, JUNIOR

TOP THREE INEXPENSIVE DATES

You have chosen to defy the hookup/FWB culture and actually ask someone out on a date. You want to impress him or her, but you're not exactly Donald Trump. What can you do to impress that special guy or girl without blowing your textbook budget for the year?

1. **Breakfast in the park.** Cheaper than a restaurant brunch, and a much better view. All you need is a blanket, bagels and coffee, and jeans for sitting on the ground. Your date will be amazed that you got so organized so early in the morning.

2. **Front-row seats at one of those freebie campus concerts.** If the concert is good, your date will admire your taste. And even if it's bad, you'll bond by making fun of the performance afterwards, over (small) cappuccinos.

4. **Athletic exertion.** Mini golf and bowling have the advantages of being fun, funny, and cheap. But don't go if you're a sore loser—on an important date, sulking is definitely not allowed.

I HAVE A CHECKBOOK AND I RECORD what I spend. As for getting a job—try to milk your parents as much as possible. It's too hard to try to do it all; don't overwhelm yourself, if possible.

—*JESSICA*
BARNARD COLLEGE, JUNIOR

• • • • • • • •

IT'S BETTER NOT TO WORK your freshman year, or at least the first quarter, because you're still adjusting. I was overwhelmed by the homework. And if you work your first year you don't get to meet as many people. But later, working helps to keep you focused. You gain skills and it helps you learn to budget your time. It's good to work on campus because they're flexible, and they'll give you time off during finals.

—*ABBY HERNANDEZ*
UNIVERSITY OF CALIFORNIA AT SANTA BARBARA, JUNIOR

• • • • • • • •

I WORK AS A WAITRESS ON CAMPUS. I work 11:30 a.m.–2:30 p.m. so it fits well into my work/study plan. My nights are open, I'm paid in cash, and I get tips. I keep a car at school, which is an expense, so I enjoy working; it's empowering. My parents are generous, but again, I enjoy having my own income and have been able to save a lot, which is important to me as I plan for my future.

—*VANESSA VALENZUELA*
SONOMA STATE UNIVERSITY, SOPHOMORE

• • • • • • • •

DON'T GET A JOB YOUR FRESHMAN YEAR. You don't know how involved in organizations you'll be or how much time you'll have to dedicate to school. But definitely work during Christmas and summer vacations, and save the money you earn.

—*SHEILA CRAWFORD*
NORTH CAROLINA STATE UNIVERSITY, SOPHOMORE

Skip the meal plan and buy your own groceries.

—*EAMON SIGGINS*
STATE UNIVERSITY OF NEW YORK AT BINGHAMTON GRADUATE

GET THE FLOOD INSURANCE

In January of my freshman year I was woken up one cold morning at three o'clock by the fire alarm going off in the hall of my dorm. I ran outside as fast as I could in my pajama shorts and T-shirt. They turned off the fire alarm, but something in the sprinkler system had malfunctioned, setting off the sprinkler in our hall, so we had a good five inches of disgusting, rusty water on the floors of our rooms. I had stored all of my schoolbooks under my bed, and they were now completely submerged in water, along with a good deal of dirty clothes strewn about, my printer, and all the electronics. The school informed me that because I hadn't bought insurance through them, they wouldn't cover any of the damage.

So keep your room neat, because you never know when you'll have gallons of rusty water flooding your room. And if the school offers insurance for a reasonable price, it's worth getting.

—MOLLY DONAHUE
SYRACUSE UNIVERSITY, SOPHOMORE

BUYING BOOKS

You can buy books online but then you have to wait two days for the shipment. I bought mine like that, but then realized how long it would take to get here, so I had to cancel the order. The problem with buying used books is that sometimes there will be pages missing. And don't get used books if there is a new edition out. I know people who did this; the page numbers don't match up and the problems don't match up. They're constantly coming to my dorm to ask me what's going on.

—MORGAN
COLUMBIA UNIVERSITY, FRESHMAN

GET A CHECK card instead of a credit card. But be careful with it. And don't use the on-campus bank—it's always the worst bank.

—ANONYMOUS
JOHNS HOPKINS UNIVERSITY, JUNIOR

• • • • • • • •

THERE ARE A LOT of good budgeting programs for your computer; that's what helped me. You have to stay on top of it. Come up with a system for tracking your bank account or you will get screwed. Those charges will add up.

—RUTH FEINBLUM
BRYN MAWR COLLEGE, JUNIOR

GET SOME FIRSTHAND office experience before you graduate. You learn how to interact with people, and you have your own money for the first time in your life. You can pay for tuition and rent; you can live on your own. That freedom can help you achieve more.

—*M.B.*
SAN JOSE STATE UNIVERSITY, GRADUATE

It's a good experience to have a job.

—*M.B.*
SAN JOSE STATE UNIVERSITY GRADUATE

❝ Whatever is left after school expenses, invest it in either money-market accounts or CDs. Within four years you have a nice little bundle saved.❞

—*NIROSHAN RAJARATNAM*
UNIVERSITY OF MARYLAND, GRADUATE

I TRY NOT TO GO OUT too much or go shopping too much and just try to keep the costs down any way I can.

—*CHANA WEINER*
BARNARD COLLEGE, SOPHOMORE

EVERY TIME YOU GO OUT, when all your friends are having that last drink, cut yourself off; don't have that last drink. Then, go home and put the money you saved in a piggy bank. You'll be surprised how quickly it adds up. And you can go out and buy a new outfit.

—*S.G.*
COLUMBIA UNIVERSITY, SENIOR

TAKE AS LITTLE FINANCIAL ASSISTANCE as possible; debts stink. Work hard and try to pay as much up front as you can. I worked in the summers and at night leading up to college, and that helped pay bills during my first year of school.

—*MICHAEL ALBERT PAOLI*
 UNIVERSITY OF TORONTO, GRADUATE

• • • • • • • •

I THINK IT'S GOOD TO WORK A FEW HOURS a week at least, and that can be your weekend spending money. I worked at a restaurant and I used my tips as my spending money. It's also a good way to meet people in your school's town, so you get away from college, so you can vent, so you can be well rounded.

—*MEGHAN*
 UNIVERSITY OF NOTRE DAME, JUNIOR

• • • • • • • •

I REFEREED FOR INTRAMURALS. I was lucky, because my parents helped me out quite a bit. But even if you do get help or are on scholarship, I would recommend getting a job at some point. I know some people who work at the library, and they just sit there and study while getting paid for it. On the other hand, I knew people who did research for work in college, and that was like adding another three- or six-hour class; that was tough.

—*JOHN BENTLEY*
 TRINITY UNIVERSITY, GRADUATE

Food For Thought: Pop-Tarts, Beer & Other Essential Nutrients

s it humanly possible to eat pizza every day for a whole semester? Is the "Freshman 15" a myth or an unhappy reality? Will your 10 a.m. history professor mind if you bring your breakfast to class? Does the maraschino cherry on top of your sundae count as one of those five fruit and vegetable servings you vaguely remember hearing about? Yes, freshman year means you must face many food-related quandaries. For possibly the first time in your life, you have total freedom to eat when, where, and what you want. Let our friendly guides steer you around the Pop Rocks.

If you drink the beer, you're gonna gain the weight.

—BRIAN ROSEN
PRINCETON
UNIVERSITY
GRADUATE

GET A GEORGE FOREMAN GRILL, or even just a toaster oven. You'd be surprised at how much you can make with those, from bagel pizzas to steak.

—JESSIE
VILLA JULIE COLLEGE, JUNIOR

· · · · · · · ·

I HAVE WEIRD EATING HABITS. I eat rice cakes and dried pineapple. I don't know why. Also, chocolate helps.

—ANONYMOUS
YALE UNIVERSITY, SOPHOMORE

· · · · · · · ·

HOW TO DECIDE IF YOU WANT THE MEAL PLAN: If you like to eat lots of food and you're not picky about quality, then eat at school. But if you care about things like taste, plan on buying your meals elsewhere. I bought the meal plan and was happy with it. You could eat tons of food cheap. Was it good? No. But as long as I was full, I didn't care.

—DON WAZZENEGER
YOUNGSTOWN STATE UNIVERSITY, SENIOR

· · · · · · · ·

THIS IS THE FOOD HERE: They have all the basic food, and then they have these huge vats of sauce. And they just slosh the sauce over the food and it becomes disgusting.

—LUCY LINDSEY
HARVARD UNIVERSITY, FRESHMAN

· · · · · · · ·

SCARF THAT FOOD DOWN! Everyone eats faster than you. I had to go to the cafeteria 15 minutes before my roommates and friends just to be finished at the same time.

—JOY HEARNDON
MICHIGAN TECHNOLOGICAL UNIVERSITY, GRADUATE

TAKE EVERY FREE MEAL you can get. Generally, the dining hall is not bad. But when you eat it seven days a week, it gets pretty old, no matter how good the food is. Every time someone wants to take you out, take them up on it. If nothing else, it's a good way to make friends or meet people.

—*JONATHAN COHEN*
EMORY UNIVERSITY, SENIOR

* * * * * * * *

THE FIRST INCLINATION when you get to college is to eat anything you want. Mom isn't there making sure you eat your vegetables. But three months and 15 pounds later you find out why a mom is a good thing when it comes to food.

—*D.R.*
UNIVERSITY OF NORTH CAROLINA, GRADUATE

* * * * * * * *

I RECOMMEND THAT ONE ACQUIRE a taste for hummus. Hummus can really be put onto anything, it comes in all sorts of flavors, it's healthy, and it's relatively cheap if bought in bulk. Seriously, try and think of something that hummus wouldn't be good on; you can't!

—*STEVEN COY*
SAN DIEGO STATE UNIVERSITY, SOPHOMORE

* * * * * * * *

DON'T THINK THAT YOU WON'T GAIN that Freshman 15 by ordering pizza while watching late-night TV (in my case, David Letterman), eating Burger King, and drinking every night.

—*K.E.R.*
FLORIDA STATE UNIVERSITY
GRADUATE

> ✓
>
> **Don't eat the food.**
>
> —*SIERRA*
> *CAL POLY SAN LUIS OBISPO, JUNIOR*

The Freshman 15 happens to everyone, and don't believe anyone who tells you otherwise.

—*AMY*
PRINCETON
UNIVERSITY
FRESHMAN

DON'T BUY THE FULL MEAL TICKET, unless you're sure you can eat breakfast every day. I made it to breakfast once the whole year. When I got up, I didn't have time to go downstairs and eat; I had to go to class.

—*JAKE MALAWAY*
UNIVERSITY OF ILLINOIS, GRADUATE

• • • • • • • •

I WOULDN'T GET ON ANY MEAL PLAN. I would fend for myself, foodwise. Cafeteria food is bad.

—*ERICA MARIOLA*
EMORY UNIVERSITY, GRADUATE

• • • • • • • •

BE CAREFUL WHAT YOU COOK in your toaster. My friend bought some frozen hot dogs—like, six of them—and then one day she was hungry so she tried to cook them in the toaster in her dorm room, and smoke came out of it and she set off the fire alarm. So she had to go to peer review, which was funny because most of the cases they get in peer review are people using excessive bandwidth from downloading too much, and then they get this interesting case. For punishment they said she had to make a few posters saying, "Be safe—don't put hot dogs in toasters."

—*J.R. MCKINNEY*
UNIVERSITY OF CALIFORNIA AT BERKELEY, SOPHOMORE

• • • • • • • •

THE HOT-DOG VENDOR will become your new best friend.

—*J.G.*
FLORIDA STATE UNIVERSITY, GRADUATE

• • • • • • • •

BUY LOTS OF TUPPERWARE CONTAINERS to take to the cafeteria and sneak food out, so you don't have to buy it. You're paying for a meal plan anyway.

—*MEG*
UNIVERSITY OF NORTH CAROLINA, GRADUATE

DON'T ASSUME YOU WON'T GAIN WEIGHT just because as a teen in high school you ate a lot. In my first year of college, I didn't understand the concept of self-control with food. The all-you-can-eat buffet seemed like a good idea at the time, especially where the cookies and brownies were concerned. I used to stash as many as I could carry under a folded napkin and was so proud of myself for being able to sneak out with it—as if it were an accomplishment! I didn't realize that all I accomplished was a good 15 pounds. I was convinced that I couldn't fit into my clothes anymore because the dry air in the dorm room shrunk them all.

—*VERONICA*
QUEENS UNIVERSITY, GRADUATE

• • • • • • • •

GET YOUR OWN MINI-FRIDGE and buy your own food. Buy Easy Mac—it's microwaveable maca-roni and cheese—so you don't need a stove.

—*SIERRA*
CAL POLY SAN LUIS OBISPO, JUNIOR

• • • • • • • •

DON'T EAT THE EGGS IN THE DINING COMMONS—they're fake. Anything you can eat from a bowl, like cereal and salad, is good. Don't eat a lot of fast food just because it's there and it's cheap. Jamba Juice is the way to go: it won't make you fat, it's kind of healthy, and it doesn't smell bad so you can take it to class and no one will yell at you. You get these people who go to class with a burger and onion rings and sit there for an hour in class and it's gross.

—*KYM*
SAN JOSE STATE UNIVERSITY, SOPHOMORE

BEST THINGS TO COOK UP IN A DORM KITCHEN

Brownies (from a mix)

Instant noodle-and-sauce packages

Pasta and sauce in a jar

Precooked chicken meat

Store-bought cookie dough

The dining hall was good. But I'm glad I don't eat there anymore.

—CHRIS MCANDREW
UNIVERSITY OF
DELAWARE, JUNIOR

AFTER I COULD NO LONGER AFFORD a meal plan, my friend and I would scour the campus paper and fliers for events with free food. Then, we would fill in our own "Free Food Calendar" with all the times and places of those events. We would end up at academic speeches, random barbecues, or various group meetings, none of which we belonged to or knew anything about. But they put out free food at these events. We wound up eating for free at least three to four times every week. You can't beat that!

—CHAVON MITCHELL
XAVIER, GRADUATE

. . . .

❝You're going to gain weight and you're going to take it off the next summer. Don't worry about it. Buy some fat pants. Everybody I know gained a lot of weight.❞

—HANNAH
EMORY UNIVERSITY, JUNIOR

. . . .

I HAVE A LOT OF SNACKS IN MY ROOM—macaroni and cheese and peanut butter and jelly. You might want to bring that kind of stuff, in case you can't make it to the cafeteria or don't want to go, for whatever reason.

—ANONYMOUS
UNIVERSITY OF MARYLAND
FRESHMAN

TOP THREE ZERO-EFFORT HEALTHY SNACKS

1. **BANANAS:** Requiring no preparation and no utensils, these wonders of nature are also easy to carry in a backpack.

2. **NATURAL YOGURT:** Try to avoid the brands full of artificial sweeteners and other chemicals, and you're all set. Spoon is recommended but not absolutely mandatory.

3. **FROZEN ORANGE JUICE:** No, not the concentrate that comes in a can. Instead, buy the smallest cartons you can get at the campus store, wedge them in the freezer section of your mini fridge, and pry them out the next day for frosty deliciousness.

YOU SHOULD ALWAYS have chips in the dorm room when you're up at four in the morning writing a paper.

—*DAN AMERMAN*
  YALE UNIVERSITY, SOPHOMORE

MOST IMPORTANT PIECE OF ADVICE I ever received about college food: If you find a hair in your food in the dining hall, just assume it's yours and move on.

—*MATT LACKNER*
PRINCETON UNIVERSITY, GRADUATE

• • • • • • • • •

DON'T BE FOOLED by the Freshman 15. Real men go for the Freshman 30; at least that's how I cope with it.

—*ADAM*
ELON UNIVERSITY, SOPHOMORE

Ready to Wear: Fashion & (Eventually) Laundry

gnore what the fashion magazines tell you to wear this season; those people don't know anything about your lifestyle. You don't have a laundry service, dry cleaner, tailor, personal dresser, makeup artist, stylist, and airbrush technician greeting you in the morning with a cup of herbal tea. Instead, you have a pile of semiclean clothes and 10 minutes to get dressed and get to class. This chapter will give you some handy tips for looking (and smelling!) good, despite all that. And why not read it in the laundry room? Could be a conversation starter.

You can wear your pajamas around campus; you won't be the only one.

*—Amy Forbes
Mississippi State University Graduate*

NOBODY LIKES THE PREPSTERS. They're done all up; that's just pretentious. You've got to find your own style.

*—Molly
Brown University, Sophomore*

• • • • • • • • •

BIG FASHION FAUX PAS—the lanyard with the ID in it. We have what is called a "one-card." It gets you into the dorms and some other buildings. The sure sign of a first-year is the lanyard with the one-card, especially the "Wellesley College" lanyard in your class color. Some first-years don't catch on and the poor dears wander around with them all year.

*—Sarah
Wellesley College, Sophomore*

• • • • • • • • •

I DIDN'T OWN A VERA BRADLEY and that's a faux pas at UVA. Vera Bradleys are these quilted bags, kind of like if your grandma made you a present, except more expensive. I swore I would never ever own one. Well, now I have one with two matching belts, and I want the umbrella.

*—Jo
University of Virginia, Senior*

HISTORY CORNER

Oberlin College has long been known for its progressive ideals, and admitted women students as well as men back when higher-education opportunities for women were rare. But all was not equal, even at Oberlin. In the 19th century, female students were responsible for the male students' laundry.

IF YOU LIVE IN A DORM AND YOUR BATHROOM is down the hall, get good shower shoes. If you go barefoot, by mid-October they'll be studying the stuff on your feet in biology class.

—*J.T.*
UNIVERSITY OF FLORIDA, GRADUATE

• • • • • • • •

DO NOT BRING CLOTHES that require ironing or dry cleaning or special handling. And do not loan your favorite shirt to a party-happy friend if you want it back in the same condition. If you are female, leave your handbag at home. No one brings a purse to a party, and during the day your backpack is your bag.

—*J.*
UNIVERSITY OF GEORGIA, GRADUATE

• • • • • • • •

"No one will really notice if you wear the same two or three (or one) pair of jeans or khakis— it's the shirt that people notice. So get plenty of shirts and one or two pairs of jeans and you can cut laundry efforts in half."

—*DAN*
MIAMI UNIVERSITY, FRESHMAN

• • • • • • • •

GUYS, BRING KHAKIS in the fall and then cut them off in the spring.

—*STEVE DAVIS*
FLORIDA STATE UNIVERSITY, GRADUATE

BUY A STURDY, ROOMY BACKPACK. You'll need it to hold thick, heavy textbooks for courses like English, political science, biology, algebra, etc.

> —BRIAN TURNER
> UNIVERSITY OF GEORGIA, GRADUATE

• • • • • • • •

RESIST CONFORMITY. We have too many Gap kids and Abercrombie look-alikes running around campus.

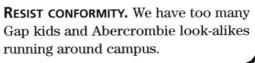

> —KHALIL SULLIVAN
> PRINCETON UNIVERSITY, JUNIOR

Just get lots of underwear and only do laundry when you run out.

—MEREDITH
BROWN UNIVERSITY
SOPHOMORE

• • • • • • • •

NEVER ATTEND A PUNK-ROCK CONCERT in a sundress and Keds sneakers. I left a Ramones concert wearing only one shoe after getting caught in the middle of a group of overeager slam-dancers. Doc Martens would have been a better choice.

> —LYNN LAMOUSIN
> LOUISIANA STATE UNIVERSITY, GRADUATE

• • • • • • • •

IF YOU FIND YOURSELF IN THE LAUNDRY ROOM and don't know how to wash your own clothes, do not push the "help" button. This button is for security purposes only; for example, if you are attacked. No little helper will come and help you wash your clothes. Instead, you will sound the alarm and call the police.

> —ANONYMOUS
> UNIVERSITY OF PENNSYLVANIA, SENIOR

• • • • • • • •

IF YOU WANT TO BE COOL, don't wear anything with your school name or colors on it. It's called Freshman Fashion Wear for a reason.

> —J.G.
> FLORIDA STATE UNIVERSITY, GRADUATE

SPECIAL HYGIENE SECTION

Thanks to all those imperfectly socialized freshmen who made this page possible—and necessary.

IF POSSIBLE, TRY TO FIND THE SHOWER IN YOUR DORM with the best pressure and the most considerate bathroom users and ask politely to share it with them. A nice hot shower under a showerhead with good pressure is a great way to unwind. Be considerate of other bathroom users! Don't leave a mess for your janitors; they are there to maintain a standard of hygiene, not to clean up your messes.

> —*ARIEL MELENDEZ*
> *PRINCETON UNIVERSITY, FRESHMAN*

EVEN IF IT DOESN'T BOTHER YOU to walk around for a few days without a shower—please, oh God, before you forgo the morning cleaning, please think of the person sitting next to you in class.

> —*ADAM*
> *ELON UNIVERSITY, SOPHOMORE*

SHOWERING EVERY DAY IS A MUST. There are college students who think they can go more than a day without showering, but they are sorely mistaken. Trust me when I say that it can be painfully (and nauseatingly) obvious when someone has not bathed properly. As a courtesy to those around you, remember to take a shower.

> —*JOSHUA BERKOV*
> *BROWN UNIVERSITY, JUNIOR*

JUST BECAUSE YOU CAN'T SMELL IT, doesn't mean it's not there. Shower at least once a day and especially after coming from the gym.

> —*KHALIL SULLIVAN*
> *PRINCETON UNIVERSITY, JUNIOR*

DON'T TURN COLLEGE into an uncomfortable place to be. There is no sense in wearing high heels to school!

—ERICA LANGE-HENNESEY
TEXAS STATE UNIVERSITY, SENIOR

. . . .

"During crunch time, you need only a few pieces of clothing: Sweatpants in school color of choice, comfy tank top or ratty T-shirt, and a hoodie."

—AMY
PRINCETON UNIVERSITY, FRESHMAN

. . . .

MY FRESHMAN-YEAR ROOMMATE and I were polar opposites. She was a city girl from D.C., really stylish, and she hated the way I dressed. When I got up in the morning to go to class, I would throw on my jeans, a sweatshirt, and my Birkenstocks, and for the first couple of weeks she would block the door so I couldn't leave. She would say, "Uh-uh, girl. You are not leaving the room like that." I would say that I was just going to class, and she would say, "Girl, you could be cute if you changed your style or did your hair. You could get yourself a boyfriend!" Finally, by Thanksgiving break, we came to an understanding: She would never wear Birkenstocks, and I would never wear tall, black, leather boots. But as I left for break, she told me, "Girl, do two things for yourself over break: Style your hair, and buy black shoes."

—SUMMER J.
UNIVERSITY OF VIRGINIA, SENIOR

LAUNDRY 101

Just about the last thing I ever feel like doing in college is my laundry. Either I don't have quarters, don't have soap, or just don't care that my clothes are more wrinkled and dank than Bea Arthur on a humid day. If this sounds like you, try sticking to the following strategies for avoiding the laundry room:

For shirts, pants and the like, divide your clothes into two categories. Category One is the stuff you wear every day. Keep these items as clean as possible and when you're done wearing them, fold them neatly, put them in your drawer, and pretend they're clean. A squirt of Febreze might help as well.

Category Two is your "going-out-to-parties clothes." This should be only one or two shirts and a pair of pants, which will stink of beer and smoke after a night out. Keep these in a trash bag on your closet floor. Wear them on Friday nights. No one will know the difference.

Tempting as it may be, you're not allowed to wear underwear twice. It's just wrong. You'll need to go to Wal-Mart and get 30 pairs of tightie-whities and 30 pairs of white tube socks. Wear each pair one day, and then once a month, throw all of them in the wash. It's all white, so you can do one load, and because it's just socks and underwear, you don't have to fold or sort anything. Just put them in another trash bag, next to your Friday night clothes. Keep two pairs of clean boxers on hand for dates.

—ADAM F.
GEORGE WASHINGTON UNIVERSITY, GRADUATE

STRANGE BUT TRUE UNDER-WEAR TALES

I WAS ON THE WAY to the laundry room and I dropped my underwear on the dorm stairs. I didn't realize until someone came up to me and said, "You dropped your underwear on the stairs." I was so embarrassed.

—*CONSTANCE A. LINDSAY*
DUKE UNIVERSITY, GRADUATE

· · · · · · · · ·

I HAD THIS GIRL who did my laundry and I would notice that I was losing underwear. I rummaged through her stuff one day and found six pairs of my Fruit of the Looms! I haven't trusted anyone with my clothing since.

—*RYAN BOWEN*
THE UNIVERSITY OF GEORGIA, SENIOR

· · · · · · · · ·

ONE TIME, THE WASHERS WERE BROKEN at the dorms. So I asked my new guy friend, who was six years older, if I could wash some clothes at his place. I finished washing and left but had forgotten a load at his place. His friends came over that night and saw my yellow thongs and pink granny panties. Needless to say we stopped hanging out.

—*M.T.*
GEORGIA STATE UNIVERSITY, SENIOR

· · · · · · · · ·

I HAD GIRL'S UNDERWEAR in my laundry one time; she must have left it in the dryer. They had her name in them, so I went to her room to give them back. It was kind of awkward, at least for me.

—*ALEX*
EMORY UNIVERSITY, SOPHOMORE

· · · · · · · · ·

KEEP TRACK OF THE TIME when you are doing your laundry. During my freshman year I was late to take my clothes out of the dryer and someone stole my Victoria's Secret underwear and left my granny panties. I was so mad!

—*DANIELLE*
DUKE UNIVERSITY, GRADUATE

SWEATS ARE ALL THE RAGE, especially if they have Greek letters on them or a logo of an organization that you are in. But don't wear the ones that simply have the school logo. I heard someone say that they were able to identify all of the freshmen because they wore our school's logo on everything.

—*SUSAN MORGENBESSER*
PENNSYLVANIA STATE UNIVERSITY, GRADUATE

"*Laundry is expensive, and you have to be careful because people will steal your stuff. I had a problem with that. I had to take my homework down there and do it while doing laundry.*"

—*B.M.*
UNIVERSITY OF MARYLAND, JUNIOR

WARNING: DON'T WASH DOWN COMFORTERS. You'll flood the laundry room and ruin your blanket.

—*ETHAN WASSERMAN*
BOSTON UNIVERSITY, JUNIOR

I HAVE NOT USED MY COMB YET. I have not worn any college shirts, either. A lot of the kids do that, but I haven't worn one, and my mom packed 15 of them.

—*BAYLESS PARSLEY*
UNIVERSITY OF VIRGINIA, FRESHMAN

I'VE BEEN DOING MY OWN LAUNDRY since I was 12, but in college, I got a really big laundry bag and saved it and took it home, an hour and a half away.

—*MELISSA K. BYRNES*
AMHERST COLLEGE, GRADUATE

• • • • • • • • •

GET A LAUNDRY SERVICE. People will take your clothes out of the washer and dryer.

—*J.G.*
GEORGE WASHINGTON UNIVERSITY, SENIOR

• • • • • • • • •

I HAD NEVER DONE LAUNDRY before in my life, but it's not that bad. Wash in cold water.

—*KATHY*
UNIVERSITY OF DELAWARE, FRESHMAN

• • • • • • • • •

FOR LAUNDRY, I WAIT until I have no clothes left, and then I do two big loads all at once and I'm done with it in a couple of hours.

—*ANONYMOUS*
UNIVERSITY OF PENNSYLVANIA, SOPHOMORE

• • • • • • • • •

COLLEGE IS A GREAT PLACE TO MEET all kinds of new people. But sometimes you can get into a rut—your daily routine becomes so regimented that you don't encounter as many new people as you did in the beginning. That's when it's time to try something new or go someplace different. In my case, this was the laundry room. I found that on the rare occasions I went to the laundry room, I would make friends with one or two of the people waiting for their clothes to dry.

—*BRANDON WALKER*
JAMES MADISON UNIVERSITY, SOPHOMORE

Never wear anything from your high school. I mean, we all went to high school, but you don't have to advertise it.

—*J.T.*
UNIVERSITY OF FLORIDA, GRADUATE

IF YOU HAVE A LIMITED CLOTHES BUDGET, spend it on jeans. Jeans never go out of style. If you have some extra cash, buy socks and underwear. They seem to disappear between the dorm rooms and the Laundromat.

—*DON WAZZENEGER*
YOUNGSTOWN STATE UNIVERSITY, SENIOR

• • • • • • • •

IF AT ALL POSSIBLE, GO TO A SCHOOL in a state where your grandmother lives an hour away and just take your laundry there. You need to visit her every once in a while, anyway. So take your laundry there; she'll cook you dinner.

—*ANONYMOUS*
UNIVERSITY OF VIRGINIA, SOPHOMORE

• • • • • • • •

FIND SOMEONE WHO REALLY KNOWS how to do laundry. You get here and you realize that you don't understand how not to dye all your clothes pink.

—*LUCY LINDSEY*
HARVARD UNIVERSITY, FRESHMAN

• • • • • • • •

BEWARE OF WHAT YOU PUT in the communal washing machines. When I was a freshman, I decided to wash my orange rug. There was so much lint on it that it got on everyone else's clothes in that washing machine. Everybody knew it came from me.

—*GLENDA L. RICHARDSON*
DUKE UNIVERSITY, GRADUATE

• • • • • • • •

I FIND MYSELF BUYING UNDERWEAR instead of actually doing laundry. My advice is to wait until after the holidays and get the holiday packs of boxers for $1.99 at the Gap. I do that a lot. I have a lot of boxers with holly on them. And you can get a lot of free T-shirts from clubs.

—*MARTIN*
GEORGETOWN UNIVERSITY, SOPHOMORE

If it doesn't smell bad or have stains on it, it's not dirty.

—*HASSAN*
UNIVERSITY OF TULSA, GRADUATE

READ THE LABELS! Whenever I did laundry, I made it a point to read the directions on the detergent boxes and the labels on the clothes. I also read the directions on the washing machines. I didn't want anything going wrong; clothes are too expensive!

> —*JOSH*
> *MISSOURI STATE UNIVERSITY, GRADUATE*

• • • • • • • •

NEVER, EVER MOVE SOMEONE'S LAUNDRY from the dryer. I did this once. When I came to pick up my clothes, I found a girl sitting in a chair she'd dragged into the laundry room, waiting for me to come back so she could give me a piece of her mind.

> —*ALLISON GRECO*
> *MONTCLAIR STATE UNIVERSITY, GRADUATE*

• • • • • • • •

HANG UP CLOTHES IF THEY'RE NOT REALLY, really dirty. It keeps them from getting wrinkled.

> —*JOEL*
> *PRINCETON UNIVERSITY, GRADUATE*

• • • • • • • •

MAKE FRIENDS WITH KIDS whose parents live close by and do laundry at their parents' house. I lugged laundry home on a two-hour train ride just so I didn't have to do it. It was a real pain. And do the essentials so that you don't run out of underwear and towels.

> —*J.P.G.*
> *UNIVERSITY OF PENNSYLVANIA, SOPHOMORE*

• • • • • • • •

BUY A LOT OF UNDERWEAR before you go. You can wear jeans until they walk. But you have to wash your underwear.

> —*CHRISTINE*
> *UNIVERSITY OF RHODE ISLAND, SOPHOMORE*

FRESHMAN FACTOID

At the Graffiti Party at the Rose-Hulman Institute of Technology (Indiana), the dress code is simple: a plain white T-shirt, that is, so your artsy school-mates can decorate you with Magic Markers.

WHEN TO DO IT

DO YOUR LAUNDRY IN THE MIDDLE OF THE WEEK, not on the weekends.

> —KELLI
> UNIVERSITY OF DELAWARE, SOPHOMORE

• • • • • • • •

DO LAUNDRY IN THE MIDDLE OF THE NIGHT or early in the morning— no one's there.

> —CASEY
> GEORGETOWN UNIVERSITY, SENIOR

• • • • • • • •

DO NOT DO LAUNDRY ON FRIDAY, SATURDAY, OR SUNDAY. Wait until Monday, midday, when most people are at class. The maintenance staff has already fixed the machines from the weekend, and you don't have to worry about people taking your laundry out.

> —H.D. BALLARD
> UNIVERSITY OF VIRGINIA, FRESHMAN

• • • • • • • •

I DO LAUNDRY A LOT, BETWEEN CLASSES in the morning or afternoon, during the week, and on the weekend. I do it whenever I can, to get it out of the way.

> —JENNIFER A. SICKLICK
> GEORGE WASHINGTON UNIVERSITY, FRESHMAN

• • • • • • • •

DON'T DO LAUNDRY ON SUNDAY. Everyone does it that day.

> —ANONYMOUS
> UNIVERSITY OF MARYLAND, SOPHOMORE

• • • • • • • •

I DO MY LAUNDRY SUNDAY MORNING. I set my alarm clock early. By the end of the week, all my clothes are dirty, and during the week I don't have time.

> —AMY HOFFBERG
> UNIVERSITY OF DELAWARE, FRESHMAN

I HEARD SOME HORROR STORIES about people's roommates forgetting to wash their sheets. That will keep people out of your room.

—*MIKE PARKER*
GEORGETOWN UNIVERSITY, SOPHOMORE

• • • • • • • •

I'M THE GIRL IN JEANS, a university T-shirt, and flip-flops. At the beginning of every fall semester I would see freshman girls walking around campus in high heels; and I would always smile and nod because I knew by the end of the day their feet would be in so much pain. The only advice I can give about fashion is to be comfortable in whatever you are wearing.

—*QUONIAS*
UNIVERSITY OF WEST GEORGIA, SENIOR

• • • • • • • •

SOME FRESHMEN TRY TOO HARD. They try to be too radical, or too preppy. I mean, fashion is part of who you are. But don't try too hard.

—*THEODORE SCHIMENTI*
COLUMBIA UNIVERSITY, FRESHMAN

SAFE SCIENCE

One day a freshman chemistry major flounced into my office after being sent out of lab for inappropriate attire. To participate in lab, students are required to be fairly well-covered in case the odd chemical splashes up, or someone drops a beaker. This freshman was wearing a tube top, micro-miniskirt, high-heeled sandals, and dangly jewelry.

"Why'd they make me leave?" she wailed. "I was wearing my safety goggles!"

THE LAUNDRY ROOM is a pretty competitive spot. Stay with your clothes while they are in the washer and dryer. Bring homework with you, your phone, your laptop, whatever. Don't leave! If you do, there is a significant chance you will come back to find your underwear strewn all over the room because someone wanted your machine. This will probably happen as you enter the laundry room with a member of the opposite sex.

—*LAURA TRUBIANO*
HAMILTON COLLEGE, JUNIOR

"Shower. Don't go to class in your sweaty gym clothes. I know your mom is not at college with you to dress you, but get cleaned up; it's distracting."

—*MOLLY*
BROWN UNIVERSITY, SOPHOMORE

HOW TO MANIPULATE YOUR PARENTS into doing your laundry: When my mom was scheduled to visit, I'd throw practically all my clothes—clean or dirty—around the room. I knew that she wouldn't be able to take the sight of it. She'd take my stuff, clean it, fold it, and bring it back. That's a service you just can't beat!

—*JENNY PRISUTA*
YOUNGSTOWN STATE UNIVERSITY, SENIOR

The popped collar thing is too much. Do not pop your collar—that's out.

—*Jarrod Timothy Young*
North Carolina A&T State University, Senior

YOU KNOW IT'S TIME to do laundry when you run out of underwear. I know guys who said it was time to do laundry when you've worn your underwear inside out. That's pretty gross.

—*Nat*
University of Rhode Island, Sophomore

• • • • • • • • •

AS LONG AS YOUR WARDROBE doesn't consist of only leather pants and tiger print shirts, fashion isn't a big deal.

—*Jo*
University of Virginia, Senior

• • • • • • • • •

I NEVER DID MY OWN LAUNDRY before college, so I had no idea what to do. I felt embarrassed because I thought that I should know how to do this and I was the only one at college who didn't. But that isn't true; most people don't do their laundry at home. My roommates were more than happy to help me. My roommate and I pooled our laundry into one big laundry bin. The first couple of times, he did it. Then I took over.

—*Dan Amerman*
Yale University, Sophomore

• • • • • • • • •

IF YOU SEE A FREE LAUNDRY MACHINE, be on the ball and grab it. I have a little card I keep with me that says, "Dibs on these machines—Molly." If I see a free machine, I put the card on it, run upstairs and get my clothes.

—*Molly*
Brown University, Sophomore

CONTRARY TO THE LAUNDRY INDUSTRY'S CLAIMS, all clothes can be washed and dried in one load. Over time, this will amount to a considerable saving, as well as create more time for partying.

—*BRIAN TURNER*
UNIVERSITY OF GEORGIA, GRADUATE

• • • • • • • •

GET BACK TO THE LAUNDRY ROOM on time! Time your cycles and don't be late. There were way too many times when people took my clean clothes out of the washing machine or dryer and put them on the dirty folding table.

—*RENE*
DUKE UNIVERSITY, GRADUATE

• • • • • • • •

IT WAS AN EXCITING ACCOMPLISHMENT that I was able to take care of things like laundry by myself. I would wash my clothes at two in the morning. It was a relaxation thing. After I spent the whole night studying, I could just put my laundry in and watch it spin. I also realized I didn't have time to separate my clothes, so I just did everything in one cold batch.

—*ELIZABETH ROTH*
UNIVERSITY OF PENNSYLVANIA, SENIOR

• • • • • • • •

MY WORST LAUNDRY EXPERIENCE happened during my freshman year; someone stole all but four pairs of my jeans out of the laundry in my dorm. I was pissed off, but my parents gave me money for new clothes, so that was a plus.

—*M.G*
VALDOSTA STATE UNIVERSITY, SENIOR

Pajamas are okay for 8 a.m. class but not for 4 p.m. class.

—*DANIELLE*
DUKE UNIVERSITY
GRADUATE

LEARN ABOUT YOUR campus before you decide to wear high heels! I've seen a girl fall down a hill in her stilettos—not a good look!

—*JANELLE*
UNIVERSITY OF GEORGIA, JUNIOR

• • • • • • • •

Always dress a cut above the rest. College has a lot to do with image.

—*SEAN CAMERON*
PRINCETON
UNIVERSITY
SOPHOMORE

AT STANFORD, the majority of students ride bikes around campus. I attempted to wear a miniskirt and ride a bike. I immediately realized the awkwardness of it. I tried to push my skirt down and cover my underwear with my hand, but I don't think it really worked.

—*TIFFANY*
STANFORD UNIVERSITY, SENIOR

• • • • • • • •

DOING LAUNDRY CAN BE REALLY VICIOUS, especially Saturday and Sunday nights. That's when everybody wants to do their laundry, because they're going out. At 6 p.m. everyone wants to wash their clothes. You've got to do it in the morning, or on a weekday.

—*MOLLY*
BROWN UNIVERSITY, SOPHOMORE

• • • • • • • •

DON'T OVERSTUFF the incredibly small dorm washers. Your clothes won't get washed and you'll end up with detergent stains all over your white tank tops. Just pay the extra dollar and do another load.

—*SAMANTHA STACH*
DUKE UNIVERSITY, JUNIOR

• • • • • • • •

USE MOM'S LAUNDRY detergent and fabric softener to make your dorm room smell a little bit more like home!

—*LAURA WOLTER*
UNIVERSITY OF TEXAS AT AUSTIN, GRADUATE

Free Time & How to Spend It

T wo factors will help you make the free time of your college years the most varied and interesting free time of your life. First, you can participate in activities even if you have no background or skill whatsoever: one student joined his school's fencing team with no experience other than having watched a few old swashbuckling movies on TMC. Second, you're surrounded by hundreds of other creative personalities, so at any given moment, at least a few people around you are dreaming up crazy schemes of adventure and enjoyment. For proof, read on.

SPORTS—I PLAYED A LITTLE BIT OF EVERYTHING in college. I had never played water polo in my life and I played that in intramurals and it was great. I played flag football, softball, volleyball; all that stuff. Sports are a great release. I played competitive sports in high school but I wasn't good enough to play on the college level, so it was a good way for a frustrated athlete to get out there and keep alive and be active. Intramurals were a way to be competitive, but it wasn't so competitive that you had to deal with the pressures.

—*JOHN BENTLEY*
TRINITY UNIVERSITY, GRADUATE

* * * * * * * * *

A DAILY NAP IS A GOOD IDEA. Come back from class and take a nap and you wake up and feel like it's a whole new day. An hour-long nap, or even a 15-minute power nap, is good.

—*WHITNEY*
YALE UNIVERSITY, FRESHMAN

* * * * * * * * *

IT'S NEVER TOO EARLY TO GET INVOLVED. Don't think, "But I'm just a freshman." If you join as a freshman, you could have enough experience to be president of the club by junior or senior year. That will look great on your résumé. In my freshman year, I got involved with the campus radio station, the campus newspaper, and the campus magazine. Since I was a journalism major, I wanted to get as much experience in the field as possible. My junior year, I became the editor-in-chief of the campus magazine.

—*LAUREN TAYLOR*
UNIVERSITY OF GEORGIA, GRADUATE

Keep your hobbies—you'll have lots of free time that you'll otherwise waste.

—*D.D.*
UNIVERSITY OF PENNSYLVANIA GRADUATE

FREE TIME: USE IT. Don't waste a drop. Don't sleep your life away either! Enjoy any good weather you get; study outdoors, play some Wiffle ball, anything to keep you busy. Or, use the time to get ahead or catch up in classes. This will help your GPA immensely. Learn to balance your free time between recreation and schoolwork and you can be guaranteed a great college experience.

> —*ARIEL MELENDEZ*
> *PRINCETON UNIVERSITY, FRESHMAN*

• • • • • • • •

DON'T BE A WUSS YOUR FRESHMAN YEAR or you will have few friends. If you are the kind of kid who goes to bed at 10 o'clock, you will be in trouble. Learn to stretch yourself. Push yourself to be a late-night party person or you will have no social life. Everyone walks around here deprived of sleep, but misery loves company. We have weekends to catch up.

> —*TEJ SHAH*
> *CARNEGIE MELLON UNIVERSITY, SOPHOMORE*

• • • • • • • •

IT'S OK TO SAY NO. You don't have to do everything the first semester of your freshman year; you have seven more semesters to go. There's time. Pick one or two things that you're really passionate about. Then, go to your classes. Believe it or not, it's why we're here.

> —*H.D. BALLARD*
> *UNIVERSITY OF VIRGINIA, FRESHMAN*

• • • • • • • •

CHECK THINGS OUT, PARTYWISE, when you first get to college, because after a while it gets too crowded with work. You get too busy, so it's important to have fun at first.

> —*PATRICK*
> *UNIVERSITY OF RHODE ISLAND, FRESHMAN*

Never underestimate the power of a Tuesday night game of cards in the dorm room.

> —*AMY FORBES*
> *MISSISSIPPI STATE UNIVERSITY GRADUATE*

HEADLINES
Best Advice and Top Tips

- Go out and have a good time—as long as your work is done.
- Physical exercise is a great way to relieve stress.
- Spend your free time on things that don't involve school..
- If you have nothing else to do, take a nap!

Use the gym as much as possible, because when you get out, it's not free anymore. It's in your tuition so you're paying for it.

—SANI G.
UNIVERSITY OF CALIFORNIA AT IRVINE, JUNIOR

IT'S REALLY HARD TO PAY ATTENTION freshman year because of all the new influences. A lot of people are meeting every day and wanting to hang out every day. I couldn't balance all the work I had to do and still hang out with people, so I had to stop hanging out with so many people.

—R.S.
HOWARD UNIVERSITY, SOPHOMORE

THE GREATEST THING WAS TAKING MUSIC; the camaraderie in general is great. I'm in a quartet and I'm in the orchestra. The orchestra was great in that you can play lots of different pieces that are new and keep up stuff that you've been doing for a while. In the quartet you get to know people on a very individual level and get to know how they play. You get to hang out with them at different times, so it just makes it that much more special. That was a big highlight of my year.

—IAN MOK
HARVARD UNIVERSITY, SOPHOMORE

DO STUPID STUFF. One time our R.A. randomly said, "I'm going to the beach to go swimming, you want to go?" It was 2 a.m. in the fall and it was freezing cold. But we said, "OK." So we all went swimming in freezing water at 2 a.m. in the ocean—and I've never felt more alive. You'll never remember staying up and studying for a midterm. What you'll remember is staying up and doing something instead of studying.

—*MIKEY LEE*
STANFORD UNIVERSITY, JUNIOR

SO MANY PEOPLE ARE SLEEP-DEPRIVED that they become zombies. Once I woke up and went to class in the afternoon thinking it was morning; this is not unusual. People are always confused about dates and times. Learn how to survive without sleep and you will thrive in college.

—*LINDSEY SHULTZ*
CARNEGIE MELLON UNIVERSITY, SENIOR

IF YOU'RE AN ATHLETE, YOU HAVE TO LEARN to manage your time. Learn to rest, and learn when you can socialize.

—*JOHNATHAN J.*
GEORGIA INSTITUTE OF TECHNOLOGY, JUNIOR

I TRY NOT TO WASTE TIME. Work hard, play hard, is my attitude. Get your work done, then go out and have fun. There's definitely enough time in college to do what you need to do, as long as you're not watching TV.

—*JONATHAN GIFTOS*
BOSTON COLLEGE, SENIOR

Take fun classes. I took yoga and aerobics. I also joined the salsa-dancing club. These things break up the monotony of the usual classes.

—*EMILY TUCK*
CALIFORNIA STATE UNIVERSITY GRADUATE

WHEN YOU HAVE FREE TIME, enjoy things that are nonschool-related and healthy: Join a really random club, be in a play, volunteer, run a marathon, become a film noir enthusiast. Your free time can really give you a chance to meet people of similar mind-set and interest, and can also expose you to interests and ideas you can't find in the lecture hall. Also, make sure you watch a little bit of TV now and then, to prevent college "bubble" syndrome.

—*AMY*
PRINCETON UNIVERSITY, FRESHMAN

● ● ● ● ● ● ● ●

" Try new things. I never acted in high school, but I tried out for a play and got one of the lead roles. It's a lot of fun. I'm going to do a lot more of that now. "

—*CONOR MCNEIL*
EMORY UNIVERSITY, SOPHOMORE

● ● ● ● ● ● ● ●

HAVE FUN DOING ANYTHING, and just smile and laugh at least once a day. You've got to find ways to have fun and relax every day, or else you'll go nuts. You can tell the kids that don't: they just suck at life and are no fun to be around.

—*ANONYMOUS*
UNITED STATES MILITARY ACADEMY AT WEST POINT
JUNIOR

FIND A WAY TO RELAX AND GET AWAY; know when to let go. There are things that are hard to deal with and overwhelming. Know when to detach and say "whatever," and take it in stride.

> —*MICHAEL GAY*
> *ST. LAWRENCE UNIVERSITY, SOPHOMORE*

• • • • • • • •

NOTHING IS BETTER THAN PLAYING FLAG FOOTBALL with a bunch of other washed-up, untalented, former high school football players. Another benefit to intramural sports: you can show up to the game drunk and nobody says anything!

Do things you never thought you would do. Ride the mechanical bull in that redneck bar, drink too much, and participate in karaoke. Do all these things while you can. Before you know it these behaviors will be frowned upon, so you need to get it out of your system.

> —*P.G.*
> *UNIVERSITY OF GEORGIA, GRADUATE*

My freshman year I tried archery and karate for the first time. I wasn't good at either of them, but it was fun being bad at something new.

> —*AMY FORBES*
> *MISSISSIPPI STATE UNIVERSITY GRADUATE*

MASCOT MADNESS:

According to USA Today, there are over 1,700 college mascots and nicknames. With that many choices, colleges that are trying to be original tend to push the envelope from traditionally impressive symbols . . . and toward names that are, well, odd. Here are a few of our (strange) favorites:

Scottsdale Community College Artichokes
Randolph Community College Armadillos
Grays Harbor College Chokers
Southern Arkansas University Tech Varmits
Whitter College Poets

DOING A SPORT HELPS ME GET MY WORK DONE. It has given me more friends, and I got to start freshman year with a set group of friends.

—*SUSAN LIPPERT*
EMORY UNIVERSITY, JUNIOR

• • • • • • • •

IF YOU ARE INVOLVED in an extracurricular activity, you need to learn time management. Since I was a student-athlete in college, I found out first-hand what time management was. I had to keep up my grades and coursework in addition to practicing three hours a day, plus having games or meets to compete in. It was hard, but it was worth it in the long run. I can't tell you how good it looks on my résumé that I competed in an NCAA sport while keeping up my grades.

—*JAMESE JAMES*
UNIVERSITY OF TULSA, GRADUATE

• • • • • • • •

It's very important to do something physical. That's how I release all my stress.

—*B.M.*
UNIVERSITY OF MARYLAND, JUNIOR

IT'S REALLY HARD TO FIND TIME to be alone in college. You're always surrounded by people: your roommates, your friends, your classmates. In high school you have your own room; in college I always shared a room. It's important to find time to be alone so that you can reflect on everything you're going through. Go on walks, and write in a journal. If you go through your routine every day, the days pass so fast; if you don't think back on your day, it doesn't seem as meaningful. You don't treasure the memories that you make if you don't record them in a journal. In the future you'll be able to look back and see how your freshman year was. Try to find yourself and think about your experiences.

—*MEGHAN*
UNIVERSITY OF NOTRE DAME, JUNIOR

VOLUNTEERING AND SERVICE LEARNING: WHAT'S THE DIFFERENCE?

Although quite different, both volunteering and service learning are important and valuable!

Volunteering	Service Learning
Volunteers give their time and energy to the community.	In a reciprocal arrangement, service learners help the community and receive the opportunity to hone their skills and deepen their learning.
Not connected with academic credit.	Often built into an academic course, and supervised by the professor.
Volunteers walk away with feelings of pride and virtue because they helped others.	Service learners also walk away with new knowledge.
Typically does not require extensive preparation.	The activity is bracketed by classroom learning of specific skills and/or background information.
Example: Students get together to clean up a local park.	Example: Based on what they've learned in class, environmental studies students design and implement energy-saving initiatives on and off campus.

I RECOMMEND SELF-DEFENSE CLASSES if they're offered. It makes you feel more aware and comfortable and confident. The more you're like that, the less likely it is that you'll be a target.

—*MELISSA K. BYRNES*
AMHERST COLLEGE, GRADUATE

• • • • • • • •

INTRODUCE YOURSELF TO EVERYONE; it makes a difference. If you continue to say hi to people, you'll get to know people. Not everyone will be your best friend, but you'll get there. You'll have new friends.

—*J. DEVEREUX*
GEORGETOWN UNIVERSITY, GRADUATE

• • • • • • • •

How do you survive freshman year? Nap. Get up for class. Go to class. Then nap. That's how you survive.

—*MIKEY LEE*
STANFORD UNIVERSITY JUNIOR

WALK TO CLASSES WHEN YOU CAN. It's good for you and it will give you a chance to get to know the campus. Notice the people around you. Take time out of your day to sit on a bench and look at your surroundings. Be friendly; make the effort to say hello, even if the other person looks grumpy.

—*J.S.*
UNIVERSITY OF GEORGIA, GRADUATE

• • • • • • • •

I WAS INVOLVED WITH THE CRISIS HOTLINE. The most common call that we had by far was what we called the loneliness call. It would be a person on a huge campus who felt lonely—a person who doesn't know how to meet people, who's away from home the first time.

My college has more than 250 student organizations—fraternities and sororities, hang-gliding club, bungee-jumping club, weight-lifting club, all kinds of ethnic organizations, every religious group. There has to be a group out there that has your interest.

—*MICHAEL A. FEKULA*
UNIVERSITY OF MARYLAND, GRADUATE

ON FREEDOM

I had a really smooth transition. My parents had given me a lot of independence at home, so I was used to not having very much supervision, and when I went to college it wasn't much different.

I know a lot of people who had really strict parents, and sometimes when your parents are too strict or too overbearing you don't learn how to deal with things yourself. So when you're left on your own and your parents aren't there—I mean, some parents still try to control you from really far away through the phone or whatever—you should really know what your values are and what you want to do. You need to know what your goals are, and be disciplined to do what you want and get what you want.

There are so many other distractions and there's nothing to really stop you—there are no parents—so have in mind what you're going to college for, and never lose sight of that.

First semester I was really there for the experience, because I had gotten straight A's in high school and I thought, "I'm not really going to worry about getting straight A's in college." So I took the first semester a lot more easily, and when I had the opportunity to go out and do something or have fun, I would do that rather than study. After I did that for a semester, I got more serious.

It's really about knowing when to draw the line. Every time you're faced with a decision you have to realize what it means.

—*Eric Cheng*
  Harvard University, Sophomore

GET FOOTBALL TICKETS when they are offered to you, even if the team did terribly the year before and you have never been a fan. There's so much more to the game than the actual game.

—*SUSAN MORGENBESSER*
PENNSYLVANIA STATE UNIVERSITY, GRADUATE

• • • • • • • •

DON'T BE AFRAID TO USE THE HEALTH CENTER, for both medical and mental problems. It's cheap, it's confidential, and it really can help if you get the blues.

—*ANONYMOUS*
UNIVERSITY OF GEORGIA, GRADUATE

BEATS STUDYING

While you're cramming in the library, here's how some other freshmen around the country are spending their time:

- Race track—Washington State University

- Toy design department—Otis College (California)

- Professional golf courses—Purdue University (Indiana), Augusta State University (Georgia), Kent State University (Ohio)

- Massage therapy room—Baker College (Michigan)

- International gaming institute—University of Nevada-Las Vegas

- Cross-country ski trails—SUNY Oswego

- Dance studio—University of Tampa (Florida)

- Rodeo arena—Oklahoma Panhandle State University

THERE'S ALWAYS SOMEBODY AWAKE in the dorm that you can go talk to. We had 300 people in our dorm, so there was always somebody awake, doing something.

If you go out at night, your whole day the next day is killed. So we started doing different things. We started running races on Saturday mornings and things like that. It was more fun than going out and getting trashed.

—*S.L.R.*
UNIVERSITY OF VIRGINIA, SOPHOMORE

"People need to go out and party. Not necessarily go out and get drunk, but go out and have fun with friends. Do something you like to do. Don't do work all the time; there's more to life than that."

—*GREG*
JAMES MADISON UNIVERSITY, JUNIOR

STUDYING IN COLLEGE IS VERY HARD, so be careful to take care of your health. It's important to have time to refresh your mind. Find a social outlet. Do your work with friends; it makes it easier. Go to the gym, go hiking, meet other people. You talk about other topics and it takes your mind off your studies. You need that.

—*H.N.*
HARVARD UNIVERSITY, SENIOR

I FOUND MYSELF, FRESHMAN YEAR OF SCHOOL, suffering from Seasonal Affective Disorder due to my first experience in a location that featured long, cold winters. Having depression when you're at college (supposedly the best years of your life) sucks. Don't be afraid to check into the local tanning booth for some sun treatment. Don't be embarrassed about trying antidepressants. Or transfer to a college somewhere warm. I swear, my grades would have been better if I had gone to school somewhere less environmentally challenging.

—*ANONYMOUS*

• • • • • • • •

"Cold weather fun: Take lunch trays and go sledding. Build giant snow sculptures; if you pour water over them, they won't melt until spring."

—*JACKIE*
STATE UNIVERSITY OF NEW YORK AT BINGHAMTON, GRADUATE

• • • • • • • •

AT MY SCHOOL, one of the freshman traditions is to go in this fountain. By the end of my freshman year, I still hadn't gone in that fountain. One night, one of my guy friends and I decided to go. The fountain wasn't turned on, but we sat up at the top of this dry fountain for three or four hours. It was one of the best experiences. We talked about everything—our expectations for college and for life. I think we started to understand what life is really about.

—*KERRY*
GEORGETOWN UNIVERSITY, GRADUATE

IT'S TOUGH TO BALANCE doing a sport and being at school. You practice three hours a day, and you go to school all day. When you get home you're tired, and you have to find time to study. A lot of times you don't want to, but you have to learn how to do it. It took me all of first year to learn how. I mean, we're normal students in some ways, but in other ways we're not, because we're always doing something. We don't have the free time a lot of people do when they get out of class. When we get out of class, we have to go here and go there; we're traveling, we're on the road, we're in hotels. It's tough to make the grade when you play sports.

—*RUSTY BENNETT*
GEORGIA STATE UNIVERSITY, SOPHOMORE

. . . .

I GOT SICK MY FIRST YEAR. I didn't have anyone to supervise when I went to bed and what I ate. That's a learning-by-doing thing.

—*A.G.H.*
UNIVERSITY OF VIRGINIA, SENIOR

If your college has sports events, go to them. It's part of the college experience.

—*ANONYMOUS*
UNIVERSITY OF MARYLAND SOPHOMORE

THE COMPLETE STUDENT-ATHLETE

The college existence provided endless opportunities for me to display my athletic talent:

- Track and Field = Running to class, hurdling benches, hedgerows, and midget freshmen on the way.
- Football/Rugby = Getting into a pool-cue swinging, bottle-throwing, table upending bar brawl over a $5 billiards game.
- Swimming = Jumping naked into frigid Lake Mendota (Wisconsin) during the middle of November and frantically trying to reach the shore before hypothermia claimed my life.
- Beer-pong.

—*JOHN*
UNIVERSITY OF WISCONSIN AT MADISON, GRADUATE

ANGELA AND THE MAGIC VENDING MACHINE

In 1977, Meatloaf recorded "Paradise by the Dashboard Light." Many years later, one of my advisees met her first college boyfriend in front of the blinking green light of a campus vending machine.

Angela and her friend Casey had gone down to the lounge in search of chocolate at the end of a very, very long day of classes. The college's vending machines offered so many delicious options that the ladies sat down to ponder them more fully—and once they sat down, they couldn't get back up. And within seconds, their weary brains were captivated by the little green light next to the dollar slot.

Blink. Blink. Blink. How long they sat there, mesmerized, is unknown, but their reverie was interrupted when the tall strawberry-blond kid from across the courtyard said,

"Uh, hi."

He had seen them through the windows and come over to find out what was so interesting. "I thought maybe you were watching TV. But … there's no TV in here."

The girls hastened to explain, and romance bloomed for Angela and the strawberry-blond kid. Casey didn't find love that semester, but she did eventually decide what she wanted from the vending machine.

The moral of the story: some of the best things in college come from wasting time.

Road Trip! Vacations & Studying Abroad

Five years from now, some of your best college memories may be of journeys you took off campus. Picture yourself on a beach, enjoying tropical drinks with your best friends from the dorm; driving cross-country with the windows down and the music turned up, creating your own personal montage of carefree adventure; sipping coffee in a Paris sidewalk café, flipping through an impressively intellectual text before your afternoon class at the Sorbonne. These students did all those things and more, and you can, too.

Advice to the guys: Go on a cruise for spring break. The odds are unbelievable! You will be amazed at the ratio.

—*JIMMY LYNCH*
AUBURN UNIVERSITY
GRADUATE

I WENT HOME FOR THE HOLIDAYS my freshman year, and I think it was a good thing, because it can just get really crazy. Everything is so new and so exciting and there are so many people that you feel like you're at camp for an extended period of time. It depends on what your home situation is like, but it's important to keep in touch with your parents; it helps remind you that you're actually here to do something. For me, keeping in touch with my parents kept a balanced view; you should explore, but keep your feet on the ground, too.

—*SHANNON*
STANFORD UNIVERSITY, SENIOR

• • • • • • • • •

THE LESS OFTEN YOU GO HOME your freshman year, the better. The more you're at school your freshman year, the more you're going to make friends and have people to hang out with after that. Your ties from home are going to break anyway. The sooner you do it, the better off you are.

—*BETHANY*
JAMES MADISON UNIVERSITY, SENIOR

• • • • • • • • •

GO TO ITALY. Spend a semester there. I did, and it completely changed my outlook on life. Before I went, I was only interested in the American college existence: partying, getting by, attending football games. After I got back, I wanted to learn more, to be more.

—*M.A.*
FLORIDA STATE UNIVERSITY, GRADUATE

• • • • • • • • •

STUDYING ABROAD WAS A FANTASTIC EXPERIENCE: learning the culture of the British people, learning so much about a different way of studying, a different school system, and a different language in England. It's a valuable opportunity and experience.

—*C.W.*
RHODES COLLEGE, SENIOR

IF IT'S NOT YOUR THING TO DRINK A LOT and do all that stuff, you probably won't enjoy spring break. You only get four spring breaks while you're in college. If you don't enjoy partying all the time, you're not going to enjoy it in Mexico after you spent $1,000.

—*JONATHAN COHEN*
EMORY UNIVERSITY, SENIOR

. . . .

" When you go to school overseas, you get a better perspective on the world. You don't see the world from an American point of view. It will help anybody. "

—*MICHAEL LANDIS GOGEL*
NEW YORK UNIVERSITY, SOPHOMORE

. . . .

I GOT INVOLVED IN SERVICE WORK, traveling to other countries. I've been to Mexico and down south to North Carolina for Habitat for Humanity. That's defined my college career, my transformation. It gave me a better appreciation for my position in the world and at the same time for others in the world who don't have as much as I do. It's been an enlightening experience. But I've still had plenty of time to party.

—*JONATHAN GIFTOS*
BOSTON COLLEGE, SENIOR

Go home for the holidays your freshman year.

—*SHANNON*
STANFORD UNIVERSITY, SENIOR

I WOULD RECOMMEND DRIVING your parents' van, with a nice bed in back, coast to coast, 3,000 miles. It doesn't take too long. I did that with my girlfriend. I learned to surf once I got to California. My parents didn't know I had taken the van until I was in another state. But when I called them, they said, "We've been waiting for you to do something like that." It was great.

—*STEVE BAKER*
COLUMBIA UNIVERSITY, SENIOR

● ● ● ● ● ● ● ●

MY JUNIOR YEAR, I TOOK ADVANTAGE of the "terms abroad" program and lived in Ecuador for a year. It was a phenomenal opportunity to study abroad. Life had seemed sort of small before that experience.

—*CALE GARAMANDI*
UNIVERSITY OF CALIFORNIA AT BERKELEY, JUNIOR

● ● ● ● ● ● ● ●

TAKE A FUN JOB IN THE SUMMER after your freshman year; you deserve the break. I couldn't stand the thought of being at home all summer, living with a curfew, so a friend and I went to Orlando for the summer and got a job at Disney World. We didn't make any money, after paying our apartment and expenses, but we met lots of people and had a good time.

—*K.E.R.*
FLORIDA STATE UNIVERSITY, GRADUATE

Bring friends home for the holidays. Your family and your friends will remember it forever.

—*D.D.*
UNIVERSITY OF PENNSYLVANIA GRADUATE

● ● ● ● ● ● ● ●

BEST WEEKEND GETAWAY—CAMPING. It's cheap, it's fun, and all your friends will want to join you. Get a map of state campgrounds; a great weekend of hiking, nature, romance and s'mores may be just an hour's drive away.

—*WENDY W.*
UNIVERSITY OF GEORGIA, GRADUATE

I WENT ON A SEMESTER-LONG TRIP on a cruise ship. It's a program where professors from around the country come and teach everything from anthropology to music to economics. We went to 10 countries around the world. It's the most amazing opportunity ever. You get to learn about countries from a very non-Western point of view. I went to a wild game reserve in South Africa and visited the sand people who live on the outskirts. We learned about them and they sold us their wares. We went skydiving. We went to Carnival in Rio. When you're a freshman you should plan to do something like that; it had such an impact on me.

—*MAYTAL AHARONY*
GEORGE WASHINGTON UNIVERSITY, SENIOR

I WENT TO NIGER FOR A SEMESTER. It was amazing. The academics are not a priority, but the cultural experience shifted my direction of what I want to get involved in.

—*MAYA MOORE*
GEORGETOWN UNIVERSITY, SENIOR

STUDY ABROAD

I studied abroad for a semester, in Santiago, Chile. It was a fantastic experience, breaking out of the Princeton bubble. Going out and meeting new people, seeing a new culture, and learning from a different perspective was absolutely integral to my collegiate experience. We went on weekend trips, and one weekend we went to the south of Chile to Patagonia. We climbed a volcano and went camping. It was awesome.

—*JOSH*
PRINCETON UNIVERSITY, SENIOR

SETTING AN EXAMPLE

One of the most memorable times I had in college was a road trip to New York City with about five pals, an idea hatched at 10 p.m., executed immediately, and celebrated in Central Park in the wee hours. We all flopped on the floor at a friend's place at Columbia University, partied some more with him, and woke up in a stupor. The highlight was a morning visit to the home of one of the pals, the only son of a working-class couple in Queens. In that cramped apartment, during the time it took to eat a carefully pre-pared breakfast, we observed in utter awe the incredible, unfettered love of a mother and father for their

son. They were so proud of their boy. It wasn't so much in what they said, but the ambience, the pictures on the mantle, the beam in dad's eye, the doting by the mother. There was nothing overpowering or unbalanced or pushy about it; it was a natural pride and confidence in their son. For me, there have been few times when I was inspired by the human condition; this was one of them.

—*R.S.*
GEORGETOWN UNIVERSITY, GRADUATE

GOING HOME AFTER FRESHMAN YEAR was a big adjustment; not being surrounded by all my friends, being
the only one awake after 10 p.m. I don't think I had
much fun that summer, which is why the last few
summers I've stayed at school. But I think all the
vacations and other chances you have to go home
are a good time to reflect on your freshman year.

—*T.P.*
STANFORD UNIVERSITY, SENIOR

" Don't go home on the weekends.
Stay at college as much as you
can as a freshman, to get to
know people and get a feeling
for what's going on. "

—*MATT BIGGERSTAFF*
EMORY UNIVERSITY, SENIOR

DOESN'T FEEL LIKE SCHOOL

*Where can you get that vacation feeling without having to
leave campus?*

- Beach house—The Citadel (South Carolina)
- Wilderness cabin—Linfield College (Oregon)
- Research boat—Hawaii Pacific University
- 2 private beaches and a private dock with a fleet of
  sailboats—Mitchell College (Connecticut)
- 20-foot boat "for marine studies"—Muhlenberg College
  (Pennsylvania)
- 29,000-acre experimental forest—University of Montana

SPRING BREAK

FOR SPRING BREAK I WENT TO EUROPE with my good friend Dave. We went to Switzerland and France with backpacks and thoroughly enjoyed getting to know the cities and each other. I think this was valuable because we are now greatly connected and also learned so much about the cities we explored. In particular, it was nice to be with a fellow student because this attracted other student travelers over the break.

—*GERALDINE SARAH COWPER*
CUNY/MACAULAY HONORS COLLEGE, SENIOR

• • • • • • • • •

I TOOK AN ALTERNATIVE SPRING BREAK to Honduras with a bunch of friends. We helped build latrines in an underdeveloped village. It was a great experience. At college there are amazing extracurricular service volunteer opportunities.

—*ELIZABETH ROTH*
UNIVERSITY OF PENNSYLVANIA, SENIOR

• • • • • • • • •

MAKE SURE YOU GO SOMEWHERE FOR SPRING BREAK. I knew some guys who didn't go anywhere, and it's just not fun. If you go to school in Texas, like I did, you can go to Mexico for Spring Break. It's great. There's cheap alcohol and they let you do anything. My freshman year, I went to this really sketchy border town. We actually stayed in a motel on the U.S. side and then walked across a bridge and partied down, and stumbled back every night.

—*KYLE*
UNIVERSITY OF TEXAS, AUSTIN, GRADUATE

MANY OF MY FRIENDS HAVE BEEN TO CANCUN or did the "crazy" Spring Break thing. They've inevitably been disappointed. I found that leaving those weeks unplanned has been a big blessing. I've gotten in shape, caught up on work and (what I miss most in college) sleep. That said, I've also gone to Liverpool, London, and Oxford for Spring Break when I was studying abroad. My girlfriend went with me. We're huge Beatles fans and we loved staying in hostels and visiting all the haunts and museums dedicated to that awesome band.

— *RON Y. KAGAN*
CUNY/MACAULAY HONORS COLLEGE, SENIOR

. . . .

SPRING BREAK IN MEXICO freshman year was the best. There was this one guy who imitated a dancer at a club we went to, by putting on a thong and carrying a torch. He did this dance for 500 people at the pool and everyone loved it. He became a hero at our school and girls loved him. Go to spring break and distinguish yourself, and you will develop a reputation.

— *JAKE DENNE*
CARNEGIE MELLON UNIVERSITY, JUNIOR

When you
see the
world from
a different
perspective,
you realize
what you
can be.

—*M.A.*
FLORIDA STATE
UNIVERSITY
GRADUATE

IF SOMEONE YOU KNOW OFFERS to have you stay with her over a break, take her up on it. One of the most interesting experiences I had was staying with the parents of a roommate or friend, and discovering what her life was like before I met her. It is really mind-expanding, and allows you to get to know someone in your life even better. You also have the added bonus of a personal tour guide to show you around. Nothing is more fun than rediscovering where you have lived for your whole life by showing your college friends all of the tourist destinations.

—*AMY*
    PRINCETON UNIVERSITY, FRESHMAN

Friends: Good, Better, Best, or Former

Research shows that one in 10 babies is blessed at birth by a good fairy, and grows up with the ability to make and keep perfect friendships with no effort whatsoever. The rest of us, on the other hand, could use a few suggestions on how to find those new, lifelong friends in college while still holding on to the high school friendships that matter. Read on for down-to-earth wisdom on everything from casual connections to kindred spirits.

It takes time to meet good friends.

—*Zak Amchislavsky*
Georgetown
University, Senior

IM is the only way I stay in contact with some people. It's an amazing invention; I use it all the time. But it can suck you in. Yesterday, I stayed off it for the first time in a week; I guess I realized I needed to do some college stuff. But it helps you adjust to college life. Back home, I have a lot of friends I want to stay in touch with. I have one life back home and now I'm starting up a new life. In the beginning it's hard; you want to maintain your old life. But you also have to realize that you're maturing and changing. IM is kind of a bridge between these two worlds.

—*Matt Monaco*
George Washington University, Freshman

• • • • • • • •

Make real efforts to be with your friends, even if you're just doing dumb stuff like watching a movie or painting your nails. This is the only time in life where you'll be living with all your friends, and you'll miss it when it's gone. One of my best friends and I make a date every week to do our nails and talk; it's something you need to do anyhow, and it's so much more fun if you get to spend quality time and gossip with one of your favorite people. College can get really hectic: it's nice to know that some things can stay constant.

—*Julie*
Princeton University, Sophomore

CHECK YOUR E-MAIL EVERY DAY. And IM is a must; I message all my friends. It's one of the first things you do when you meet someone. You exchange room numbers and phone numbers, and then after you start talking, you ask for their screen name so you can tell each other about parties or when you're going to dinner. It's on all the time. I leave an away message: I'm at class, I'll be back at 2 p.m. That way, people don't call you worrying where you are.

—*AMY HOFFBERG*
UNIVERSITY OF DELAWARE, FRESHMAN

• • • • • • • • •

WHILE MY HIGH SCHOOL FRIENDS are not as involved in what I am trying to do as my Curtis friends, they remain my truest of friends. They represent a place where I can come anytime and be comfortable. They pick me up from school, they sit through concerts full of music they don't really like—they are my true friends.

—*N.*
CURTIS INSTITUTE OF MUSIC, SOPHOMORE

• • • • • • • • •

REMEMBER THAT YOU'RE NOT THE ONLY ONE who's starting from scratch with few or no friends. Most of the people there are in the same situation. And most colleges have events for freshmen, especially if you live in a dorm. They will usually involve free food or a movie. Go, even if you don't like the food or the movie. At least you'll have the opportunity to meet people. That's the whole point! It'll give you something to talk about with the person later ("Wasn't the food last night horrible?").

—*LAUREN TAYLOR*
UNIVERSITY OF GEORGIA, GRADUATE

WHAT KIND OF FISH ARE YOU?

Little pond?
California's Deep Springs College has 27 undergraduates.

Big pond?
The University of Texas at Austin has 37,155 undergraduates.

HEADLINES
Best Advice and Top Tips

- E-mail and IM are great ways to stay in touch with high school friends.
- Reuniting with your old friends can be strange when you realize you all have new lives.
- Be open to meeting new people, but remember it's the quality not quantity of people around you.
- It can take some time to make new friends at college, be patient.

Stay open. You are going to meet so many different people every day. Just stay open.

—*Lina J.*
  Georgia State University Sophomore

Going home for the first time is a combination of the best and worst feelings you will ever have. Although it is fabulous to hook back up with the old crowd, party where you used to, and possibly rediscover that old flame, it is also very hard to realize that every one of your friends now has a life that is completely separate from your experience. Sometimes reuniting is not the celebration you thought it would be. Acknowledge your differences, and enjoy your friends for who they are. Look at photos, hear crazy stories, and go out and have fun together, but always remember that things have changed (which is not necessarily a bad thing). And never go back to the old ex; it only ends in trouble.

—*A.*
  Princeton University, Freshman

I HANG OUT WITH ABOUT FIVE PERCENT of the people that I hung out with freshman year. You hung out with them because you had to spend time with them; they were on your floor. But then you figure out whom you like.

—*ZAK AMCHISLAVSKY*
GEORGETOWN UNIVERSITY, SENIOR

. . . .

" Don't spend too much time with your high school friends. Half my high school ended up going to my college. I was fortunate enough to live on the other side of campus. They're still hanging out with each other. They've never met other people and they all live together. "

—*R.S.*
UNIVERSITY OF MARYLAND, JUNIOR

. . . .

IT'S VERY EASY FOR A GIRL to find guy friends. My freshman year all my friends at first were guys. I loved the attention and they were cool to hang out with. But while other girls were making friendships with girls that were solid, I was not. So when I hit a rough time and needed a female shoulder to cry on, it was not there. This was a big mistake I paid for dearly.

—*KAROLINE EVANS*
CARNEGIE MELLON UNIVERSITY, JUNIOR

Surround your-self with good people. It's more about quality than quantity when it comes to friends.

—*JESSICA*
   BARNARD COLLEGE
   JUNIOR

DEFINITELY KEEP IN TOUCH with your high school friends. You can always count on them for support and good laughs. This may be stating the obvious, but when you return home, they'll be the first ones (aside from your family) who will want to spend time with you and with whom you will most likely socialize, so why fall out of touch?

—*ARIEL MELENDEZ*
   PRINCETON UNIVERSITY, FRESHMAN

. . . .

IT'S FAR TOO EASY TO MAKE FRIENDS in college. What is difficult is weeding through the self-serving jerks and spending as much time as possible with your true crew. But make it your first priority. These select people are the key to eternal happiness and enlightenment.

—*JOHN*
   UNIVERSITY OF WISCONSIN AT MADISON, GRADUATE

. . . .

WHEN I MET MY BEST FRIEND, she was crying in her bed in our freshman dorm. She had a long-distance boyfriend. She was from the mountains of Georgia. I'm from St. Louis. I went to a private Catholic girls' school. She went to a public school with rednecks and people with gun racks on their cars. We couldn't be more different. But we had a class together and one day, after I found her crying, she overslept. So I was like, "Oh, I'll call you in the morning," and we started walking to class together, and we got breakfast after class. We became friends.

—*J. DEVEREUX*
   GEORGETOWN UNIVERSITY, GRADUATE

Make sure you have some good friends around.

—*LAURA GZYZEWSKI*
   DESALES
   UNIVERSITY, JUNIOR

WHEN FRIENDSHIPS END

"We like all the same music."
"She's just like me!"
"We're best friends already."
"I wish there had been more people like him in high school."

One of the most exciting things about starting college is making new friends. And because of all the freedom you have—to go to the cafeteria together for every meal, to meet up for coffee between classes, to stay up all night talking or playing air hockey in the lounge—everything gets accelerated.

People get used to seeing you and your friends together. *You* get used to going everywhere together. You thought that starting college not knowing anyone would be scary, but now you're set!

But. The quick-blooming friendships of Welcome Week don't always last. Intellectually, you know that college is a time to reinvent yourself, try new things, shed some old habits. Still, it's incredibly painful when *you* are the "old" habit getting shed. Suddenly, your new BFF doesn't want to stay up talking about bands—she's got other plans. And it's not just the two of you anymore eating huge stacks of waffles on Sunday mornings; you're sharing a big table with 10 other kids from your hall.

So what can you do? Go ahead and feel the pain. Mourn the friendship just like any other breakup, and know that things will never go back to the way they were with that person. Write a bad poem if you must, then get rid of it (not much privacy in the dorm).

And open yourself up to new friends.

ONE OF MY BIGGEST MISTAKES was trying to keep in touch with everyone from my small high school graduating class. Bill Cosby once said, "I don't know the key to success, but the key to failure is trying to please everybody." If I could go back and change one thing, I would not try as hard to keep in touch with everyone. I would have focused more on securing more meaningful relationships in college and on my studies.

—*DAVID*
     ANDERSON UNIVERSITY, SENIOR

INVITE YOUR HIGH SCHOOL FRIENDS over for a couple of days. The ones who stay in touch are the ones worth keeping for a lifetime.

—*KHALIL SULLIVAN*
     PRINCETON UNIVERSITY, JUNIOR

Family Ties: Keeping in Touch & Setting Boundaries

Leaving home was all about the big break, but now you've got to figure out how to live your life as both a member of your family and an independent adult. (Although if you're taking your laundry home every weekend, you won't get your "Independent Adult" merit badge just yet!) How can you stay close when you're far away? And how can you grow as a person without growing apart from your loved ones back home? It's a tricky balancing act that every freshman has to work out for him- or herself—but these stories will help.

My relationship with my parents has improved a lot over the phone versus in person.

—*Chana Weiner*
Barnard College
Sophomore

The thing with parents is that, nine times out of ten, they love you and they want to help you. If they get a little protective when you go away, it's because they don't know how to deal with it. Help them through it. Be patient with them.

—*B.*
George Washington University, Senior

You've got to be honest with your parents. You've got to break them in. If you do bad stuff, you've got to let them know; they're going to find out anyway, so you might as well be honest about it. If you tell them the way it is, they'll get used to it.

When you're visiting your parents you have to go by their rules in their house, but at the same time you can't be expected to follow every rule, especially if you're a college student.

—*Beth*
Diablo Valley College, Freshman

· · · · · · · ·

I have Caller ID on my cell phone. If my parents call, I can see it's them and let it ring. But they e-mail every day, too. They don't do IM because I haven't taught them that yet and they haven't figured it out. They say, "When you talk to people online, what does that mean?" And I say, "Oh, I just e-mail them."

—*W.*
Yale University, Freshman

· · · · · · · ·

I became a lot closer with my parents after going to college; I think a lot of students do. When you leave home, you hit a point of self-sufficiency. Parents start to respect your opinions more—once they come to grips with the fact that you're growing up, and once *you've* come to grips with the fact that you're growing up. I saw this chart once that showed that parents know everything when you're a little kid, then they start to not know as much. And by the time you get to high school, you hate them.

MAKE IT CLEAR TO PARENTS and grandparents that surprise visits are not a good idea, given how often you will be at the library.

—*D.D.*
UNIVERSITY OF PENNSYLVANIA, GRADUATE

. . . .

" Do a lot of things your mother would disapprove of. Tattoos, body piercing, spring break trips; as long as you can act like an adult, the sky's the limit. "

—*ANONYMOUS*
MISSISSIPPI STATE UNIVERSITY

. . . .

CALL YOUR PARENTS EVERY SINGLE WEEK, but you don't have to tell them everything. I call my mother on Sundays and talk to her for an hour and I'll catch her up with the things she will not be judgmental about. And the other stuff, I just don't tell her anymore. Pick and choose what you tell your parents.

—*CATE*
BROWN UNIVERSITY, JUNIOR

. . . .

I HATE TO ADMIT IT, but freshman year I learned that when my parents tell me something, they may actually be right, and I realized that I should start to listen to what they say, especially since they have much more life experience than I do.

—*STEPHANIE KLEINER*
UNIVERSITY OF DELAWARE, SENIOR

When your parents visit, just let them baby you.

—*M.A.*
FLORIDA STATE UNIVERSITY GRADUATE

HEADLINES
Best Advice and Top Tips

- Surprise visits from the family are off limits!
- Scheduling a weekly phone call with your parents will help with homesickness.
- Don't tell your mom everything that goes on!
- Staying connected to your family can help get you through the stressful times.

I'M FROM **L.A.** and I have no family up here, so the transition from having a lot of family to not having anybody was tough. My mom used to call me twice a day—once at noon and once around 9 or 10 at night, just to check in on me, and say, "Where are you?" And I'd say, "I'm out." She'd be okay as long as I wasn't doing anything bad. When I think about it, I think it was a good thing that she gave me a call every day, even though sometimes it was an invasion.

—*EDUARDO CHOZA*
SAN FRANCISCO STATE UNIVERSITY, SOPHOMORE

• • • • • • • •

MY MOM CALLS ME THREE TIMES A DAY. It's good to use the excuse that you're studying if you don't feel like talking. When I was a freshman, my roommate and I had this deal where we'd say, "Oh, my roommate didn't tell me you called." You invent little lies to keep them at bay.

—*J.*
BARNARD COLLEGE, JUNIOR

I'M CLOSE TO MY PARENTS. We talk on the phone every other night and my mom IM's me. I don't think you should keep your parents at bay; my parents really helped me. They're very supportive, and when you don't have anyone else there for you, they help you through your hard times. In college it's important to have your parents in your life, because we may think that we're really mature and know everything, but a lot of times they give you really good advice. They've been there before. In college, your parents are finally honest with you. In high school, they're like, "I never drank." Then in college, they're like, "This one time, I did this. You never want to do that." They become more human and less authoritarian. They help you.

—*ALYSSA*
JAMES MADISON UNIVERSITY, SOPHOMORE

> My parents get their two calls a week and that's about all they're going to get right now. It's the best way to do it.
>
> —*WALTER*
> *UNIVERSITY OF MARYLAND– COLLEGE PARK SOPHOMORE*

• • • • • • • •

SET UP ONE NIGHT A WEEK when you call your parents. Then they're not calling you every day and you're not calling them every day; that's not healthy for anyone.

—*J.G.*
GEORGE WASHINGTON UNIVERSITY, SENIOR

• • • • • • • •

I'M HISPANIC and I have really close ties with my family. I get along well with my parents and my little brother is my best friend. It was hard to say goodbye. I talk with them a lot. I call them on my cell phone every other day, and talk for 45 minutes to an hour. And I e-mail my little brother.

—*CESAR*
YALE UNIVERSITY, FRESHMAN

MY DAD IS KIND OF OLD-FASHIONED. Before I went to school he didn't even want me to have an ATM card. Then in the dorms, everyone had a mini-fridge. My dad said no to that, too. But I eventually won on both counts. College has changed so much that you should be patient with your parents, as they don't always understand the needs of today's freshmen. It might even be a good idea to give them a list of must-haves for freshmen: cell phones, computers, Internet, beepers, etc.

—*A. ROSEN*
UNIVERSITY OF FLORIDA, GRADUATE

• • • • • • • • •

ONCE I GOT TO COLLEGE, I curtailed all contact with home. I didn't call home as often as we agreed; sometimes I just wouldn't call home at all. My parents really worried. In retrospect I really regret that, because I put them through a lot of shit doing that. That's definitely a resolution for next year—to be more up on it when it comes to communication with back home.

—*F.S.*
STANFORD UNIVERSITY, SOPHOMORE

WHEN TO CALL MOM AND DAD

Kids shouldn't feel pressured to call their parents (or not call them at all). They should call them when they want to talk to them, even if that's five times in a day because it's a really exciting day. I was ready to move out of the house when I came to college, but that doesn't mean you can't talk to your parents just because you don't live with them.

—*TOBIAS*
HARVARD UNIVERSITY, FRESHMAN

IT'S GOOD TO SHARE YOUR EXPERIENCES with your parents, but not all your experiences. Part of becoming your own person is having your own secrets and your own personal business. But if you share with your parents the things that fascinate you about growing up and being an adult, then that strengthens your bond. And they remember that they were kids once, too; they remember how it was.

—*SHELBY NOEL HARRINGTON*
UNIVERSITY OF CALIFORNIA AT SANTA BARBARA, FRESHMAN

I NEVER GOT HOMESICK, but staying close to my parents and siblings definitely kept me sane over the course of freshman year.

—*PETE*
PRINCETON UNIVERSITY, SOPHOMORE

Only tell your parents a fourth of what's really going on. They're on a need-to-know basis.

—*J.G.*
FLORIDA STATE UNIVERSITY GRADUATE

" Whenever you think about old friends or family, call them or write them right then. If you put it off you'll get preoccupied with a million other things and never get to it. So every time you think of someone, let them know— make it a first priority and do it—even if it's been a long time. "

—*AUBREY WALKER*
SANTA BARBARA CITY COLLEGE, SOPHOMORE

GRANDMA KNOWS BEST

It was the second half of my freshman year and I had my first hangover. My friends and I were at a concert and we were all drinking. I couldn't tell exactly what I drank and how much, but I tried anything and everything. It's all about discovering what you like and what you don't like, right? The next morning when I woke up, before I even opened my eyes, my head was throbbing. I hadn't eaten anything and my stomach and I were definitely not on speaking terms. I called my grandmother and asked her if she had ever experienced a hangover. She said, "Yes." I then told her I was having one. She laughed and came over to my apartment to comfort me. It's funny; I was 18 and thought I knew it all, but once I got my first hangover, whom did I go running to? My grandmother! Keep close ties with your family as you may need them at any time.

—STEPHANIE M. MCKNIGHT
FROSTBURG STATE UNIVERSITY, SENIOR

IF YOU GO HOME FOR THE SUMMER, make sure you go on vacation. I had to take trips by myself because I cannot be around my parents all the time. I realize they are real people and not all their habits are ones I want to live with.

—S.
UNIVERSITY OF CALIFORNIA AT SANTA BARBARA, FRESHMAN

I TALK TO MY PARENTS A LOT AT NIGHT. Last night was the season premiere of *The West Wing*. I used to watch that with my dad a lot, so I called him before and after. And besides that, I talk to them twice a week just to catch up and see how it's going. It was my little brother's birthday and I wished him a happy birthday.

> —*MATT MONACO*
> *GEORGE WASHINGTON UNIVERSITY, FRESHMAN*

• • • • • • • •

ASK FOR CARE PACKAGES. I loved receiving cookies and photos every now and then, and this lets your parents remain part of your life even if you are far away.

> —*AMY*
> *PRINCETON UNIVERSITY, FRESHMAN*

• • • • • • • •

I'M REALLY CLOSE TO MY FAMILY. They drove me up here and we all cried. After they left, I was excited to be at school. I was ready to get away from my parents, experience life by myself, and be able to make my own decisions. I immediately had 25 friends, which were the girls on my hall, so I didn't miss them at first. But by mid-semester I was extremely homesick. I suddenly realized that my life was never going to be the same. I called home a lot and talked to my parents all the time. My dad e-mailed me every single day, and he always said, "P.S. Take your vitamins, go to church, and pray." Talking to them really helped me.

> —*A.G.H.*
> *UNIVERSITY OF VIRGINIA, SENIOR*

• • • • • • • •

YOUR PARENTS WILL LET GO of a lot once you leave for college, but swearing (especially f-bombs) when you're home on visits won't be well received.

> —*D.D.*
> *UNIVERSITY OF PENNSYLVANIA, GRADUATE*

Go to school away from home and away from your parents. But let them into your life. Be friends with them.

> —*GINGER M.*
> *BRODTMAN*
> *SPRING HILL*
> *COLLEGE*
> *GRADUATE*

THE GENIUS OF ELECTRONIC GREETING CARDS

You're busy, and you're broke. The odds that you'll remember Great-Aunt Susan's 85th birthday are not good. And you don't particularly want to shell out $3.95 for a card, plus whatever ridiculous amount they're charging for stamps these days. Luckily, the Web provides the perfect solution.

Bookmark your favorite electronic-greeting-card site, and write reminders in your planner when it's time to send birthday greetings.

And if you have a few extra dollars, find one of the sites that lets you design a greeting card now but specify that it be sent on a future date. (They usually charge you for that.) Make cards for all your family's and friends' birthdays for the whole year.

Congratulations! You are now officially *the* most considerate son/daughter/friend/brother/sister/niece/nephew ever. And don't forget to check the box for the Web site to remind you when those birthdays come around next year, so you can keep your title.

Going Out, Getting Serious: Dating & Sex

O*ne thing you can count on; relationships get more complicated, not less, in college. With plenty of like-minded new students all interested in getting to know one another, romance is definitely in the air—and in the dorm and in the classroom. There are far more choices, and the decisions are all yours. Don't be surprised if you find yourself on an emotional roller-coaster ride. Read this chapter for some insight about college students in love, out of love, looking for love, or looking for something other than love.*

You need to go out and party and meet lots of people.

—ANONYMOUS
YALE UNIVERSITY
SOPHOMORE

AS A FRESHMAN you can still get women to hang out with you despite the competition from the older guys. I talk to the woman to get to know her—you have to know about the person you want to go out with. Most guys try pick-up lines and the like, which women can see right through. When I know what they are like, I can go further and ask to be with them in a more private setting. My method is mainly to get a woman to get acquainted with me, and I with her, before we hook up.

—Y.H.
UNIVERSITY OF VIRGINIA, JUNIOR

• • • • • • • •

I'M REALLY HORRIBLE at talking to a hook-up afterwards. I just avoid them because I feel it would be awkward. I always kind of want to talk to them and apologize for avoiding them, but I never get around to it. To avoid this, just think before you act.

—NATHANIEL SCHIER
POMONA COLLEGE, SOPHOMORE

• • • • • • • •

I WASN'T A VERY PROMISCUOUS GUY in high school so the thought of going to a frat party with two kegs, tons of twenty-one year old frat guys who knew what they were doing and a bunch of scantily clad women was terrifying. I went though, and eventually got used to it. You have to be proactive or else you won't get what you want. Do anything—talk to girls, talk to guys, dance, or have a drink. I swallowed my pride and accepted that there is nothing wrong with someone saying to you, "I'm not interested." If you can't accept that, you might as well not even bother.

—MICHAEL
NORTHWESTERN UNIVERSITY, SOPHOMORE

DON'T BELIEVE THAT AN UPPERCLASSMAN is going to call you for a date, like he says he's going to. Don't wait by the phone. He gets drunk at frat parties and hooks up with the first thing he sees; that's how guys "date" in college.

—*K.E.R.*
FLORIDA STATE UNIVERSITY, GRADUATE

· · · · · · · ·

" "Our dorm was arranged in suites; there were 18 people sharing a living room and a restroom. It was pretty much understood that you don't have a relationship with a suite mate because that was bad. That would cause horrible conflicts for everybody else in the group." "

—*D.H.*
UNIVERSITY OF CALIFORNIA AT BERKELEY, GRADUATE

· · · · · · · ·

I HAD A BOYFRIEND FROM HOME, which was a big mistake. It kept me tied to home a little too much. I went a full year before we broke up. And I didn't party that much because of the boyfriend. I didn't drink at all in high school and that took a year to kick in, too. Then I was just like, screw it, I'm going to go out and have fun.

—*LYNN SNIFFEN*
BOSTON COLLEGE, JUNIOR

HEADLINES
Best Advice and Top Tips

- Don't leave a high school sweetheart waiting at home—you'll miss out on a lot of dating.
- Frat parties are not the best places to look for long-term relationships.
- Avoid dating someone in your dorm—breakups can be very messy.
- Ladies: be smart, use good judgment, and always keep yourself safe.

LADIES, BE SMART, be safe, and remember that the university health centers are a great place to go in situations of need.

—*ERIN*
SUFFOLK UNIVERSITY, GRADUATE

• • • • • • • • •

YOUR FIRST SEMESTER, DON'T DATE. You're still trying to get settled in college, you're making some new friends, you're dealing with all the anxiety of being away from your family and high-school friends, you're trying to get into classes that are much harder than you've had before. There's a lot of stress that first semester. Whether you're a guy or girl, you've got four or five years, and maybe after college, to meet the right person. Enjoy the freedom and you'll have a lot more fun that way.

—*C.W.*
RHODES COLLEGE, SENIOR

A GREAT PLACE TO MEET GIRLS is at the bookstore. Upon receiving the class syllabus, you have to buy books. If you're in the bookstore and you see a girl buying books, it's an easy entrance: "Oh, are you taking history?"

—*J.R.*
COLUMBIA UNIVERSITY, GRADUATE

• • • • • • • •

TURKEY DROP: This is the time around Thanksgiving when freshmen break up with their significant others they "promised" to date for life. This is typical. Expect it.

—*RAE LYNN RUCKER*
BIOLA UNIVERSITY, GRADUATE

• • • • • • • •

DON'T EVER LISTEN to what any college guy says. They all lie—about everything. Especially if they say, "Let's go for a walk." That's the worst: Run screaming.

Every girl needs to know how to punch so she can stick up for herself. Girls have to be tough: physically tough to kick someone's butt if you have to, and mentally tough to be able to say no.

—*JENNIFER SPICER*
FOOTHILL COLLEGE, GRADUATE

• • • • • • • •

DON'T COME WITH A GIRLFRIEND from home. There are several reasons. First, this is the first time you will really taste freedom and you do not want to be limited and restrained by someone from home. Second, there is booze and parties everywhere. You will feel like you are in a candy store. And you will see girls who are not the girl you grew up with. Everyone is insecure and looking for a connection.

—*DEREK LI*
CARNEGIE MELLON UNIVERSITY, JUNIOR

Roller-skating, bowling, and getting ice cream cones are still great dates in college. In fact, you get major points for being bold enough to do them with gusto.

—*BRIAN TURNER*
UNIVERSITY OF GEORGIA GRADUATE

ADVICE FOR THE DATELORN

It's a mistake to start dating the first few weeks of college. I mean, compared to high school, college is paradise for dating: you're surrounded by people with your interests, you can stay up late, go to parties whenever you want, you can sleep together and not worry about parents—it's amazing. But be patient. There's this huge rush to date someone, but it's important to make friends first. That way, when you break up with someone, you still have your friends. If you start dating someone right away, you may miss out on making real friends, and that's more important.

Date someone who is also a freshman. In the first few months of school, it's hard to really relate to someone who's older. Plus, if you date someone who's older, it takes you away from your dorm and first-year activities; it almost makes you skip your first year. If you date someone who is also a freshman, you can go through freshman year together.

—SUMMER J.
UNIVERSITY OF VIRGINIA, SENIOR

SOME GUYS ARE GREAT; some guys are not so great. Coming to school, no one has a past; people are going to be pushing the image they want you to see. So many people put up a front. They are who they're not. You can't possibly trust someone if you've just met them, so take time to get to know people. And don't have a relationship your first semester.

—*KERRY*
GEORGETOWN UNIVERSITY, GRADUATE

. . . .

"If someone gets you alone, and gets the room all comfy and dim, and asks if you like Beefeater, please run screaming for eight miles in the opposite direction. They don't just mean gin, no matter what they say."

—*KARLA SAIA*
SAN DIEGO STATE UNIVERSITY, JUNIOR

. . . .

BE PREPARED TO MEET NO WOMEN your freshman year who want to date you. They are just not available. Either they have boyfriends, or hang-ups, or they like girls. Whatever the reason, as a freshman you will have no girlfriend. If I knew why, I would not be alone.

—*JOE MAYAN*
CARNEGIE MELLON UNIVERSITY, SOPHOMORE

YOU WANT TO KNOW HOW TO GET GIRLS? Respect them. Be nice to them; it's that simple. Forget pickup lines or getting them drunk. In fact, warn them about guys like that. It sounds silly, but be their hero by being nice and thinking of them. Also, never, ever, ever try a pickup line, unless you're just kidding around. They never work. The only pickup line that works is, "Hi. How are you?" It's a legitimate start to a conversation.

—*R.B.*
MASSACHUSETTS INSTITUTE OF TECHNOLOGY, JUNIOR

• • • • • • • •

66 The biggest thing I told myself was to put the whole boyfriend thing on hold. I figured it would be too much of a distraction to have a significant other. That helped. 99

—*JERI D. HILT*
HOWARD UNIVERSITY, SENIOR

• • • • • • • •

⭐ **GIRLS, YOU'VE GOT A ZONE.** The first month, you're automatically going to fall in love with someone. Just keep your eyes open and don't get locked into anything.

My perception of college came from everything I saw on TV. I thought, it's going to be easy to get girls. It turns out it is easy, but you've still got to work. I thought being at college, girls would just flock to you, but it's not really the case.

—*KENTON*
UNIVERSITY OF VIRGINIA, SENIOR

DON'T DATE SOMEONE you're good friends with. If you go to a small school, it becomes a thing where everyone knows about your business, everyone knows everything about your relationship.

—*CONOR MCNEIL*
EMORY UNIVERSITY, SOPHOMORE

• • • • • • • •

BE FRIENDS UNTIL YOU KNOW you really want to take it to the next level. I see so many girls having sex right away because they need reassurance. They later regret it.

—*SARAH LOLA PALODICHUK*
RIVERSIDE COMMUNITY COLLEGE, GRADUATE

• • • • • • • •

NEVER TRY TO TWO-TIME ANYBODY, because you always get caught. Don't do that. Two-timing is bad; that's a tough lesson to learn. I was with this girl, and I didn't think it was serious, but she thought it was. Then I got with another girl and the first one found out from someone she knew. She confronted me, and I was in the doghouse. But I talked my way back into the relationship, and that is hard to do. I learned my lesson: If you've got someone, you better take care of her. College is a small world; smaller than you think. So respect the women.

—*ANONYMOUS*
BROWN UNIVERSITY, SOPHOMORE

• • • • • • • •

I LEFT A SERIOUS RELATIONSHIP hanging when I left high school, so I didn't date anyone seriously my whole freshman year. I just hooked up and had one-night stands. I enjoyed being single in college—true love will come eventually, and until then, you should have some fun.

—*P.*
PRINCETON UNIVERSITY, SOPHOMORE

More Wisdom

Be careful about dating too many older men when you're 18. Make sure they're actually going to your school.

—*ANONYMOUS*
CALVIN COLLEGE
GRADUATE

Avoid meeting people at frat parties when you're looking to date. It's hard to tell how sincere they are when you're a freshman.

*—Ann Malipatil
Emory University
Senior*

THE SINGLE-ROOM BATHROOMS in the college library are the best place to have quickie sex on campus.

*—J.
University of Georgia, Graduate*

• • • • • • • •

IT MAY LOOK LIKE THE GIRLS who are out partying, and doing who knows what with who knows who, are the girls getting the guys. But they're not, really. Also, the nice boys are not on sports teams. I don't know where they are, but they're not on sports teams.

*—Ebele Onyema
Georgetown University, Senior*

• • • • • • • •

I'VE SEEN THE MISTAKE OF PEOPLE staying with their high-school boyfriend or girlfriend, then breaking up with them senior year. That's a terrible experience. You lose the entire novelty of being in college. I would recommend meeting new people and going out with different types of people, whether they're from other states or countries, or whatever.

*—Mike
University of Texas at Austin, Graduate*

• • • • • • • •

HOOKING UP—DON'T DO IT ON HALLOWEEN unless you really know who is behind that costume. I had a lot to drink and ended up with a very big surprise once we got comfortable. I ran out of there quickly: it was a very homely girl.

*—Jamie Jasta
Carnegie Mellon University, Senior*

SADDER BUT WISER

I met my girlfriend in my freshman year. All year long I had been active with my dorm. It was coed and very community-oriented. Then my friend moved into my dorm, and things changed. We started dating and did the whole isolation thing, and it was especially dumb because of the community feeling on our floor. As it turned out, I dated her until spring of senior year, and in the process, I stopped really doing the whole college scene thing; this is something one should definitely not do.

Breaking up with my girlfriend was the hardest thing I have ever done: Basically, you grow up with the person in college, and you go through your whole college experience with just them. I found myself almost at the beginning of the cycle; having to develop friends and cultivate relationships, and trying to bring back friendships with people I had deserted over the years.

—*D.*
AMERICAN UNIVERSITY, GRADUATE

WHEN YOU'RE NOT PAYING ATTENTION, that's when someone will be looking at you.

—*SARAH*
GEORGIA INSTITUTE OF TECHNOLOGY, GRADUATE

MY SISTER IS A FRESHMAN. I told her not to hook up with a lot of guys, not to get a bad reputation, because you can't shake it; it follows you everywhere. I'm a senior now, and some of the people that in my opinion have had bad reputations for whatever reason, when I look at them now, that's what I think of. Some people have been away for a year, studying abroad; some people, I haven't seen them since freshman year. But the reputation sticks.

—*TIM JOYCE*
GEORGETOWN UNIVERSITY, SENIOR

• • • • • • • •

66 Try to avoid feeling committed to anyone the first year. Don't get too serious about dating any particular person. Spend some time. And I wouldn't go in with too much baggage from high school, either. 99

—*RYAN A. BROWN*
UNIVERSITY OF NORTH CAROLINA AT CHAPEL HILL, GRADUATE

• • • • • • • •

DON'T DO ANYTHING WITH A GIRL who's not making rational decisions; that's a good way to get thrown in jail. It's better to be extremely modest in that situation. If a girl wants to do something with you, you can do it the next time or three times down the road.

—*NICHOLAS BONAWITZ*
UNIVERSITY OF ROCHESTER, GRADUATE

SEASONAL AFFECTION DISORDER

Take full advantage of all of the social opportunities that college offers a freshman, and avoid any serious relationships that may hamper or deter you from enjoying all of the rites of passage of being a college freshman. There is no better time than fall on a college campus, with fraternity/sorority rush, parties, and football games to enjoy and revel in. If you have a significant other, or meet someone who could quickly become a significant other, find any reason to put that relationship off until winter when it gets cold and the social life slows down a bit. Keep in mind, however, that after winter comes spring break, when once again, all ties must be broken.

I learned this lesson the hard way; I had a serious girlfriend who attended Auburn while I was attending Georgia Tech. Not only did I put many unnecessary miles on my car, I also missed the opportunity to meet many other interesting coeds with a lot to offer. While my fraternity and college experience was certainly not without its share of fun, a serious long-distance girlfriend did not enhance it. And to make matters worse, I actually dropped a Naval ROTC scholarship (and an opportunity to become a pilot) after my freshman year because I thought I would rather marry the Auburn coed than cruise the Mediterranean on an aircraft carrier. Needless to say, we broke up less than a year after this very forward-looking decision. That's another reason for stalling those serious entangling relationships early in college; they hamper logical decision-making.

—*S.A.H.*
GEORGIA INSTITUTE OF TECHNOLOGY, GRADUATE

At a party, you usually ask a girl for her cell phone number, but asking her if she has a screen name isn't bad either.

—*PATRICK*
 UNIVERSITY OF
 RHODE ISLAND
 FRESHMAN

ASK PEOPLE OUT. It takes guts but you'll never know unless you try. And everyone appreciates a little more courtship and a little less of the senseless hookup culture.

—*SEAN CAMERON*
 PRINCETON UNIVERSITY, SOPHOMORE

• • • • • • • • •

I HAVE A FRIEND WHO STARTED DATING her boyfriend about a week after they got to college. She never really did freshman year like some people do, and it's affecting her now. She feels like she didn't go through the crazy freshman stuff before getting into a serious relationship.

—*HANNAH*
 EMORY UNIVERSITY, JUNIOR

• • • • • • • • •

I TRANSFERRED TO ANOTHER SCHOOL because my girlfriend couldn't get into my school. After I transferred there, we dated for another six months, then broke up. I felt like an idiot, because I had transferred to an easier school.

—*JUAN GONZALEZ*
 CLEMSON UNIVERSITY, GRADUATE

• • • • • • • • •

AS A FRESHMAN, a male friend of mine invited me to his room to "watch a movie." I had a boyfriend back home and was not promiscuous at all, so I honestly thought this guy was a friend. Halfway through the movie, I turned around to realize he had pulled out his penis and was sitting there looking at me. After a few confused and startled words, I got my stuff and left. He later apologized and said he thought we were on the same page when he invited me to his room. He thought I knew what the words "watch a movie" meant in college, especially at 10 p.m. on a Friday night. I did not!

—*CHAVON*
 XAVIER UNIVERSITY, GRADUATE

STAY AWAY FROM THE BOYS on the athletic teams; they're players in the dating scene. They think they're really cool, and they take advantage of the freshman girls. The freshman girls come in and they're in awe, and the athletes hit on them and take advantage of them. Beware.

— *A.*
GEORGETOWN UNIVERSITY, SOPHOMORE

If you're looking for love, be patient.

—*KHALIL SULLIVAN*
PRINCETON UNIVERSITY, JUNIOR

• • • • • • • •

"Advice on dating: Don't. It costs too much. Go out with friends and meet new people. If you do date, don't date one person exclusively. It only leads to trouble."

—*JIMMY LYNCH*
AUBURN UNIVERSITY, GRADUATE

• • • • • • • •

YOU DON'T EVER WANT TO MOVE IN with a girl-friend. If you do, your lifestyle becomes limited; you always have to come home with her and you always have to deal with her. I had roommates who were a couple living together in my house and I saw them fighting all the time. The reason was that they were together too much, and the expectations grow and grow and if they don't meet those expectations for one moment, they get in a fight.

—*STEPHAN*
UNIVERSITY OF CALIFORNIA AT SANTA BARBARA, GRADUATE

YOU COME TO COLLEGE and there are women everywhere; that's probably the best thing about it. But you have to have your act together. If you don't have your obligations in order, you're never going to make it. I've seen people fail out of college in the first year. But if you have your time managed right, there's nothing you can't do.

—*CHRIS MCANDREW*
UNIVERSITY OF DELAWARE, JUNIOR

* * * * * * * *

"College is when dating really begins. In high school I had boyfriends, but I never really dated. It was in college that I began to better understand the concept."

—*HEATHER POLLOCK*
CALIFORNIA STATE UNIVERSITY, GRADUATE

* * * * * * * *

HERE'S HOW THE IM THING WORKS with dating: You hang out with a bunch of friends and there's this one person you have an interest in and you want to improve that. It used to be that you would have to call them. Now the IM is an icebreaker. You ask for their IM name and you chat a little and get to know them. Then you call them.

—*CHRIS PROVENCHER*
JAMES MADISON UNIVERSITY, FRESHMAN

LATE-NIGHT HANGOUT: top of the parking deck at the medical center. Great views, quiet, good for making out. For the thrill factor: the 50-yard line in the football stadium.

> —*MARGOT CARMICHAEL LESTER*
> *UNIVERSITY OF NORTH CAROLINA AT CHAPEL HILL*
> *GRADUATE*

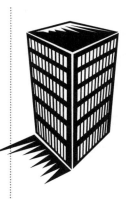

• • • • • • • •

DON'T TRUST PEOPLE as quickly as you might want to. As a freshman girl, you could get in a lot of trouble if you don't watch yourself. Listen to your friends when they say you shouldn't do something. They probably know something more than you. You probably won't listen to them; but you should.

> —*LAUREN*
> *GEORGETOWN UNIVERSITY, SOPHOMORE*

• • • • • • • •

☆ **I DIDN'T REALLY DATE.** I went to clubs a lot; danced and partied, but all for fun. I gave guys fake phone numbers (that was fun). Just remember, dancing with a guy and going home with a guy are two different things. Kissing a guy at a club and going home with a guy are two different things. One thing does not always need to lead to the other. Be patient. And no, boys will not die if you don't "help them out."

> —*LESLIE M.*
> *UNIVERSITY OF FLORIDA, GRADUATE*

• • • • • • • •

USE REQUIRED P.E. CREDITS to your advantage in meeting potential dates. Girls, try bowling or weight lifting. Boys, go with ballroom dancing or walking.

> —*WENDY W.*
> *UNIVERSITY OF GEORGIA, GRADUATE*

Don't give in to pressure. I am glad that I didn't and stayed true to myself.

> —*ALLISON*
> *UNIVERSITY OF*
> *NORTH CAROLINA*
> *AT GREENSBORO*
> *SOPHOMORE*

UNIVERSITY HEALTH CENTER

It's not just for treatment of minor cuts and sprains. Your college's health center may provide some or all of the following services:

Advice nurse
Alcohol and drug treatment, counseling, prevention
Allergy injections
Birth control
Emergency contraception (the morning-after pill)
Ergonomic evaluations (especially for computer setup)
Flu shots
Health classes
HIV testing/prevention/care
Nutritional counseling
Physical exams
Physical therapy
Rape/sexual assault prevention/response
Referral to medical services in the community
Sexual health education
Smoking cessation assistance
TB testing

Various other vaccines and immunization, such as:

Gardasil (for HPV)
Hepatitis A
Hepatitis B
Meningitis
Travel shots
Weight management

Services are confidential, and are typically offered at no or low cost to you (other than the health fee typically built into the cost of college).

IF YOU GENUINELY WANT TO BE SINGLE so you can party hard your freshman year, that's great. However, if you're in a serious relationship that you don't want to lose just because you're going to college, don't let anyone pressure you into ending it. Yes, many high school relationships fail during the freshman year of college, but the good ones can stand the test of time and distance. I have two friends who are now married to their high school sweethearts, and two more who are engaged.

> —*ANONYMOUS*
> *ILLINOIS WESLEYAN UNIVERSITY, JUNIOR*

• • • • • • • •

IF YOU KEEP YOUR BOYFRIEND BACK HOME, you must learn to trust each other. My boyfriend lives in Maryland and I'm at school in North Carolina. My freshman year, we talked on the phone every night, and he would always tell me how much he missed me and how hard it was to be that far away. We visited each other, but he would complain that it wasn't enough. It was also hard to see the other girls go to parties and dance and kiss other boys. But I didn't want to break up; I love my boyfriend. Over the past year, he has learned to trust me. I have told him a million times that I would never do anything to hurt him; he finally believes me.

> —*ALLISON*
> *UNIVERSITY OF NORTH CAROLINA AT GREENSBORO,*
> *SOPHOMORE*

• • • • • • • •

Guys, be aggressive meeting girls. It's not going to come to you. You've got to make it happen yourself.

—*ALEC*
BOSTON COLLEGE
JUNIOR

TWO RULES: Don't date three guys at the same time who are all on the soccer team together. And don't date anyone on your dorm floor.

> —*HEATHER POLLOCK*
> *CALIFORNIA STATE UNIVERSITY, FULLERTON, GRADUATE*

If you have a boyfriend at home, get rid of him: You're going to stay in your dorm, you're not going to do anything, you're not going to meet new people; you're not going to live your life.

—*AMBER WITTEN*
LOS MEDANOS
COLLEGE
SOPHOMORE

DON'T DATE SOMEONE IN YOUR HALLWAY; I did. Not only are you living together, but you also have shared counselors and shared activities; you can't escape them. Anytime I went anywhere, or anytime he went anywhere, we would know about it. We'd have fights over IM, and sometimes we'd have to run down the hallway to go yell at each other. And even if we were to break up, there was no chance of having our own lives without the other person knowing about it. So I basically continued to date him for the whole year, regardless of how happy I was, in order to not deal with the issues involved with having him around.

> —*CATE*
> *BROWN UNIVERSITY, JUNIOR*

• • • • • • • • •

IF YOU'RE TALKING TO SOMEONE at a party and you hit it off, an easy way to talk to him again and not wait for the next party is to ask him if he wants to IM. You can tell him that you're so addicted to IM; make a joke about it. Get his screen name; I've done that.

> —*EDITH ZIMMERMAN*
> *WESLEYAN UNIVERSITY, SOPHOMORE*

TOP 5
COED-BUT-MOSTLY-FEMALE SCHOOLS

1. Parsons School of Design   (75% female)
2. Sarah Lawrence College   (73%)
3. Adelphi University   (71%)
4. Bennington College   (70%)
5. Goucher College   (70%)

IN THE FIRST TWO WEEKS OF MY FRESHMAN YEAR, I met a senior. We started dating and were soon an official couple. It was good while it lasted, but a year later, after he graduated, we broke up. All of the friends I had before going out with him had already moved on to hang out with other friends. They all had their own groups, and I wasn't included because I thought that I was so cool going out with a senior. Yeah, right! I was left in the dust.

—*LYNDSEY WENTZ*
KUTZTOWN UNIVERSITY, JUNIOR

• • • • • • • •

THE SUMMER AFTER MY FRESHMAN YEAR, I met this guy who lived hundreds of miles from my school. We dated for a year and a half: I drove to his town, five hours away, almost every single weekend of my sophomore year; it really got old. Long-distance relationships suck. Don't try it.

—*KATHERINE*
AUBURN UNIVERSITY, GRADUATE

Advice to the guys: know that she's just waiting for you to come up to her and say hi. I'm now in grad school; it took me seven years to figure that out.

—*KAMAL FREIHA*
UNIVERSITY OF OREGON GRADUATE

TOP 5
COED-BUT-MOSTLY-MALE SCHOOLS

1. United States Naval Academy   (85% male)
2. United States Air Force Academy   (84%)
3. United States Military Academy   (84%)
4. Rose-Hulman Institute of Technology   (80%)
5. Worcester Polytechnic Institute   (77%)

DO NOT GET INTO A SERIOUS RELATIONSHIP your freshman year. I started dating a girl in October. We had a very passionate, exclusive relationship, which was great until we broke up at the end of the year. I realized that I did not meet any new people after meeting her and I was left with no new friends, only acquaintances.

—*GREGORY MOGILEVSKY*
UNIVERSITY OF NORTH CAROLINA-CHAPEL HILL, GRADUATE

. . . .

DON'T DATE PEOPLE IN YOUR DORM, especially if you're just hooking up after a party, because there will be a breakup and, therefore, awkwardness in the dorm. It's impossible to avoid someone in your building. You'll step into the elevator and they'll be there and everything gets silent.

—*REID ATTAWAY*
JAMES MADISON UNIVERSITY, FRESHMAN

. . . .

DO NOT HAVE SEXUAL RELATIONS with anyone in your dorm, because if you have a one-night stand, you don't necessarily want to see them the next day; that creates tension. Dating isn't a bad idea; it just depends on whether you can handle a relationship. I recommend dating; it's healthy.

—*N.*
EMORY UNIVERSITY, JUNIOR

. . . .

FOR SOME REASON, I thought that I was going to find my husband in the first month of college. I was wrong. This belief was my biggest misconception about college because in terms of dating, it gave me tunnel vision. College is about experience and experimenting. Work on building friendships; relationships will come later.

—*E.S.*
DUKE UNIVERSITY, GRADUATE

Don't be afraid to be alone; take a class, meet strangers, join a club by yourself.

—*WENDY W.*
UNIVERSITY OF GEORGIA GRADUATE

HOOKUP ETIQUETTE

Keep condoms readily available. If the time comes, you'll have them local. And your RA should have condoms, if it comes down to it. Ultimately, it's up to the couple to use them. If the thought of sex is out there, it is important to talk about condoms. The last thing you want to happen is there to be a "miscommunication" mid-hookup.

After hooking up, stay awhile. Spend some time after talking. Don't zip up and run.

How you meet usually determines how your relationship will go. If you meet one drunken night, most likely it's a one-night thing. If you met in class while discussing the last lecture, you most likely owe the girl a call after the hookup, since the relationship began on something less superficial.

—E.F.
CLAREMONT MCKENNA COLLEGE, SOPHOMORE

DURING MY ORIENTATION, I met a girl who ended up on the same floor in the dorms. We became best friends and a month later we started dating. We're about to celebrate our fourth year of that. I strongly advise incoming freshmen to look for friends, not dates. You'll want them as you make the transition into and eventually out of college. Also, the connection that comes from being intimate with someone you're friends with makes being in a relationship worthwhile and takes away what might otherwise be awkward or even dangerous.

—RON Y. KAGAN
CUNY/MACAULAY HONORS COLLEGE, SENIOR

ENJOY COLLEGE AND DON'T DATE TOO SERIOUSLY. I entered college with a boyfriend. We met in high school at the Model U.N. conference, and then he went on to Tufts University in Boston, while I came to the Macaulay Honors College at CUNY. While I did enjoy my frequent trips to Boston and to a "real" college campus (CUNY is urban), I feel that I could have experienced more in college. It is now senior year and we just broke up. We were together all through this time when we both should have been dating and experiencing life, without being bogged down in a long distance relationship. This is not the time to settle down, so just enjoy getting to know yourself and who you are. The more you date, the better. See what's out there.

—*GERALDINE SARAH COWPER*
CUNY/MACAULAY HONORS COLLEGE, SENIOR

• • • • • • • •

THERE IS EXTRAORDINARY COMPETITION. The first semester of school is tough because the guys and girls are looking for the "true college experience." The upperclassmen are able to show the freshmen a good time. There is nothing really anyone can do about that. After time, however, this fades. People find their groups of friends and date within them, usually.

—*E.F.*
CLAREMONT MCKENNA COLLEGE, SOPHOMORE

Parties 101: How to Have Fun & Be Safe

Y*ou don't see them on the college Web site or featured in the glossy viewbook, but you and your friends know that parties are a crucial part of the college experience. And everyone else in your life knows it too: your parents, your RA, your high school principal, your professors. You know they know because they've all been giving you advice on how to have a great time without getting yourself into too much trouble. So be honest— did you really pay attention? Just in case you didn't (and even if you did), read this chapter.*

YOU HAVE TO LEARN that the week is for studying and the weekend is for partying. You can't think that you just party every day. That's what I thought: I thought that college was a never-ending party, without work. I thought it was going to be easier than high school, without busy work. But it's overwhelming.

—*AMY HOFFBERG*
UNIVERSITY OF DELAWARE, FRESHMAN

• • • • • • • •

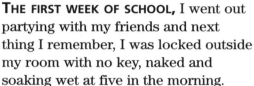

THE FIRST WEEK OF SCHOOL, I went out partying with my friends and next thing I remember, I was locked outside my room with no key, naked and soaking wet at five in the morning.

—*S.*
HARVARD UNIVERSITY, SOPHOMORE

• • • • • • • •

BEST PARTY SCHOOLS

1. University of Wisconsin-Madison

2. Ohio University

3. Lehigh University

4. University of California-Santa Barbara

5. State University of New York-Albany

WHEN YOU'RE AT A PARTY, TRY TO THINK about the next morning. Ask yourself the question: Will I be able to look at myself in the mirror?

—*G.*
UNIVERSITY OF NORTH CAROLINA AT CHAPEL HILL
SOPHOMORE

• • • • • • • •

FOOTBALL GAMES ARE SO MUCH FUN HERE—everyone is drunk in the stands. On game day, the whole campus is up by 9 a.m. You can't get students up at 9 a.m. for school, but they'll get up early to start partying before a game.

—*M.M.*
BOSTON COLLEGE, JUNIOR

• • • • • • • •

IF YOU'RE GOING TO DRINK, drink *before* you go out. It saves tons of money. Use the money you save to buy an Xbox or PlayStation to keep you occupied.

—*JIMMY LYNCH*
AUBURN UNIVERSITY, GRADUATE

IF YOU WANT TO DRINK FOR FREE, head to a bar and pretend you don't want to drink alcohol. You'll suddenly be everyone's pet project. As the efforts to convert you mount, give in slowly; not only will everyone have a good time, but you'll have a good buzz to match.

—*BRIAN TURNER*
UNIVERSITY OF GEORGIA, GRADUATE

• • • • • • • •

I SMOKED A LOT OF POT; that was something entertaining that came with college. I had smoked before, but not to the extent I did my first year, which could very likely be a reason it is so unmemorable.

—*K.*
SAN DIEGO STATE UNIVERSITY, JUNIOR

• • • • • • • •

DON'T DRINK HARD LIQUOR—stick to beer. You have better control with beer. I had bad experiences with liquor. If you wake up the next morning and you don't remember what you did, you've had too much to drink.

—*REID ATTAWAY*
JAMES MADISON UNIVERSITY, FRESHMAN

• • • • • • • •

IF YOU'VE NEVER FUNNELED THREE BEERS after going shot for shot with some guy in your bio lab, don't do it the first night on campus; you will end up throwing up in the washrooms, and it is just not pretty. Yes, college is a time for experimentation and partying, but don't screw up what you worked 12 years for just because the opportunity is there.

—*AMY*
PRINCETON UNIVERSITY, FRESHMAN

No matter how desperate you are for a daiquiri, do not use blueberries.

—*MARGOT CARMICHAEL LESTER*
UNIVERSITY OF NORTH CAROLINA AT CHAPEL HILL GRADUATE

Don't drink the punch. There's a lot more alcohol in there than you think.

—*ANONYMOUS YALE UNIVERSITY SOPHOMORE*

HEAD**LINES**
Best Advice and Top Tips

- In college the words "party" and "beer" go hand in hand.
- If you set your drink down and walk away, don't go back for it—it's too risky.
- Never drink and drive—DUIs go on your permanent record.
- As long as you're staying on top of your work, you're not partying too much.

GO TO PARTIES. I didn't party at all in high school. When I went to college, my R.A. took me to a frat party the second night I was there. I wouldn't say overdo it, but you should experience that part of college life.

—*ERIC FRIES*
BOSTON UNIVERSITY, GRADUATE

IF A MAN APPROACHES YOU and your friends at a garden party offering strange-looking mushrooms in a baggie, tell him you're not hungry.

—*D.D.*
UNIVERSITY OF PENNSYLVANIA, GRADUATE

A LOT OF PEOPLE COME IN HERE and they don't have experience drinking, and they just sort of explode. My friend had a freshman roommate who failed out the first semester because he had spent all his time drinking. Don't get in over your head.

—*LEE ROBERTS*
UNIVERSITY OF NORTH CAROLINA AT CHAPEL HILL, SENIOR

ALCOHOL IS A REALLY BIG FACTOR in what goes wrong with freshmen. Everything is new, you're getting a lot of attention from other people, and when you're under the influence of alcohol you don't make the best decisions. And there's peer pressure: A lot of people think they're above peer pressure, but when you get in a scene with a hundred other people having a good time, you don't do things you would normally do.

—*A.G.H.*
UNIVERSITY OF VIRGINIA, SENIOR

❝❝Don't try to drink all the beer on campus. You can't, trust me. And not having a car your freshman year is a good safety measure.❞❞

—*STEVE DAVIS*
FLORIDA STATE UNIVERSITY, GRADUATE

DON'T FEEL LIKE YOU NEED to funnel beers to have a good time, and know that if you choose not to drink, there are tons of other people who don't either. But don't lecture other people—if they wanted you to be their mom, they would've asked. Exceptions: your close friends, people who are being offensive to you, people you are close to, and girls who are about to be taken advantage of because of their state.

—*JULIE*
PRINCETON UNIVERSITY, SOPHOMORE

Don't party before tests. It really does impair your ability.

—*H.K.S.*
OXFORD COLLEGE JUNIOR

FRESHMAN DRINKING PRIMER

1. Every college student needs to know the old mantra, "Liquor before beer, never fear. Beer before liquor, never sicker."

2. It helps to have a glass of water with, or in between, drinks. And don't drink on an empty stomach.

3. If you close your eyes and you can't keep your balance, it's probably time to stop drinking for the night.
   —*D.R.*
   UNIVERSITY OF NORTH CAROLINA AT CHAPEL HILL, GRADUATE

· · · · · · · · ·

TO PREVENT SERIOUS TROUBLE—and perhaps even death—you must follow some simple rules. First, you need to do the stand-up test: The first time you drink a lot of liquor, don't do it all sitting down. You won't feel what it's doing to you. But the first time you stand up, hit the floor, and eat some carpet, you will suddenly feel what it is doing to you. So, stand up often while drinking liquor, to better measure the effect. Also, drink a lot of water when drinking alcohol; you've got to dilute that stuff.
   —*R.S.*
   GEORGETOWN UNIVERSITY, GRADUATE

· · · · · · · · ·

THE BEST WAY TO GET OVER A HANGOVER is water and bread. Bread is your best friend: It helps take care of your stomach, and it fills you and soaks up anything. The water makes you not dehydrated anymore. The next day, just make it a Blockbuster night; that's all you need to do.
   —*BETH*
   DIABLO VALLEY COLLEGE, FRESHMAN

· · · · · · · · ·

DRAMAMINE is an incredible cure for a horrible hangover.
   —*J.*
   UNIVERSITY OF GEORGIA, GRADUATE

HOUSE PARTIES ARE THE WAY TO GO! Forget frats, clubs, or fancy bars. Drink cheap, fast, and with friends. It's all about the people, not the place. The most fun I had was spending the night at a friend-of-a-friend's house partying, and then taking the party back to my apartment. We hung out until the wee hours of the morning. The fun is right where you are.

—*JACKIE*
STATE UNIVERSITY OF NEW YORK AT BINGHAMTON GRADUATE

Go to places
with free beer.

—*JOEL*
PRINCETON UNIVERSITY GRADUATE

. . . .

"If you're a bunch of girls and you go to a frat party, which you will, be aware of your surroundings and keep track of each other. Be in charge of yourself, and keep track of your girls, and they'll keep track of you."

—*TRACY*
UNIVERSITY OF COLORADO, GRADUATE

. . . .

YOU END UP IN PRETTY WEIRD SITUATIONS. Once I went to a party of all Indians. Everyone in the room was Indian except me. The food, the conversations, the dress—everything was Indian. By the end of the night I thought I was Indian and was ready to give up beef forever.

—*JOE MAYAN*
CARNEGIE MELLON UNIVERSITY, SOPHOMORE

I DON'T DRINK. It's not hard to socialize if you don't drink, because everyone needs a designated driver. If I go, they usually buy my dinner. So it works for me.

—*B.M.*
UNIVERSITY OF MARYLAND, JUNIOR

* * * * * * * *

66 Alcohol makes some people seem more attractive than they will look the next morning. So, think a little more about your decisions at frat parties or anything like that. 99

—*H.K.S.*
OXFORD COLLEGE, JUNIOR

* * * * * * * *

THERE ARE LOTS OF PARTIES THE FIRST YEAR and you meet a lot of eager goofs: people who want to make a bold statement and show you who he/she is. It seems like they're in high school again, trying to compete to be cool. Take these poseurs with a grain of salt!

—*MICHAEL ALBERT PAOLI*
UNIVERSITY OF TORONTO, GRADUATE

* * * * * * * *

HERE'S SOME ADVICE that my brother left me on my answering machine the first week I was in college: "If you smoke pot in your room, make sure to put a towel under the door."

—*B.K.*
CORNELL UNIVERSITY, GRADUATE

Stay on top of your stuff, and regulate your drinking habits.

—*BRETT STRICKLAND*
GEORGIA STATE UNIVERSITY FRESHMAN

AS FAR AS DRINKING GOES, I had a closed mind. I thought, I don't want to go through four years of school drunk and not experiencing everything. I didn't realize you could balance those things. So I didn't drink at all. Then I gradually started with friends here and I was like, you know what? Going out with friends on Friday night and partying doesn't mean you're wasting four years. It just means you're experiencing different things.

—*LYNN SNIFFEN*
BOSTON COLLEGE, JUNIOR

• • • • • • • •

I DON'T DRINK. When I go to parties, people ask why I'm not drinking and I'll just tell them I decided I don't want to do it. Ninety percent of the people I talk to about it—even the people who are completely drunk—think it's cool and say I should stick with it.

—*REID ATTAWAY*
JAMES MADISON UNIVERSITY, FRESHMAN

• • • • • • • •

NEVER, EVER DRIVE AFTER DRINKING any amount of alcohol at all. A DUI will give you a police record and cost you thousands in legal fees and fines; don't even chance it. I had friends who did, and once it happens, all you can do is regret what you've done.

Be wary of hard liquor. Don't drink it or let others guzzle it like weak beer. That can easily be a quick slide to alcohol poisoning, coma—even death.

—*WENDY W.*
UNIVERSITY OF GEORGIA, GRADUATE

• • • • • • • •

YOU'RE AHEAD OF THE CURVE once you accept that the upperclassmen get all the hot girls at parties. The football players do, too. Instead of worrying about this, work on building friendships.

—*MICHAEL*
GRADUATE

How can you tell if you're partying too much? If you're doing fine in classes, you're not partying too much. If you don't do well in classes, you're partying too much.

—*NOURA BAKKOUR*
GEORGETOWN UNIVERSITY SENIOR

I DON'T PARTY A LOT NOW. The first couple of years, I partied too much. I realized, this is a lot of work, trying to party and go to school, and it's expensive. So, I decided I didn't need it; it's too much effort.

—*ADAM PENA*
AMERICAN REPERTORY THEATER AT HARVARD, JUNIOR

• • • • • • • •

YOU'RE GOING TOO FAR with the drinking when you have to drink every time you want to go out. When you "pregame" for everything: "Let's go to the diner, let's pregame first!"—that kind of thing. Some people have an obsession with it.

Don't become an alcoholic; that screws up everything. I've seen people screw up their whole school career. They do too many drugs or drink too much, they're not in school anymore, and they're working hard to get back in.

—*DANIEL RUSK*
UNIVERSITY OF MARYLAND, SOPHOMORE

• • • • • • • •

DON'T DRINK TOO MUCH; at this school, it can cost you a lot of money. My freshman year, my roommate got alcohol poisoning. She came home early one morning and passed out. We couldn't wake her up so we called campus security and an ambulance came and took her to the hospital. She was fine afterwards, but the school fined her $2,000; plus, she had to pay her hospital bill.

—*LIANA HIYANE*
SANTA CLARA UNIVERSITY, JUNIOR

• • • • • • • •

GIRLS, BE ESPECIALLY CAREFUL of what you drink while at clubs or house parties, because an uncovered drink could mean a lost night and a trip to the gynecologist the next day.

—*ANONYMOUS*

WISDOM FOR WOMEN

WHEN YOU GO OUT, HAVE SOMEONE WITH YOU that you trust—I don't care if you're just going over to a guy's house, you don't want to be left alone. You need a friend who knows when to take you home. I have a friend and we do that for each other; we don't let each other out of sight. Sometimes I'll get pissed off and get in a full-on fist fight, saying, "No, I can handle this!" and she's like, "No, I'm taking you home right now." We have to be strict with each other, but it's good to have someone looking out for you.

The best place to hide from guys is in the bathroom. Just make puking noises and they'll run. That's all you have to do to be left alone.

I don't care where you go to school, you have to be tough; two girls were raped in my dorm. Take a kickboxing class so that you know you can protect yourself.

> —*MOLLY SELMER*
> *SONOMA STATE UNIVERSITY, GRADUATE*

· · · · · · · · ·

WHEN YOU'RE DRINKING, know your limits. Girls don't know how much they can drink, because they don't drink as often as guys. So girls will play drinking games with guys, thinking that they're cool and tough; then all of a sudden they're messed up, throwing up, or passed out.

> —*JENNIFER SPICER*
> *FOOTHILL COLLEGE, GRADUATE*

· · · · · · · · ·

THERE ARE A LOT OF SCUMBAGS OUT THERE who try to take advantage of girls, especially freshmen. Don't put your drink down or let someone else get you a drink, because they could put something in it. Never walk around campus alone at night. Be careful.

> —*KATHERINE*
> *AUBURN UNIVERSITY, GRADUATE*

DRINKING: I GOT WRITTEN UP BY THE POLICE multiple times for stupid reasons. It caused me some problems with housing for my sophomore year. And I lost housing for my senior year. I'm pretty liberal about drinking, but you've got to watch yourself. Blackouts are never too good.
—*M.M.*
BOSTON COLLEGE, JUNIOR

"I worked in the bars on the weekends, which was cool because you're still in the social scene and you can see everyone, but you're making money instead of spending money."

—*STEVEN RILEY*
STATE UNIVERSITY OF NEW YORK AT BINGHAMTON, GRADUATE

DON'T GET TOO CAUGHT UP IN ALCOHOL. I personally believe that college is the time to experiment with stuff like this; but if you do plan on getting drunk, try to set a reasonable limit and abide by it. If you pace yourself, this isn't too hard to do. And definitely try to confine it to the weekend. If you start drinking Thursday or even Wednesday nights, your studies and your grades will suffer. There's nothing like coming home inebriated at 2 a.m. and still having homework to do for the next day, especially when your responsible friends already did it together as a group and have gone to sleep.
—*ANONYMOUS*
UNIVERSITY OF VIRGINIA, SENIOR

TRY TO LIMIT THE DRINKING to three times a week. Work hard Monday through Thursday, and party Thursday, Friday, and Saturday nights; that's what worked for me.

—*NICK DOMANICO*
UNIVERSITY OF CALIFORNIA AT SANTA BARBARA, SENIOR

• • • • • • • •

IF YOU GET DRUNK, don't throw chairs at your dorm neighbor. My neighbor had the same major as mine and I saw her for the next four years. She remembered that.

—*CASEY*
GEORGETOWN UNIVERSITY, SENIOR

• • • • • • • •

I WENT TO A SMALL JESUIT COLLEGE, but it was pretty cool. We had crazy frats and sororities, because we had a wet campus. I think a wet campus is good; you learn responsibility. If you hadn't had a drink before, it was very supportive. A lot of people knew what they were doing and helped the people who didn't. Every party we ever had was bused; no one ever drove to parties or to go out. If you drove to go out, you drove because you were stupid.

—*GINGER M. BRODTMAN*
SPRING HILL COLLEGE, GRADUATE

• • • • • • • •

GO TO FRAT PARTIES with a bunch of girlfriends, and make sure you all go home together. Don't listen to any of the crap the guys try to hand you. They're looking for freshmen; they're waiting for them. Freshmen are so naïve and gullible and they think everything the guys say is true, and it's not. The guy will say anything: he'll say all these nice things and make a girl feel special, but it doesn't matter. He won't know your name the next day. He probably doesn't know your name right then.

—*KRISTIN THOMAS*
JAMES MADISON UNIVERSITY, JUNIOR

At parties, never set a drink down and walk away.

—*SWEETS*
GEORGIA STATE UNIVERSITY, JUNIOR

TRY TO STEER CLEAR OF THE DRINKING as much as possible. It's easy to get too fixed on the drinking of beers each night. That usually ends up causing trouble.

—*DAVID BLANEY*
WILLIAMS COLLEGE, GRADUATE

• • • • • • • •

"Don't be a fool and party and act like an idiot. That happened to a bunch of girls on my hall and they all did poorly."

—*ERICA MARIOLA*
EMORY UNIVERSITY, GRADUATE

• • • • • • • •

 I DID SOME DUMB THINGS and I'm still paying for them. I did something illegal that I got caught for. Looking back now, I wish I could change some of the partying to more studying.

Don't get stupid; people remember that. People will say, "Oh, I remember that party when you were passed out on the stairs." Whatever you do, it will follow you around the rest of your life. You want to have a good time, but you don't want to get carried away.

Everyone does stupid things, but don't get caught doing something illegal. You pick up habits in your freshman year where you say, "Oh, I didn't get caught then, so I might as well do it now." Then you get caught, and you're like, "Oh, that's how the real world works."

—*JOSH H.*
PURDUE UNIVERSITY, GRADUATE

FRESHMAN FACTOID

44 percent of college students "binge-drink" (defined as drinking at least 5 [for men] or 4 [for women] drinks in a row, at least once in the previous two weeks).

IF YOU GO TO A SCHOOL WHERE IT GETS COLD, get a somewhat fashionable jacket that can stand the wear and tear of a party. You'll want a jacket that's cheap, that will stand up to dirt, spit, beer, the weather, and your friend's drool.

—*JOSEPH S. SMITH*
PENNSYLVANIA STATE UNIVERSITY, GRADUATE

• • • • • • • •

IN MY FRESHMAN YEAR I would go out every night on weeknights and stay out until 5 a.m., when I had to be in class at 9 a.m. I wasn't making it. That was the last semester I didn't live at home.

—*ODELL*
HUNTER COLLEGE, SENIOR

STAND BY YOUR DRUNK FRIENDS

One of my girlfriends was really injury-prone. She would hurt herself constantly, usually while drinking. She almost died three or four times. One night we were out at a strip of bars and we got really drunk. She was standing 30 feet away from me at the end of the street, and I'm standing with five people. She called my name and I saw her running towards me. Then, she's sprinting at me. She gets five feet from me and leaps at me—she wanted me to catch her, or something. I sidestepped her and she met the concrete. Her entire face was bruised and cut and it was Parents Week next weekend and everyone thought her boyfriend did it to her. Our guy friends almost beat him up. She was called Scarface from that point on. The moral of the story is, don't sidestep your friends. Break their fall or something. But I blame the alcohol.

—*CASEY*
GEORGETOWN UNIVERSITY, SENIOR

MORE WISE WOMEN

THERE WERE A LOT OF FRESHMAN GIRLS that I took home from bars; they thought they had friends. They got too drunk, and their friends left. We used to find girls drunk in the bathrooms of bars all the time. They didn't know where their friends were and they would need someone to take care of them.

Girls, don't put down your drink. I think I went to a great school, but you don't know who is around. I had a friend who was drugged her sophomore year. She had two beers and all of a sudden she's out of her head and can't stand. And we thought she must have done shots and we didn't know about it. But the next day, she was in bed and couldn't get up. And she'd had hardly anything to drink. You don't know who's out there; you have to be careful.

You don't want to go to bars when you're a freshman, anyway. You're not going to meet anyone that you want to meet. I mean, who do you meet at a bar? Alcoholics and weirdos.

—*J. DEVEREUX*
GEORGETOWN UNIVERSITY, GRADUATE

• • • • • • • • •

YOU HAVE TO BE CAREFUL. We went to frat parties where they kept trying to give us drinks and beers. They went into the bathroom and then came out with a cup of beer. We were like, "Wow, no. Can I watch you pour it, please?" Some girls don't know better.

—*CHRISTINE*
UNIVERSITY OF RHODE ISLAND, SOPHOMORE

I WENT TO SCHOOL ABOUT THREE HOURS from the Mexican border. My freshman year, I was kind of an idiot. I went down to Mexico, and coming back across the border, I had had a few beers. Well, they stop you and ask if you have anything to declare. So I said, "Nothing to declare, except for my automatic weapons." It was a joke, but it wasn't taken well by the border patrol. A couple of hours later, after being strip-searched and interrogated, I was told never to come into the country again.

—JOHN BENTLEY
TRINITY UNIVERSITY, GRADUATE

. . . .

"Don't drink to get drunk. You're not cool if you're drunk. Better to get a social buzz that keeps you in a jovial and rhythmic mood all night."

—RICHARD
GEORGIA SOUTHERN UNIVERSITY, GRADUATE

. . . .

ALWAYS GO TO PARTIES with people you know, and be careful with your alcohol, wherever you put it down. And don't drink so much, because there are cops around. And don't do anything stupid, if you can help it. And don't run across the busy street, and don't be stupid in front of cops, and don't drive drunk. But have fun.

—ANONYMOUS
JAMES MADISON UNIVERSITY, SOPHOMORE

IF YOU DON'T WANT TO DRINK, then it's all about the people you find. If you surround yourself with people who drink and who will pressure you, it will be a difficult situation. If you surround yourself with people who are hesitant to drink or who are responsible, it won't be such a problem.

—*ANONYMOUS*
UNIVERSITY OF VIRGINIA, SENIOR

• • • • • • • •

66 Don't feel that you need to be at every party all the time. It's perfectly OK to be at home sleeping on a Saturday night; there's nothing wrong with that. More people do it than you think. If you get too caught up in the social scene, you lose sight of other things. 99

—*HANNAH SMITH*
HARVARD UNIVERSITY, JUNIOR

• • • • • • • •

MAKE SURE YOU GO out with reliable people. When you party and get trashed in college, you need a support system. If you're passed out, you need someone to drag you home. Always party with people you trust.

—*KYLE*
UNIVERSITY OF TEXAS, AUSTIN, GRADUATE

WORDS OF WARNING

DON'T MAKE DRINKING A COMPETITIVE ACTIVITY. If you find your-self trying to prove how much you can drink to impress others, then it's going to end badly. You'll get alcohol poisoning, whether you believe you're immune or not. Or, you'll end up puking your guts out in front of your friends and people you don't even know. Also, drinking should not be the main activity of your night. If you go out just to drink, you're going to get drunk. If you go out to meet people at a party, or to dance, play a game, or bowl, focus on the main activity first, and then just let the drinking be an additive; it should never be the focus of your night. The funny thing is, the people who make it the focus of their night can't understand why everyone else might not want to do the same thing. But watch those people; they're all cool and everything when they're playing quarters and making jokes and doing shots, but they'll end up puking or acting like idiots.

—*ANONYMOUS*
VILLANOVA, GRADUATE

• • • • • • • •

IF YOU DO DECIDE TO EXPERIMENT WITH ALCOHOL and drugs in col-lege, be prepared to accept the consequences of your actions; what you're doing may be illegal and, as such, a poor decision. Alcohol and drugs are only a temporary escape from the dullness of life. If you find yourself consumed by these substances, you may need to reevaluate the directions your life is going in and realign yourself. If you're drinking to be more social, then maybe you're too self-conscious. If you're smoking marijuana to relax and be happy, then maybe you need a hobby. There are plenty of people and activities on campus to keep you busy without having to resort to drugs and alcohol on too regular a basis.

—*ARIEL MELENDEZ*
PRINCETON UNIVERSITY, FRESHMAN

Just because the beer is being served in Dixie cups doesn't mean you can drink 40 cups and still drive home.

—Scott Woelfel
University of Missouri
Graduate

If you're going to drink, get to know your bartender personally. Big tipping, right off the bat, is a good way to do this.

—J.G.
Florida State University
Graduate

ALWAYS PUT YOUR HAND over your drink, to keep people from putting something in your drink. Obviously, you shouldn't just leave your drink and come back to it. But also, cover your drink when you carry it. That was the overwhelming advice I got from everybody when I came to college.

> *—Bethany*
> *James Madison University, Senior*

• • • • • • • •

A FRESHMAN GUY FINDS A GOOD PARTY by finding some hot freshman girls and going where they go. Or, you can hook up with an upperclassman; they know where the good parties are.

> *—Dave*
> *University of Rhode Island, Junior*

• • • • • • • •

YOU KNOW YOU'RE AT A GOOD PARTY when you get slammed against the wall trying to get to the keg in the corner. And guys try to get girls to go in for them. Girls get alcohol more easily than guys do.

> *—Whitney*
> *Yale University, Freshman*

• • • • • • • •

WHEN YOU FIRST START COLLEGE, the phrase "three-day weekend" takes on a whole new meaning. The more social students tend to go out on Thursday night for the sole purpose of drinking themselves into a stupor. Friday night is a rest-and-recuperation night, and then the partying resumes Saturday night. By the time you wake up on Sunday it's already mid-afternoon. This trend fades by the time you start sophomore year. If it doesn't, you are officially an alcoholic and/or a stoner.

> *—Joshua Berkov*
> *Brown University, Junior*

SCARY STORY

It was Halloween of my freshman year. We were having a party in the dorm—not a costume deal or anything, just partying in random rooms. I was drinking mainly screwdrivers out of one of those 42-ounce, McDonald's cups. A friend of a friend, who came up to visit with her meathead boyfriend, got into a fight with him and ran away. She was about to get us written up—at Westfield State, "written up" means getting kicked off campus for five weekends—so my friend and I split up to find her. I found the psycho tucked under a stairwell, crying. I put my hand out to help her up, and the crazy girl bit me really hard. The mark she left looked like ringworm!

I said, "Whatever," gave up on that problem, and proceeded to get fizzled for rizzle—drunk, that is. The vodka I was drinking was good old Poland Springs vodka, the cheapest form of the stuff around. Let's just say that at the end of the night I puked in my roommate's garbage and passed out face down on my rug. It does not end there: I woke up outside, crying, to the sound of a fire alarm. My friends told me they had come into my room, where I was just walking around in circles; they put my jacket on me and brought me outside. This is where I allegedly was crying to call my mother. Fortunately, I don't think that many people saw my scene. Anyway, my friends ended up bringing me to my other friend's dorm and putting me to sleep. That is what I like to call Alcoholism.

Lessons learned: 1) Screw your friend who is about to get written up, and 2) Drink beer—it could save your life.

—B.
WESTFIELD STATE COLLEGE, GRADUATE

ASK THE ADVISOR

Everyone knows that college students drink. Am I really going to get into trouble for having a couple of beers in the dorm?

You're half right—all college administrators know that *some* college students drink. Plenty of students don't drink at all, or drink very moderately. But your question is about getting into trouble.

The answer depends on your college. Some colleges have almost supernatural powers when it comes to sniffing out that kind of rule breaking, whereas others operate on a purely human skill level. The second half of the story is what happens to students who are caught drinking. There will always be consequences, but they may vary in type and severity. Read your dorm handbook to find out your college's policy, and don't be fooled by other students who tell you that "they don't really mean it"; if it's on the books, it could happen to you.

JUST BECAUSE YOU can do every drug and drink everything, it doesn't mean you have to or you should. It'll take you a while to figure that out.

—*A.W.D.*
GEORGIA STATE UNIVERSITY
GRADUATE

QUITE A FEW FRESHMEN, me included, got way too drunk during orientation week before classes began and did something stupid. Those stories spread and stay alive. It took about a year for me to live mine down, and I got lucky because other people involved in the story left the school, making it a lot less interesting to tell. If I had known this would happen before I started school I could have saved a year of embarrassment.

—*ANONYMOUS*
WASHINGTON AND LEE UNIVERSITY, JUNIOR

• • • • • • • •

CALL YOUR FRIENDS before you go on a road trip to see them. My friends and I went up to Providence. We were having a good time, and then we decided we wanted to go to Newport. When we were driving, it was pretty late at night, so my friend in Newport wouldn't pick up his phone. So we had to keep on driving. When we got to Connecticut, we tried to call my friend there, and he didn't pick up either. Then we passed New York City and none of our friends would pick up the phone. They were all asleep. We ended up down at the Jersey Shore at four in the morning, after five hours of driving from Providence.

—*THEODORE SCHIMENTI*
COLUMBIA UNIVERSITY, FRESHMAN

GRADUATION REQUIREMENT

If the smoke doesn't get you, the exhaustion will: During homecoming weekend at Dartmouth, the graduating class does a Senior Sweep—running around a 70-story bonfire in the center of the green. The class of 2008 has to circle it 108 times, the class of 2009, 109 times, and so on.

If you're going to buy weed, don't buy it from the drunk on the street. What you'll end up with is oregano held together by glue.

—*J.G.*
FLORIDA STATE UNIVERSITY GRADUATE

BE RESPONSIBLE FOR YOUR FRIENDS. Make your own drinks. Watch where your friends are at all times. Don't be naïve about guys; know that they don't have your best interests in mind. I know several girls who were very trusting and were taken advantage of. It's really easy to do when everyone is under the influence of alcohol.

—*A.G.H.*
UNIVERSITY OF VIRGINIA, SENIOR

20

Animal House: Fraternities & Sororities

*I*n days of old, every college student knew Greek and Latin. Today, you just know enough Greek to tell Psi Chi from Alpha Delta. But what do fraternities and sororities really do, besides throw parties? You know there's more to the whole Greek thing than what you've seen in movies. In this chapter, Greeks and non-Greeks tell the story behind the letters.

Don't bother going to frat parties. It's a bunch of stupid people who are drunk, and there are too many of them.

—*Robin Jaleel*
  Emory University
  Graduate

I joined a frat the spring semester of my freshman year. It was a great experience; the best thing I ever did. I was against fraternities completely, I got dragged into it, and now the brothers are my best friends. I was that guy who said, "Frat guys suck!" But things change.

—*Chris McAndrew*
  University of Delaware, Junior

• • • • • • • •

Be sweet as pie during your sorority pledge period and wait until after you're active to tell off the snots who were mean to you. Better yet, just steal their boyfriends.

—*Lynn Lamousin*
  Louisiana State University, Graduate

• • • • • • • •

I went to a large school where you didn't have to be Greek to have a life. But I wanted both, so during my sophomore year I decided to pledge. This gave me time to make other friendships with people who weren't necessarily going Greek. And as it turned out, not all of my closest friends from freshman year decided to go Greek. My advice: Don't jump into pledging. Get to know the campus, get to know friends outside of Greek life, and get used to what life is like without it. That way you can decide if it's right for you. At my school, sororities were very competitive, and many women never got invited to join any sorority. So this was tough for some people.

—*Anonymous*
  Indiana University, Graduate

• • • • • • • •

Be a part of the Greek system. It is a great place for networking down the road. People get hired because they were in the same sorority as the boss.

—*Heather Pollock*
  California State University, Fullerton, Graduate

FRESHMAN GIRLS SHOULD GO through sorority Rush, but don't take it too seriously. If you take it to heart, people can tell. You run the risk of getting really hurt. It's just a group of girls; there are other things in life.

> —ANONYMOUS
> UNIVERSITY OF VIRGINIA, SOPHOMORE

JOIN WHATEVER FRATERNITY ATTRACTS THE HOTTEST chicks—that's all frats are good for, anyway.

> —J.G.
> FLORIDA STATE UNIVERSITY, GRADUATE

If you decide to rush, take the whole experience with a grain of salt.

—D.
DUKE UNIVERSITY
SENIOR

"At least try Rush. You don't have to pledge, but going through Rush is a really good time to meet other girls who are going through what you're going through. It's a really great bonding time."

> —DENISE O.
> UNION COLLEGE, JUNIOR

THE STUFF YOU HEAR about wild frat hazing is mostly college lore; in fact, some of the pranks or "rituals" are most likely obsolete. Like, you hear about the "ookie cookie," but again, it's a myth—it's not all like *Animal House*.

> —JAMES WILLIS
> UNIVERSITY OF CALIFORNIA AT DAVIS, SENIOR

I'M IN A SORORITY, and it's the best thing I've ever done in my life. I'm such a better person for being in a sorority. But it's way too early to pledge freshman year; I pledged sophomore year. You need to establish yourself at your college first. You meet your freshman group of friends; then you can pledge sophomore year. I did, and I didn't feel like I was pledging too late. The year I pledged, there were 450 sophomores, versus like 50 freshmen. It's just too much for freshmen.

—*KRISTIN THOMAS*
JAMES MADISON UNIVERSITY, JUNIOR

• • • • • • • •

THE FIRST FRAT PARTY I went to as a pledge, they told us not to wear anything nice. First thing that happens when I walk in, a girl throws an entire beer on me. It was called Beer Splash. I was like, "This is where I want to be."

—*A.G.S.*
UNIVERSITY OF TENNESSEE, DID NOT GRADUATE

• • • • • • • •

THE WHOLE PROCESS TRULY IS SUPERFICIAL. Sorority members judge rushies based slightly on appearance and primarily on a five- to 10-minute conversation that takes place within the most fake and uncomfortable environment. With all this in mind, if you want to join a sorority, you take it for what it is. Don't go into Rush believing that the girls you meet have the final say (or any say, for that matter) on who you are, or how "cool" or desirable you are. They're judging you based on a glimpse of who they think you are.

—*D.*
DUKE UNIVERSITY, SENIOR

Even if you don't want to be in a frat, you should do Rush; you'll get free drinks and have fun.

—*J.D.*
EMORY UNIVERSITY SENIOR

SCIENCE EXPERIMENT?

In my fraternity house, we had a very old iron stove in the kitchen, which was original to the house. The stove was huge, and completely useless—it hadn't worked in decades. But nobody could move it because it was so heavy, and no trash disposal company or dumping ground would accept it—not even if we paid them to take it! It seemed as though our house was stuck with this old relic for another 80 years.

Then one night we had a brainstorm. In the middle of the night, about 10 of us hoisted this piece of useless iron onto a dolly, and rolled it across campus to the Science Center. Now, in the lobby of the college's Science Center was a small museum of scientific artifacts (you know, like a 200-year-old microscope, or a skeleton of a 1 million-year-old small rodent). So, we found a nice little nook for the stove (right in between some relics) and placed a professional-looking sign on the stove which said: "Random Kinetic Energy Enhancer, circa 1842." Only a science geek would know that that is another way of saying: "This is an old stove."

The relic stayed for about a week, then was hauled off by the university. We didn't pay a dime.

—I.L.S.
WESLEYAN UNIVERSITY, GRADUATE

GREEK 101

Choose one from Column A and one from Column B to find the group that's right for you.

A: WHAT	B: WHO
Social—If you want to make friends	**Fraternity**—All guys
Service—If you love volunteering	**Sorority**—All ladies
Professional—If you're looking to do some career networking	**Coed**—You know what this means
Academic/Honor—If you're smart, want everyone to know you're smart, and prefer hanging out with other people who are just as smart as you are	

AFTER A WHILE, YOU GET KIND OF BORED with college, and it's good to meet people and network through fraternities. I've met a lot of people from different walks of life. I've learned a lot about people. There were some people that I met while pledging, and I had a feeling I might not like them. But then I got to know them and I ended up liking them.

You shouldn't rush frats the first semester. Get acquainted with the university. The second semester, it's a good thing to do. It's something to complement your academics. It helps keep you focused.

—*RON SILVER*
UNIVERSITY OF MARYLAND, JUNIOR

If you're in a frat or sorority, be prepared for people to put you down for being Greek.

—*SHEILA CRAWFORD*
NORTH CAROLINA
STATE UNIVERSITY
SOPHOMORE

❝❝I ended up going Greek in the spring semester of my freshman year. I had never planned on it in the past, but you really just have to try it out and see if it's right for you.❞❞

—*MELANIE*
PENNSYLVANIA STATE UNIVERSITY, SOPHOMORE

I DID NOT JOIN A FRAT because I did not want to do chores. I did chores at home and left that behind; who needs it? But to meet girls, the frat guys do have an advantage.

—*INSU CHANG*
CARNEGIE MELLON UNIVERSITY, JUNIOR

DON'T PLEDGE YOUR FIRST YEAR. You will limit your experiences as a freshman. And it takes up a lot of time. I pledged my sophomore year, and I know people who did it their junior year. Don't be in a hurry: Greek life isn't going anywhere!

—*NIROSHAN RAJARATNAM*
UNIVERSITY OF MARYLAND, GRADUATE

• • • • • • • • •

BEFORE COLLEGE, I WAS VERY ANTI-SORORITY; I thought they were evil. But now, even though I'm not in a sorority, I live with sorority girls, and they're all my good friends. I go to lots of their functions and have a great time. It's not a big deal if you're not in a sorority. It's only a big deal the first few weeks of the year and then the five days of Rush. During Rush I just remind myself that I do have friends; they're just all busy this week. If you're not sure whether you want to join a fraternity or sorority, remember that you can still join and it doesn't have to be the top priority in your life. Join; just don't become president. Sororities and fraternities are a great way to make a big school seem smaller.

—*SUMMER J.*
UNIVERSITY OF VIRGINIA, SENIOR

BIG FRATERNITY/SORORITY SCHOOLS

- Washington and Lee University (Virginia)
- Depauw University (Indiana)
- Indiana University - Bloomington
- University of Colorado–Boulder
- Birmingham-Southern College (Alabama)

"I HAVE TO PAY TO BE YOUR SISTER?" That was the first question that popped in my head after accepting an invitation to join my dream sorority house. My whole family had been Greek in college, but I couldn't get past the fact that I was paying to have friends. Now, I understand that the friends I made in my sorority are forever, and even when I no longer pay for room and board and T-shirts, my sisters will still be there. I never bought my friends—I just put down a deposit.

—*AMANDA SOUKUP*
UNIVERSITY OF NEBRASKA, SOPHOMORE

· · · · · · · ·

"I avoided frat parties until I was a senior. That's when I knew better."

—*ANONYMOUS*
UNIVERSITY OF RHODE ISLAND, SOPHOMORE

· · · · · · · ·

FRATS ARE FOR IDIOTS. But if you really feel like you have to pay dues to make friends, or spend a month scrubbing toilets and performing idiotic stunts so people will like you, then I guess frats are for you. If you don't care about individuality, or respect for yourself or for women, sign up. If you want to bypass all opportunity for meaningful relationships and skip right to drinking buddies and one-night stands, go for it. Don't get me wrong: I was good friends with some frat boys and sorority girls in college, just like I'm friends with some Republicans now. But it was despite their affiliations, not because of them.

—*EAMON SIGGINS*
STATE UNIVERSITY OF NEW YORK AT BINGHAMTON
GRADUATE

IF YOU'RE GOING TO JOIN A SORORITY, bail after the first year—two years at most. The whole sorority-fraternity thing inhibits having a rich and diverse college experience. You're lumped together with a small percentage of the campus population, and you cheat yourself of the opportunity to meet interesting people who wouldn't be caught dead on Greek Row. At first, a sorority or fraternity can be comforting. You just left home for the first time, and being around people who are like you can put you at ease; that's OK. But after the first year or two, it's not doing you any favors. Get out. Find the best in the bunch, keep them as friends, then bail. You may catch flak, and you won't be a lifetime member of your frat or sorority. But you will be better off, finding your own way on your own terms.

—*B.P.*
FLORIDA STATE UNIVERSITY, GRADUATE

· · · · · · · · ·

WHILE I DIDN'T JOIN A FRATERNITY, I did decide to join an engineering society at my school. This one was pretty hell-bent on getting drunk every weekend, like most fraternities at my school. This naturally became my attitude in my freshman year, and even continued into my second year. Try to keep school your priority during the week (as much as possible) so that your weekend social life doesn't intrude on your studies, when drinking affects grades. Also, ask yourself if it's worth $1,000 a semester to be in one of these groups. (Mine was only about $160 a year, which was very appealing.) You'll probably also come to a point when you're a senior and you realize that these groups aren't as exciting as they were when you were a freshman.

—*ANONYMOUS*
UNIVERSITY OF VIRGINIA, SENIOR

THE CAT IN THE FRAT?

Dr. Seuss (Theodore Geisel, class of 1925) studied at Dartmouth. Internet legend has it that he decorated his fraternity house walls with drawings of his strange characters; we're not sure it's a true story, but who cares?

SORORITY SISTERS

I'M IN A SORORITY called Kappa Kappa Gamma. I've become really close with my big sister—she's someone I wouldn't normally expect to meet, except that she's in a sorority. She's become one of my mentors at school.

> —MACKENZIE LUZZI
> PRINCETON UNIVERSITY, SOPHOMORE

• • • • • • • • •

SORORITIES PROVIDE YOU with an instant group of people you can get to know. You won't necessarily be good friends with everyone, but you will find someone you can get along with.

> —CHRISTINE SHIRINIAN
> AMERICAN UNIVERSITY, GRADUATE

• • • • • • • • •

I JOINED MY SORORITY on a whim—I was in a suite of eight girls my freshman year, and a lot of them were rushing. They encouraged me to come along for the fun experience. They said it's a great way to meet people, etc. And I went, but I didn't think I would join. But I found one sorority where I met a bunch of girls and had a lot of great conversations, so I figured I'd try it. I don't think it's right for everyone, or that everyone would feel that it's worth the time commitment. But I've had a great experience.

> —COLLEEN
> PRINCETON UNIVERSITY, JUNIOR

Imagine it is just some elaborate *Saturday Night Live* skit in which you are grudgingly playing along.

—*Anonymous*

THE FIRST FEW PARTIES OF THE YEAR, they'll let pretty much anyone in just to get themselves known for killer parties. After a few weeks, though, they start patrolling their parties by placing a few brothers in the driveway to tell the masses that "the house occupancy is full, but try back later." If you drop the name of a brother, though, they'll let you in. So at the first party of the year, I randomly met a guy named Steve and found out he was from Louisiana. So every time I went back, I told the guys in the driveway I knew "Steve from Louisiana," and it worked like a charm. I passed Steve from Louisiana's name on to whoever wanted to hang out at that frat.

—*Ashley Leavell*
Boston University, Senior

• • • • • • • • •

DO NOT BELIEVE THE HYPE that Greek organizations feed you during your first semester in college. You will not find friends who will be there for you if you join a fraternity or sorority just as you get into college. These organizations try to get freshmen to join by saying that this is the best way to find friends. On the contrary, it is the best way to exclude yourself from people who can become your best friends, and to get a narrow view of college life. Before joining a Greek organization, find an organization that shares your interests, perhaps something where you can have a wide variety of friends.

—*D.*
Moorhead State University, Junior

More Wisdom: Good Stuff That Doesn't Fit Anywhere Else

Looking back on their first year of college, whether from a distance of ten years or ten weeks, our respondents often waxed philosophical—especially those who'd taken Philosophy 101. Like a lot of good advice, their observations just didn't fit neatly into those twenty earlier categories, but were way too important to ignore.

Think of it this way: If all the other chapters were nicely frosted cupcakes, this chapter would be the extra frosting in the bowl—still tasty, but all the sweeter for being the last lick. Bon appétit!

Don't take yourself so seriously. Enjoy this unique time in your life.

—*TREVOR*
AMHERST COLLEGE
GRADUATE

IF YOU DON'T HAVE AN OPENNESS to the situation, you're going to have trouble. You're going to meet people of different backgrounds and beliefs, some people that have been coddled and some people that haven't. You need an openness to learn and an openness to accept. If you don't have that, you won't do very well. If you do, your experience will be a lot better.

—*ZACH FRIEND*
UNIVERSITY OF CALIFORNIA AT SANTA CRUZ, GRADUATE

• • • • • • • •

MY FIRST DAY OF CLASS, a department chair said something that stuck with me. He said, "It's possible to go through four years of college unscathed by education. It's a tragedy if that happens." He went on to say that college is about challenging all of your preconceived notions; from your personal values to your religious values to your social values to your political values. If you have a real college experience, it should all be challenged. If you don't have the courage to face that, you're not getting as much out of college as you could. Be prepared to be challenged.

—*MICHAEL A. FEKULA*
UNIVERSITY OF MARYLAND, GRADUATE

• • • • • • • •

IF YOU'RE NOT CAREFUL, the first year of college will be the most unhealthy year of your entire life. The food is bad for you, you're probably not exercising as much as you were in high school, you drink tons of caffeine and even more alcohol, and you don't sleep. Freshman year, try to remember to sleep more and exercise more. That way you'll be a fully functioning human being. Sometimes it's hard to pass up parties, but remember that there will be other nights and other funny stories. Choose your night.

—*SUMMER J.*
UNIVERSITY OF VIRGINIA, SENIOR

USE YOUR GAS CARD to buy cases of beer and snacks, because gas stations don't card.

—*MATT FIELD*
SYRACUSE UNIVERSITY, GRADUATE

. . . .

KNOW WHAT YOU WANT TO DO when you go to college. I didn't know and I didn't care. I didn't go to many classes; I just spent my time meeting people and going to parties. I did everything you weren't supposed to do: I signed up for hard classes, I didn't go to them, and I went out every night. When I was 18, I acted a lot younger.

—*A.G.S.*
UNIVERSITY OF TENNESSEE, DID NOT GRADUATE

. . . .

Don't set your mind on anything the first year. Explore. That's what it's about.

—*M.M.*
NEW YORK UNIVERSITY, SENIOR

66 Have an open mind and try to see everything. Not everything will be your thing, but there is something that you'll find. **99**

—*ANONYMOUS*
UNIVERSITY OF PENNSYLVANIA, FRESHMAN

. . . .

IT'S HARD TO REMEMBER back to freshman year. There's a lesson there: It will pass, good and bad.

—*LINDSEY SHULTZ*
CARNEGIE MELLON UNIVERSITY, SENIOR

. . . .

FRESHMAN YEAR WAS NOT an endurance test—it was a friggin' celebration!

—*L.*
DUKE UNIVERSITY, GRADUATE

STUDENT TEACHERS

Here's the best piece of advice I think I got in four years: At the end of my freshman year, I set up a meeting with a professor who had befriended me. I had been considering taking more classes over the summer to get ahead towards my degree (yes, I was a little nerd) and so I asked, "Is the quality of the courses the same as during the year? Do the same professors teach during the summer?" He said, "The professors are the same, but the courses are not as good." He paused for a second to enjoy the look of confusion on my face. "It's the students that are generally worse. During the summer, there are a lot of high school students, trying to put something on their résumé. You learn from your peers more than from the professor, you know."

My professor's advice was excellent—the people I met at college were so exceptional and taught me so much, everything from literature to physics.

—NOAH HELMAN
    HARVARD UNIVERSITY, GRADUATE

I WAS NEVER A FRESHMAN. When asked, I was an "undergrad," or for those not into the whole brevity thing, I was "finishing up my lower-division classes," or "in my second semester." Did this help me? Yes and no. If you are around other freshmen, you don't really have to do it; they don't need to be impressed. It works fairly well on upper-division students, though. If you tell one of them that you are a freshman, they immediately sort of shy away from you. So, use euphemisms, but use discretion, too.

—KARLA SAIA
SAN DIEGO STATE UNIVERSITY, JUNIOR

• • • • • • • •

MAKE SURE YOU RESEARCH THE SCHOOL to see if everyone goes home on weekends. I attended a commuter college. Almost all the kids who live there go home over the weekends, so there's absolutely nothing to do. It would be a good idea to talk to current students about what goes on when classes aren't in session. This is even more important if you go to a school where none of your friends are going. If all the kids go home and you go there to get away from home, you have absolutely nothing to do on weekends.

—MATTHEW MOLNAR
QUEENS COLLEGE, JUNIOR

• • • • • • • •

ANYTHING RANDOM IS BAD. Don't allow them to pick a random roommate for you; find one and request him. Don't go into a random dorm or room; pick your own. Same thing with the meal plan; do your due diligence and find out what the options are or you will be unhappy with the choices made for you. This is true for life as well as college. Don't be a sheep: Take charge.

—ANGEL NYA
CARNEGIE MELLON UNIVERSITY, SOPHOMORE

SLEEP EARLY AND OFTEN— Don't stay up till 2 a.m. because you'll never get up for your 8 a.m. class.

EAT EARLY AND OFTEN—Don't skip breakfast, and eat three meals a day.

DRINK—but not too early and not too often.

—C.B.

Never be lazy. College only happens once and it's not long enough, so take advantage of it.

—*KERRY*
GEORGETOWN
UNIVERSITY
GRADUATE

FORM HABITS THAT WILL TRANSLATE into career traits after your schooling is complete. This does not have to be stressful. It can be simplified:

1) Find a place that's just yours where you can study comfortably.

2) Get up early a few days a week and walk, jog, or practice something physical.

3) Do something at least one day a week that's for someone else—visit a facility where you can volunteer (not with a bunch of friends; just you).

4) Write in a journal. Give yourself time to reflect and see things through someone else's eyes.

If you get into these habits, it will carry you not only through your first year, but also through your whole college career. You'll amaze yourself at how consistent you can be. And the carryover of these habits will frame your post-school life for success, no matter what you choose to do.

—*TREVOR*
AMHERST COLLEGE, GRADUATE

* * * * * * * *

66 Have your fun, but realize you're here to get an education (and, hopefully, a degree!) Make it all worthwhile—academics and social life. 99

—*KHALIL SULLIVAN*
PRINCETON UNIVERSITY, JUNIOR

MY FRESHMAN YEAR WAS GOOD, BAD, everything you could possibly imagine. The bad parts were adjusting, then readjusting, then readjusting again to leaving home and being on your own and making your life work. There was a lot to be exposed to really fast.

—*J.P.G.*
UNIVERSITY OF PENNSYLVANIA, SOPHOMORE

• • • • • • • •

I WAS EXPOSED TO A LOT OF THE SCARY SIDES of people that I hadn't come so close to before. Like the time some guys beat up and killed a raccoon outside my dorm. Or the time a dorm mate expressed to me that she often felt like committing suicide, and I felt like there was nothing I could do to help her, except let her know that a lot of people around her really cared about her.

—*K. HARMA*
WESTERN WASHINGTON UNIVERSITY, GRADUATE

Everyone searches for an identity their freshman year; that's one of your biggest struggles.

—*RYAN A. BROWN*
UNIVERSITY OF
NORTH CAROLINA
AT CHAPEL HILL
GRADUATE

COLLEGE CHANGES YOU

The college experience helped me become a leader in so many ways. I came out of high school, shy like no other, unsure of myself, quite insecure. College allowed me to find out who I am, my potential to be someone great, and put my insecurities out at the curb. I am able to voice my opinion, speak in public places, and lead a group without feeling unsure of myself. College is what you make it!

—*VIVIAN ORIAKU*
UNIVERSITY OF MIAMI, GRADUATE

Everyone searches for an identity their freshman year; that's one of your biggest struggles.

—RYAN A. BROWN
UNIVERSITY OF
NORTH CAROLINA
AT CHAPEL HILL
GRADUATE

WHAT I NEGLECTED MY FRESHMAN YEAR was taking advice from professors. In high school, I always felt like my teachers didn't know what they were talking about. But the professors really do know what they're talking about, and not just in their fields. When they give you advice, listen to it. I didn't take the advice of people who could've helped me. Most freshmen have this attitude: "I got to college, so why do I need you now?" Your pride and self-confidence get in the way of re-evaluating the situation you're in. That's what it comes down to. You've got to shed your attitude; it really gets in the way.

—ZAK AMCHISLAVSKY
GEORGETOWN UNIVERSITY, SENIOR

COLLEGE FOOTBALL'S CONTRIBUTIONS TO MANKIND

1. *Gatorade* was named for the University of Florida (football) Gators, for whom it was developed in 1965. Coach Ray Graves's Florida team—powered by the potion concocted by a UF med-school professor—came from behind to defeat heavily favored Louisiana State in 102-degree heat, and a legend was born.

2. The football huddle originated at Gallaudet University, a liberal arts college for the deaf, when the football team found that opposing teams were reading their signed messages and intercepting plays.

IF YOU GO TO SCHOOL IN A BIG CITY, you have to be more careful. Watch out for your surroundings. If you have to take a route where you might have trouble, stay away from it. Take the long way. There's nothing more important than your life.

> —B.L.
> *JOHN JAY COLLEGE OF CRIMINAL JUSTICE, GRADUATE*

• • • • • • • •

"You can graduate with decent grades, you can do nothing and just get four years older, or you can suck the marrow out of your university and garner all the knowledge, academic and other, that comes your way. The choice and your future are in your hands."

> —*ADAM*
> *ELON UNIVERSITY, SOPHOMORE*

• • • • • • • •

I'M NOT NORMALLY an advice-giving person. I don't buy giving advice; who am I to tell you how to live your freshman year? Part of being a freshman is about being away from parents and doing stupid things. Doing stupid things is the best way to learn. People learn more from their own advice than anyone else's. Plus, anything you learn from is not stupid.

> —*CAITLIN BERBERICH*
> *UNIVERSITY OF GEORGIA, GRADUATE*

DON'T TALK BAD ABOUT ANYONE. My dad told me that when I was in high school and I stuck with it. No one has a bad thing to say about you if you don't say bad things about them. If they do, you realize they're not worth your time.

—*CASEY*
GEORGETOWN UNIVERSITY, SENIOR

• • • • • • • •

"Make a plan. Write out everything you have to do, every day. Follow that plan and stick with it. Don't let anything get in the way of taking care of that plan. It's like a schedule. Write down everything that you have to do, and get it done. Social things, everything."

—*BRIAN*
JAMES MADISON UNIVERSITY, JUNIOR

• • • • • • • •

THIS IS WHAT THE REAL WORLD IS LIKE. College is diverse. Be open to new experiences. Don't judge people on whether or not they get wasted on the weekends. That's just one aspect of a person.

—*ERIC MCINTOSH*
UNIVERSITY OF NORTH CAROLINA AT CHAPEL HILL, JUNIOR

I'M FROM NEW YORK and I went to a very rural, small, homogeneous southern school my freshman year. It was a bit of a culture shock. I was in classes with white, upper-middle-class kids and that was it. On your tour they say it's diverse, but I don't know what their definition of that is; it's not the New York definition. I didn't realize how much it would affect me, not having access to plays and restaurants and jazz clubs. You had to really travel if you wanted to do anything that would stimulate you. I knew by November that it was not where I wanted to spend my college life. People make you think your decision to pick a college is the end-all of your entire life. So find a place that looks interesting, and figure out what's important to you before you check out a college. Don't be influenced by a beautiful campus or the nice people in your tour. Expect that you're going to spend four years there, but know that if you don't, it's not jail; you can transfer. College is about *you*, not the school.

> —HANNAH SMITH
> HARVARD UNIVERSITY, JUNIOR

· · · · · · · ·

REMEMBER, EVERYONE ELSE IS IN THE SAME BOAT as you. College is your first taste of freedom, but it comes with a lot of responsibility. No freshman has it all figured out, so if you find people that act like they do, they're drunk or lying.

> —ANONYMOUS
> UNION COLLEGE

· · · · · · · ·

FIND A GROUP ON CAMPUS that interests you, so you don't feel that the school is so huge.

> —STEPHANIE
> UNIVERSITY OF PENNSYLVANIA, SENIOR

I learned that college is like a big high school. It's just older people, who take being immature to another level.

> —M.G.
> VALDOSTA STATE
> UNIVERSITY, SENIOR

THE BEST YEAR OF YOUR LIFE

The experience of leaving my freshman year of college is among the most memorable times of my life, along with grad-

uating from high school. Coming to college, I was scared shitless and had no idea how I was going to survive. In May, the heat hit me hard as I was packing up my life into a few duffel bags and sweeping out the room that witnessed my first attempts at indepen- dence. I peeled off the walls the pictures of people I once saw

every day and swore always to be best friends with, who became people I only talked to once in a while on IM. It sounds sad, but my high school friends and I had gone our separate ways and discovered new lives with people we once called strangers. With these strangers I now had

inside jokes, crazy blurry memories, and new pictures to plaster

on my wall. Not to say that college is always amazing: the food sucks, your roommate will smell, your professor can be an asshole, there are morning classes, and the guy you can't believe you hooked up with will live down the hall all semester long. It's what makes college college. With all the bad, there is the good. With all your worries and all your

fears, freshman year won't suck that bad—it might even be the best year of your life.

—KAREN
STATE UNIVERSITY OF NEW YORK AT NEW PALTZ, SOPHOMORE

> "I recommend taking a year off before starting college. It gives a fantastic perspective on why you need to be sitting in classes day after day. The hard thing about it is meeting other people who have been through the same experience."
>
> —*Leah Price*
> *Georgetown University, Sophomore*

The hardest part of my freshman year was to let go of my former morals, friends, and hobbies in order to develop and grow. I was so afraid that in letting go of these things I was going to lose myself. The summer after freshman year, I went to Australia with about 50 other students. It was the first time I felt like I could be honest about my doubts, thoughts, and past mistakes. I finally had the opportunity to explore new ideas and activities. Since I have come back from Australia I have attempted to continue this growth process. Some people have been disappointed and/or surprised by some changes that have taken place in my life; others are impressed. Either way, at least I am growing as an individual. Aside from getting a degree, that is what college is all about.

—*Annie Verna*
University of North Carolina at Greensboro
Sophomore

All the trouble I got into, all the bad things that came from college, came from the social gatherings. All the good things came from people I met in the classrooms.

—*J.H.*
Widener University Graduate

I SURVIVED MY FRESHMAN YEAR

Cursed with an annoying stammer, I always scrupulously avoided doing anything at all in front of an audience. But in my first week as a freshman I was forced to come face-to-face with "the stammer."

In a business management course, we were asked to debate issues given to us by our lecturers. My group was given the ridiculous proposition that "welfare benefits assist unemployment" and told to argue against it. Maintaining my treasured high school stance of protected anonymity, I offered a few ideas to my group while steadfastly refusing to be the spokesperson for the group.

However, our dear teachers were not to be fobbed off with such an approach. They started firing questions at *all* the participants.

I waited for my turn to come. When it did, I opened my mouth to answer and . . . nothing. Zilch. I writhed and wriggled, and still nothing.

I prayed hard that the earth would open and swallow me up. I knew that I'd blown it for the rest of my college life, and all in the first week.

And then, suddenly, it came: "This form of intolerance and preconceived notions is the same that the proposers of this motion are suggesting for the unemployed."

There was total silence, then applause. I had bowled them over with an outrageous display of demagoguery. Within the month, I was a candidate for the Student Representative Council. Within the year, I was conducting workshops and making speeches before thousands. Lots of screaming, plenty of demagoguery and no end of guilt-tripping. A political career was born; I had survived my freshman year.

—PHIL CARMEL
UNIVERSITY COLLEGE–SALFORD (ENGLAND), GRADUATE

THE ESSENTIAL FRESHMAN FILL-IN LIST

Some of these answers you'll find in your new-student orientation pack or handbook, or on the college Web site. The rest you'll have to discover for yourself—sort of like a first-semester treasure hunt!

Places

Best study spot _____

Best computer lab _____

Best coffee _____

Best late-night food _____

Best inexpensive date location _____

People

For help with rules and requirements _____

For help dealing with stress _____

For answers about student activities _____

For late-night philosophical discussions _____

For fun and laughs _____

Activities

To do when you're homesick _____

To do when you're stressed out _____

To do when you need to be healthier _____

To do when you want to meet new people _____

_____

To do when you want to avoid the people you already know _____

_____

FRESHMAN FIRST-AID KIT

Feeling sick? Accident-prone? Sure, you can go to the Wellness Center (if it's open) or knock on your RA's door (if he's not out that night), or hike over to the local drugstore or 7-Eleven (if the temperature isn't below-freezing)—*or,* you can remember to pack your very own first-aid kit and really be ready for anything!

- Band-Aids
- antibiotic ointment
- thermometer
- pain reliever of your choice (ibuprofen, acetaminophen, etc.)
- travel-sized containers of any other over-the-counter medicines you use
- contact information for your doctor(s) back home
- reusable gel "ice" pack (keep it in your mini-fridge)
- Ace bandage
- antiseptic soap or wipes
- tweezers

THE NOT-TOO-EARLY STUDY-ABROAD LIST

Even though you're only a freshman, it's not too early to start planning to study abroad, especially if you want to be away for a whole semester or year. Follow these steps, and you'll be (almost) on your way.

Find out:
- Where is your college's study abroad office?
- What programs are offered?
- How much do they cost?
- Is financial aid available?
- Is there a GPA requirement?

Think about:
- Why you want to study abroad.
- Where you want to go.
- What kinds of classes you want to take.
- When you should go (fall semester of junior year is a popular choice).
- Whether there are older students who can share their study-abroad wisdom with you.

Sketch out:
- A rough, four-year plan to cover all your course requirements.
- How you'll earn/save/beg/borrow the funds you'll need.

And while you're thinking about it, check your passport—it should be valid until one year *after* you plan to get back from your adventures abroad.

USEFUL WEB SITES

Hundreds of Heads: www.hundredsofheads.com

College Connection Scholarships: www.collegescholarships.com

Scholarships.com: www.scholarships.com

College Board scholarship search: apps.collegeboard.com/cbsearch_ss/welcome.jsp

College Board AP credit policy info:
collegesearch.collegeboard.com/apcreditpolicy/index.jsp

International Baccalaureate FAQ: www.ibo.org/ibna/parents_students/dpstudents.cfm

American Medical Student Association: www.amsa.org

Music and Entertainment Industry Student Association: www.meisa.org

American Psychological Association, resources for students interested in studying psychology: www.apa.org/students

The Roosevelt Institution, "The Nation's First Student Think Tank": rooseveltinstitution.org

FAFSA (Free Application for Federal Student Aid): www.fafsa.ed.gov

Volunteer Match: www.volunteermatch.org

Idealist.org, "Action without Borders": www.idealist.org

Student Environmental Action Coalition: www.seac.org

Campus Climate Challenge: climatechallenge.org

CampusActivism.org, "Tools for Activists": www.campusactivism.org

ULifeline, "An online resource center for college student mental health and emotional well-being.": www.ulifeline.org/main/Home.html

LdPride.net, "Information about learning styles and Multiple Intelligence (MI is helpful for everyone, but especially for people with learning disabilities and attention deficit disorder." www.ldpride.net

"Healthy Minds. Healthy Lives.", from the American Psychiatric Association: healthyminds.org

CREDITS

SPECIAL THANKS

Thanks to our intrepid "headhunters" for going out to find so many respondents from around the country with interesting advice to share.

Thanks, too, to our Chief Headhunter, Jamie Allen, editorial advisor, Anne Kostick, and production editor, Gayle Green. And thanks to our assistant, Miri Greidi, for her yeoman's work at keeping us all organized. The real credit for this book, of course, goes to all the people whose experiences and collective wisdom make up this guide. There are too many of you to thank individually, but you know who you are.

ADVICE FROM:

American Repertory Theater at Harvard
American University
Amherst College
Anderson University
Auburn University
Barnard College
Biola University
Boston College
Boston University
Bowling Green State University
Brown University
Bryn Mawr College
Cal Poly San Luis Obispo
California State University–Fullerton
Calvin College
Carnegie Mellon University
Central Bible College
Claremont McKenna College
City University of New York/Macaulay
   Honors College
Clemson University
Colby College
College of San Mateo
Columbia University
Cornell University
Curtis Institute of Music
DeSales University
Diablo Valley College
Dominican University
Duke University
Elon University
Emory University
Florida A&M University
Florida State University
Foothill College
Frostburg State University
George Washington University
Georgetown University
Georgia Institute of Technology
Georgia Southern University
Georgia State University
Hamilton College
Harvard University
Howard University
Hunter College
Illinois Wesleyan
Indiana University
James Madison University
John Jay College of Criminal Justice
Johns Hopkins University
Kingsborough Community College
Kutztown College
Los Medanos College
Louisiana State University
Massachusetts Institute of Technology
Miami University
Michigan Technological University
Mississippi State University
Montclair State University
Moorhead State University
Morehead State University
Mount Holyoke College
New York University
North Carolina State University
Northwestern University
Oberlin College
Oxford College
Pennsylvania State University
Pomona College
Princeton University
Purdue University
Queens College
Queens University
Rhodes College

Rutgers University
Rice University
Riverside Community College
St. John's University
St. Lawrence University
San Diego State University
San Francisco State University
San Jose State University
Santa Barbara City College
Santa Clara University
Sonoma State University
Spring Hill College
Stanford University
State University of New York at Albany
State University of New York at Binghamton
State University of New York at Geneseo
State University of New York at New Paltz
Suffolk University
Syracuse University
Texas State University
Trinity University
Union College
United States Military Academy at West Point
University College–Salford (England)
University of California at Berkeley
University of California at Davis
University of California at Irvine
University of California at Santa Barbara
University of California at Santa Cruz
University of Chicago
University of Colorado
University of Connecticut
University of Delaware
University of Florida
University of Georgia
University of Illinois
University of Maryland
University of Maryland–Baltimore County
University of Maryland–College Park
University of Massachusetts
University of Massachusetts at Amherst
University of Michigan
University of Missouri
University of Nebraska
University of New Hampshire
University of North Carolina
University of North Carolina at Chapel Hill
University of Notre Dame
University of Oregon
University of Pennsylvania
University of Rhode Island
University of Rochester
University of South Florida
University of Tennessee
University of Tennessee at Martin
University of Texas
University of Texas at Austin
University of Toronto
University of Virginia
University of West Georgia
University of Wisconsin–Stevens Point
University of Wisconsin at Madison
Valdosta State University
Villa Julie College
Villanova
Wake Forest University
Washington and Lee University
Wellesley College
Wesleyan University
Westfield State College
Western Washington University
Western Illinois University
Widener University
Williams College
Xavier University
Yale University
Youngstown State University

WHAT THE CRITICS ARE SAYING ABOUT HUNDREDS OF HEADS®:

"Colorful bits of advice … So simple, so entertaining, so should have been my million-dollar idea."

    —*THE COURIER-JOURNAL* (LOUISVILLE, KENTUCKY)

"The books have struck a nerve."

    —CNN.COM

"If you've got a kid going off to college this year, you've got to get this book... It's kind of irreverent and fun..."

    —*WGN RADIO (CHICAGO)*

"Entertaining and informative series takes a different approach to offering advice...Think 'Chicken Soup' meets 'Zagats'..."

    —*THE SACRAMENTO BEE*

"Hundreds of Heads hopes to make life in our complicated new millennium a bit more manageable."

    —*THE RECORD* (HACKENSACK, NEW JERSEY)

CHECK OUT THESE OTHER BOOKS FROM HUNDREDS OF HEADS®

The college graduate's orientation guide to the real world. Filled with hard-won wisdom from hundreds of young adults on everything from finding your first job to renting an apartment to learning how to cook.

Featured on the Today Show and in *USA Today!*

"… the perfect gift for the newly minted college graduates on your list.
—*THE POST AND COURIER*

HOW TO SURVIVE THE REAL WORLD: LIFE AFTER GRADUATION
(204 pages, $13.95)

ISBN-10: 1-933512-03-2
ISBN-13: 978-1933-51203-7

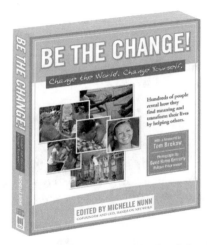

By intertwining practical advice on service and volunteerism with real-life stories of personal transformation, this book is the perfect companion for people who want to be inspired and informed and to take action to change their lives and their world. **Edited by Michelle Nunn, Co-founder and CEO of Hands On Network.**

"This is a wonderful and inspiring book."
—WALTER ISAACSON CEO, ASPEN INSTITUTE

"This is a book that could change your life … It's almost magic and it could happen to everyone. Go!"
—JIM LEHRER, ANCHOR, PBS' NEWSHOUR WITH JIM LEHRER

BE THE CHANGE! CHANGE THE WORLD. CHANGE YOURSELF.
(336 pages, $14.95)

ISBN-10: 1-933512-00-8
ISBN-13: 978-1933512-00-6

**HOW TO SURVIVE
DATING**…by
Hundreds of Happy
Singles Who Did
(and some things to
avoid, from a few
broken hearts who
didn't) (224 pages,
$12.95)

ISBN-10: 0-9746292-1-9
ISBN-13: 978-0974-62921-6

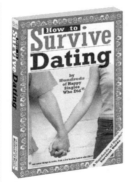

We interviewed nearly 1,000 men and women
across America to get the best straight-from-the-
trenches tips on dating.

"Great, varied advice, in capsule form … "
—SALON.COM

"… like having a few hundred friends on speed-dial."
—KNIGHT RIDDER TRIBUNE NEWS SERVICE

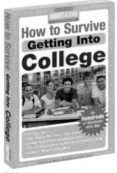

**HOW TO SURVIVE
GETTING INTO
COLLEGE:** (272
pages, $13.95)

ISBN-10: 1-933512-05-9
ISBN-13: 978-1933-51205-1

For the over two million high school students
applying to college each year, this book gives
them the inside strategies from students who've
made it in to their college picks. Perfect
companion to *How to Survive Your Freshman
Year.* **Special Editor Rachel Korn is a college
advisor and consultant.**

As seen on the Today Show!

"… a fun, fascinating read … "
—ABOUT.COM

"… chock-full of honest, heartfelt and often funny
advice … "
—CHICAGO SUN-TIMES

About the Editors

FRANCES NORTHCUTT is an academic advisor in the William E. Macaulay Honors College of the City University of New York at Hunter College. Her advising career began when she became a peer advisor at Wesleyan University, where she earned her BA in English. She went on to advise students at the University of California, Berkeley and at the University of the Sciences in Philadelphia, where she also taught classes on college skills and professional development. Frances is active in the National Academic Advising Association: she has presented at regional conferences, and was selected as the Outstanding Advisor (Primary Role) for the Mid-Atlantic region in 2006. She is currently working on a master's degree in Higher Education Administration at Temple University.

MARK BERNSTEIN graduated from the Wharton School of the University of Pennsylvania. While there, he started a business that provided students with "survival kits" consisting of unhealthy food sent by their parents, who were coping with their loss.

YADIN KAUFMANN graduated from Princeton University. He was involved in journalism and started a student agency to publish a book he wrote. He survived his freshman year by chugging Hershey's syrup, straight up. He also co-authored *The Boston Ice Cream Lover's Guide*.

Freshman Year Survival Kit!

FREE Weekly Hundreds of Heads Advicemails

Our weekly e-newsletters are packed with practical information for students, including:

- Peer-to-Peer Wisdom and "Insider" Advice
- Stories and Tips from Hundreds of College Students
- Guidance from College Experts

Sign up now for:

"HeadsUp! Freshman Year"—shares wisdom from Fran Northcutt, an expert in the freshman year experience, and an academic advisor in the Honors Program at Hunter College/ City University of New York.

"HeadsUp! Get Into College"—includes sage advice from Rachel Korn, a former admissions officer at the University of Pennsylvania, Wellesley, and Brandeis.

To see past Advicemails or to register and start receiving one or both free, go to: www.HundredsofHeads.com.

HundredsofHeads.com is All Things College

Hundreds of Heads' new website has great practical advice, the latest tips, and the best community conversation on getting into and succeeding in college.

Search, ask, discuss, and answer questions on: taking the SAT; applying to college; choosing the right school; surviving freshman year; making good grades; life after college; and much more.

Surf:

- Videos
- Blogs & Polls
- Reference Articles
- Expert Advice

Visit HundredsofHeads.com's online community of students and experts discussing all things college today.

Hundreds of Heads. Great Advice. Get it! Give it!

HUNDREDS OF HEADS